D1300955

IBM
SPSS
FOR INTRODUCTORY
STATISTICS

Use and Interpretation

Fifth Edition

IBM SPSS for Introductory Statistics:

Use and Interpretation

Fifth Edition

George A. Morgan
Colorado State University

Nancy L. Leech
University of Colorado Denver

Gene W. Gloeckner
Karen C. Barrett
Colorado State University

Routledge
Taylor & Francis Group

NEW YORK AND LONDON

First published 2013
by Routledge
711 Third Avenue, New York, NY 10017

Simultaneously published in the UK
by Routledge
2 Park Square, Milton Park, Abingdon, Oxon OX14 4RN

*Routledge is an imprint of the Taylor & Francis Group,
an informa business*

© 2013 Taylor & Francis

The right of George Morgan, Nancy Leech, Gene Gloeckner and
Karen Barrett to be identified as authors of this work
has been asserted by them in accordance with sections 77
and 78 of the Copyright, Designs and Patents Act 1988.

All rights reserved. No part of this book may be reprinted or
reproduced or utilized in any form or by any electronic,
mechanical, or other means, now known or hereafter invented,
including photocopying and recording, or in any information
storage or retrieval system, without permission in writing
from the publishers. Printed in Canada.

Publisher's Note
This book has been prepared from camera-ready copy provided by the authors.

Trademark notice: Product or corporate names may be trademarks
or registered trademarks, and are used only for identification
and explanation without intent to infringe.

Library of Congress Cataloging in Publication Data
IBM SPSS for introductory statistics : use and interpretation / George A. Morgan ...
[et al.]. – 5th ed.
        p. cm
ISBN 978-1-84872-982-7 (alk. Paper) 1. SPSS for Windows. 2. SPSS
(Computer file) 3. Social science--Statistical methods--Computer Programs. I.
Morgan, George A. (George Arthur), 1936-
HA32.S572 2013
005.5'5—dc23
2012013073

ISBN: 978-1-84872-982-7 (pbk)
ISBN: 978-0-203-12731-5 (ebk)

Contents

Appendices

Preface

This book is designed to help students learn how to analyze and interpret research. It is intended to be a supplemental text in an introductory (undergraduate or graduate) statistics or research methods course in the behavioral or social sciences or education and it can be used in conjunction with any mainstream text. We have found that this book makes IBM SPSS for Windows easy to use so that it is not necessary to have a formal, instructional computer lab; you should be able to learn how to use the program on your own with this book. Access to the IBM SPSS program and some familiarity with Windows is all that is required. Although SPSS is quite easy to use, there is such a wide variety of options and statistics that knowing which ones to use and how to interpret the printouts can be difficult. This book is intended to help with these challenges. In addition to serving as a supplemental or lab text, this book and its companion, *IBM SPSS for Intermediate Statistics* (Leech, Barrett, & Morgan, 4th ed., 2011) are useful as reminders to faculty and professionals of the specific steps to take to use SPSS and/or guides to using and interpreting parts of SPSS with which they might be unfamiliar.

The Computer Program

We used IBM SPSS, 20, in this book. Except for enhanced tables and graphics, there are only minor differences among SPSS Versions 10 to 20. In October 2009, IBM bought the SPSS Corporation and changed the name of the program used in this book to IBM SPSS Statistics. We expect future Windows versions of this program to be similar so students should be able to use this book with earlier and later versions of the program, which we call SPSS in the text. Our students have used this book, or earlier editions of it, with all of the earlier versions of SPSS; both the procedures and outputs are quite similar. We point out some of the changes at various points in the text.

In addition to various SPSS modules that may be available at your university, there are two versions that are available for students, that you can rent for 6 or 12 months online. *Statistics GradPack* enables you to do all the statistics in this book plus those in our *IBM SPSS for Intermediate Statistics* book (Leech et al., 2011) and many others.

Goals of This Book

Helping you learn how to choose the appropriate statistics, interpret the outputs, and develop skills in writing about the meaning of the results are the main goals of this book. Thus, we have included material on
1. How the appropriate choice of a statistic is influenced by the design of the research.
2. How to use SPSS to help the researcher answer research questions.
3. How to interpret SPSS outputs.
4. How to write about the outputs in the Results section of a paper.

This information will help you develop skills that cover the whole range of the steps in the research process: design, data collection, data entry, data analysis, interpretation of outputs, and writing results. The modified high school and beyond data set (HSB) used in this book is similar to one you might have for a thesis, dissertation, or research project. Therefore, we think it can serve as a model for your analysis.

The Web site, http://www.routledge.com/9781848729827, contains the HSB data files used throughout this book. Two other data sets (called college student data.sav and Chapter Seven Data.sav) are used for the extra statistics problems at the end of most chapters, and DataMales.sav and DataFemales.sav are used in Appendix A for the merging of two data files. Appendix A shows how to download these files to your computer.

This book demonstrates how to produce a variety of statistics that are usually included in basic statistics courses, plus others (e.g., reliability measures) that are useful for doing research. We try to describe the use and interpretation of these statistics as much as possible in nontechnical, jargon-free language. In part, to make the text more readable, we have chosen not to cite many references in the text; however, we have provided a short bibliography, "For Further Reading," of some of the books and articles that our students have found useful. We assume that most students will use this book in conjunction with a class that has a textbook; it will help you to read more about each statistic before doing the assignments.

Overview of the Chapters

Our approach in this book is to present how to use and interpret the SPSS statistics program in the context of proceeding as if the HSB data were the actual data from your research project. However, before starting the assignments, we have three introductory chapters. The first chapter describes research problems, variables, and research questions, and it identifies a number of specific research questions related to the HSB data. The goal is to use this computer program as a tool to help you answer these research questions. (Appendix B provides some guidelines for phrasing or formatting research questions.) Chapter 2 provides an introduction to data coding, entry, and checking with sample questionnaire data designed for those purposes. We developed Chapter 2 because many of you may have little experience with making "messy," realistic data ready to analyze. Chapter 3 discusses measurement and its relation to the appropriate use of descriptive statistics. This chapter also includes a brief review of descriptive statistics.

Chapters 4 and 5 provide you with experience doing exploratory data analysis (EDA), basic descriptive statistics, and data manipulations (e.g., compute and recode) using the high school and beyond (HSB) data set. These chapters are organized in very much the same way you might proceed if this were your project. We calculate a variety of descriptive statistics, check certain statistical assumptions, and make a few data transformations. Much of what is done in these two chapters involves preliminary analyses to get ready to answer the research questions that you might state in a report. Chapter 5 ends with examples of tables and a figure and how you might write about these descriptive data in a research report or thesis.

Chapter 6 provides a brief overview of research designs (e.g., between groups and within subjects). This chapter also provides flowcharts and tables useful for selecting an appropriate statistic. Also included is an overview of how to interpret and write about the results of an inferential statistic. This section includes not only testing for statistical significance but also a discussion of effect size measures and guidelines for interpreting them.

Chapter 7 provides examples of how to check your data for evidence of reliability and validity using several statistics provided by SPSS; e.g., Cohen's Kappa and Cronbach's alpha. The chapter also provides an introduction to exploratory factor analysis used to reduce a large number of variables to a more manageable number.

Chapters 8 through 11 are designed to answer the several research questions posed in Chapter 1 as well as a number of additional questions. Solving the problems in these chapters should give you a good idea of the basic statistics that can be computed with this computer program. Hopefully, seeing how the research questions and design lead naturally to the choice of statistics will become apparent after using this book. In addition, it is our hope that interpreting what you get back from the computer will become clearer after doing these assignments, studying the outputs, answering the interpretation questions, and doing the extra statistics problems.

Our Approach to Research Questions, Measurement, and Selection of Statistics

In Chapters 1, 3, and 6, our approach is somewhat nontraditional because we have found that students have a great deal of difficulty with some aspects of research and statistics but not others. Most can learn formulas and "crunch" the numbers quite easily and accurately with a calculator or with a computer. However, many have trouble knowing what statistics to use and how to interpret the results. They do not seem to have a "big picture" or see how research design and measurement influence data analysis. Part of the problem is inconsistent terminology. We are reminded of Bruce Thompson's frequently repeated, intentionally facetious remark at his many national workshops: "We use these different terms to confuse the graduate students." For these reasons, we have tried to present a semantically consistent and coherent picture of how research design leads to three basic kinds of research questions (difference, associational, and descriptive) that, in turn, lead to three kinds or groups of statistics with the same names. We realize that these and other attempts to develop and utilize a consistent framework are both nontraditional and somewhat of an oversimplification. However, we think the framework and consistency pay off in terms of student understanding and ability to actually use statistics to help answer their research questions. Instructors who are not persuaded that this framework is useful can skip or modify Chapters 1, 3, and 6 and still have a book that helps their students use and interpret SPSS.

Major Changes in This Edition

The major change in this edition is the new Chapter 7 on how to use SPSS to help you obtain support for the reliability and validity of your data. We also updated the windows and text to IBM SPSS 20, and we have attempted to correct any typos in the 4th edition and clarify some passages. We expanded the appendix about Getting Started with SPSS (Appendix A) to include several useful procedures that were not discussed in the body of the text. Chapter 5 has been expanded to include a figure based on descriptive statistics and how to write about it. Although this edition of our *IBM SPSS for Introductory Statistics* was written using version 20, the program is sufficiently similar to prior versions of this software that we feel you should be able to use this book with earlier and later versions as well.

Instructional Features

Several user-friendly features of this book include

1. Both words and the key **windows** that you see when performing the statistical analyses. This has been helpful to "visual learners."
2. The **complete outputs** for the analyses that we have done so you can see what you will get (we have done some editing, as shown in Appendix A to make the outputs fit better on the pages).
3. **Callout boxes** on the outputs that point out parts of the output to focus on and indicate what they mean.
4. For each output, a boxed **interpretation section** that will help you understand the output.
5. Chapter 6 provides specially developed flowcharts and tables to help you **select an appropriate inferential statistic** and **interpret statistical significance and effect sizes**. This chapter also provides an extended example of how to identify and write a research problem, research questions, and a results paragraph.
6. For the statistics in Chapters 5 and 7–11, an example of **how to write about the output** and make a table or figure for a thesis, dissertation, or research paper using the 6th edition (2010) of the *Publication Manual of the American Psychological Association.*
7. **Interpretation questions** for each chapter that stimulate you to think about the information in the chapter.

8. Several **Extra Problems** at the end of each chapter for you to run with the SPSS program.

9. Appendix A provides information about how to get started with SPSS and how to use several commands not discussed in the chapters.

10. Appendix B provides examples of how to **write research problems** and **research questions or hypotheses**.

11. **Answers** to the odd numbered **interpretation questions are provided in** Appendix C.

12. **Data sets on the book webpage** http://www.routledge.com/9781848729827 are available and are listed in Appendix A. These six realistic data sets provide you with data to be used to solve the chapter and Appendix A problems and the end of chapter Extra SPSS Problems.

13. A **Resource Web site** is available to students and instructors. To access the site please visit http://www.routledge.com/9781848729827. Some of the material is password protected and available only to instructors to aid them in teaching the course. Instructors will find the following items available for each chapter: PowerPoint slides, Additional Activities/ Suggestions for Instructors, and the answers to the even numbered Interpretation Questions found in the book (the odd answers are in the book itself). Both students and instructors can access the following material that is provided for each chapter: Chapter Study Guides, Extra SPSS Problems, and Chapter Outlines. Students and instructors, as well as researchers who purchase copies for their personal use, can also access the data files by visiting http://www.routledge.com/9781848729827.

Major Statistical Features of This Edition

Based on our experiences using the book with students, feedback from reviewers and other users, and the revisions in policy and best practice specified by the APA Task Force on Statistical Inference (1999) and the 6th Edition of the *APA Publication Manual* (2010), we have included discussions of

1. **Effect size.** We discuss effect size in each interpretation section to be consistent with the requirements of the revised APA manual. Because this program doesn't provide effect sizes for all the demonstrated statistics, we often have to show how to estimate or compute them by hand.

2. **Writing about outputs.** We include examples of how to write about and make APA-type tables from the information in the outputs. We have found the step from interpretation to writing quite difficult for students so we put emphasis on writing research results.

3. **Data entry and checking.** Chapter 2 on data entry, variable labeling, and data checking is based on a small data set developed for this book. What is special about this is that the data are displayed as if they were on copies of actual questionnaires answered by participants. We built in problematic responses that require the researcher or data entry person to look for errors or inconsistencies and to make decisions. We hope this quite realistic task will help students be more sensitive to issues of data checking *before* doing analyses.

4. **Descriptive statistics and testing assumptions.** In Chapters 4 and 5 we emphasize exploratory data analysis (EDA), how to test assumptions, and data file management.

5. **Assumptions.** When each inferential statistic is introduced in Chapters 8–11, we have a brief section about its assumptions and when it is appropriate to select that statistic for the problem or question at hand.

6. All the **basic descriptive and inferential statistics such as chi-square, correlation, *t* tests, and one-way ANOVA** covered in basic statistics books. Our companion book, Leech et al., 4th ed. (2011), *IBM SPSS for Intermediate Statistics: Use and Interpretation,* also published by Routledge/Taylor & Francis, is on the "For Further Reading" list at the end of this book. We think that you will find it useful if you need more complete examples and interpretations of complex statistics including but not limited to **Cronbach's alpha**, **factor analysis**, **multiple regression**, and **factorial ANOVA** that are introduced briefly in this book.

7. **Reliability and validity assessment**. We present some ways of assessing reliability and validity in Chapter 7. More emphasis on reliability, validity and testing assumptions is consistent with our strategy of presenting computer analyses that students would use in an *actual* research project.

8. **Nonparametric statistics**. We include the nonparametric tests that are similar to the *t* tests (Mann–Whitney and Wilcoxon) and single factor ANOVA (Kruskal–Wallis) in appropriate chapters as well as several nonparametric measures of association. This is consistent with the emphasis on checking assumptions because it provides alternative procedures for the student when key assumptions are markedly violated.

9. **SPSS syntax**. We show the syntax along with the outputs because a number of professors and skilled students like seeing and prefer using syntax to produce outputs. How to include SPSS syntax in the output and to save and reuse it is presented in Appendix A. Use of syntax to write commands not otherwise available in SPSS is presented briefly in our companion volume, Leech et al. (in press).

Bullets, Arrows, Bold, and Italics

To help you do the problems, we have developed some conventions. We use bullets to indicate actions in SPSS windows that you will take. For example:

- Highlight *gender* and *math achievement.*
- Click on the arrow to move the variables into the right-hand box.
- Click on **Options** to get Fig. 2.16.
- Check **Mean, Std Deviation, Minimum,** and **Maximum.**
- Click on **Continue.**

Note that the words in italics are variable names and words in bold are words that you will see in the windows and utilize to produce the desired output. In the text they are spelled and capitalized as you see them in the windows. Bold is also used to identify key terms when they are introduced, defined, or important to understanding.

To access a window from what SPSS calls the **Data View** (see Chapter 2), the words you will see in the pull down menus are given in bold with arrows between them. For example:

- Select **Analyze → Descriptive Statistics → Frequencies.**

(This means pull down the Analyze menu, then slide your cursor down to Descriptive Statistics and over to Frequencies, and click.)

Occasionally, we have used underlines to <u>emphasize critical points or commands.</u>

We have tried hard to make this book accurate and clear so that it could be used by students and professionals to learn to compute and interpret statistics without the benefit of a class. However, we find that there are always some errors and places that are not totally clear. Thus, we would like for you to help us identify any grammatical or statistical errors and to point out places that need to be clarified. Please send suggestions to *george.morgan@colostate.edu.*

Acknowledgments

This IBM SPSS book is consistent with and could be used as a supplement for Gliner, Morgan, and Leech (2009), *Research Methods in Applied Settings: An Integrated Approach to Design and Analysis* (2nd ed.), which provides extended discussions of how to conduct a quantitative research project as well as understand the key concepts. Or, this SPSS book could be a supplement for Morgan, Gliner, and Harmon (2006), *Understanding and Evaluating Research in Applied and Clinical Settings*, which is a shorter book emphasizing reading and evaluating research articles and statistics. Information about both books can be found at www.psypress.com.

Because this book draws heavily on these two research methods texts and on earlier editions of this book, we need to acknowledge the important contribution of three current and former colleagues. We thank Jeff Gliner for allowing us to use material in Chapters 1, 3, and 6. Bob Harmon facilitated much of our effort to make statistics and research methods understandable to students, clinicians, and other professionals. We hope this book will serve as a memorial to him and the work he supported. Orlando Griego was a co-author of the first edition of this SPSS book; it still shows the imprint of his student-friendly writing style.

We would like to acknowledge the assistance of the many students who have used earlier versions of this book and provided helpful suggestions for improvement. We could not have completed the task or made it look so good without our technology consultant, Don Quick, and our word processor, Sonia Nelson. Linda White, Catherine Lamana, and Alana Stewart, Sophie Nelson and several other student workers were key to making figures in earlier versions. Jikyeong Kang, Bill Sears, LaVon Blaesi, Mei-Huei Tsay, and Sheridan Green assisted with classes and the development of materials for the DOS and earlier Windows versions of the assignments. Lisa Vogel, Don Quick, Andrea Weinberg, Pam Cress, Joan Clay, Laura Jensen, James Lyall, Joan Anderson, and Yasmine Andrews wrote or edited parts of earlier editions. We thank Don Quick for writing appendixes for this edition. Jeff Gliner, Jerry Vaske, Jim zumBrunnen, Laura Goodwin, James Benedict, Barry Cohen, John Ruscio, Tim Urdan, and Steve Knotek provided reviews and suggestions for improving the text. Bob Fetch and Ray Yang provided helpful feedback on the readability and user friendliness of the text. Finally, the patience of our spouses (Hildy, Grant, Susan, and Terry) and families enabled us to complete the task without too much family strain.

The screen shots of the many SPSS windows are reprinted by courtesy of International Business Machines Corporation, © SPSS, Inc., an IBM Company. SPSS was acquired by IBM in October 2009.

CHAPTER 1

Variables, Research Problems, and Questions

Research Problems

The research process begins with an issue or problem of interest to the researcher. This **research problem** is a statement that <u>asks about the relationships between two or more variables</u>; however, almost all research studies have *more* than two variables[1]. Appendix B provides templates to help you phrase your research problem, and provides examples from the expanded high school and beyond (HSB) data set that is described in this chapter and used throughout the book.

The process of moving from a sense of curiosity, or a feeling that there is an unresolved problem to a clearly defined, researchable problem, can be a complex and long one. That part of the research process is beyond the scope of this book, but it is discussed in most books about research methods and books about completing a dissertation or thesis.

Variables

Key elements in a research problem are the variables. A **variable** is defined as a characteristic of the participants or situation in a given study that has different values. A <u>variable must vary or have different values in the study</u>. For example, *gender* can be a variable because it has two values, *female* or *male*. *Age* is a variable that can have a large number of values. *Type of treatment/intervention* (or *type of curriculum*) is a variable if there is more than one treatment or a treatment and a control group. The number of days to learn something or to recover from an ailment are common measures of the effect of a treatment and, thus, are also potential variables. Similarly, *amount of mathematics knowledge* can be a variable because it can vary from none to a lot.

However, even if a characteristic has the potential to be a variable, if it has only one value in a particular study, it is not a variable; it is a constant. Thus, ethnic group is not a variable if all participants in the study are European American. Gender is not a variable if all participants in a study are female.

In quantitative research, variables are defined operationally and are commonly divided into **independent variables** (active or attribute), **dependent variables**, and **extraneous variables**. Each of these topics is dealt with briefly in the following sections.

Operational Definitions of Variables

An operational definition describes or <u>defines a variable in terms of the operations or techniques used to make it happen or measure it</u>. When quantitative researchers describe the variables in their study, they specify what they mean by demonstrating how they measured the variable.

---

[1] To help you we have identified the variable names, labels, and values using italics (e.g., *gender* and *male*) and have put in bold the terms used in the SPSS windows and outputs (e.g., **Data Editor**). We also use bold for other key terms when they are introduced, defined, or are important to understanding. Underlines are used to focus your attention on critical points or phrases that could be missed. Italics are occasionally used, as is commonly the case, for emphasizing words and for the titles of books.

Demographic variables like age, gender, or ethnic group are usually measured simply by asking the participant to choose the appropriate category from a list.

Types of treatment (or curriculum) are usually operationally defined much more extensively by describing what was done during the treatment or new curriculum. Likewise, abstract concepts like mathematics knowledge, self-concept, or mathematics anxiety need to be defined operationally by spelling out in some detail how they were measured in a particular study. To do this, the investigator may provide sample questions, append the actual instrument, or provide a reference where more information can be found.

Independent Variables

There are two types of independent variables, **active** and **attribute.** It is important to distinguish between these types when we discuss the results of a study. As presented in more detail later, an active independent variable is a necessary but not sufficient condition to make cause and effect conclusions.

Active or manipulated independent variables. An active independent variable is a variable, such as a workshop, new curriculum, or other intervention, at least one level of which <u>is given to a group of participants, within a specified period of time during the study</u>.

For example, a researcher might investigate a new kind of therapy compared to the traditional treatment. A second example might be to study the effect of a new teaching method, such as cooperative learning, compared to independent learning. In these two examples, the variable of interest is something that is *given to* the participants. Thus, active independent variables are *given* to the participants in the study but are not necessarily given or manipulated <u>by the experimenter</u>. They may be given by a clinic, school, or someone other than the investigator, but from the participants' point of view, the situation is manipulated. To be considered an active independent variable, the treatment should be given <u>after the study is planned</u> so that there could be a pretest. Other writers have similar but, perhaps, slightly different definitions of active independent variables. **Randomized experimental** and **quasi-experimental** studies have an active independent variable.

Attribute or measured independent variables. An independent variable that cannot be manipulated, yet is a major focus of the study, can be called an attribute independent variable. In other words, the values of the independent variable are <u>preexisting attributes of the persons or their ongoing environment</u> that are not systematically changed during the study. For example, level of parental education, socioeconomic status, gender, age, ethnic group, IQ, and self-esteem are attribute variables that could be used as attribute independent variables. Studies with only attribute independent variables are called **nonexperimental** studies.

Unlike authors of some research methods books, we do not restrict the term independent variable to those variables that are manipulated or active. We define an independent variable more broadly to include any predictors, antecedents, or *presumed* causes or influences under investigation in the study. Attributes of the participants as well as active independent variables fit within this definition. For the social sciences and education, attribute independent variables are especially important. Type of disability or level of disability may be the major focus of a study. Disability certainly qualifies as a variable because it can take on different values even though they are not *given* during the study. For example, cerebral palsy is different from Down syndrome, which is different from spina bifida, yet all are disabilities. Also, there are different levels of the same disability. People already have defining characteristics or attributes that place them into one of two or more categories. The different disabilities are characteristics of the participants before we begin our study. Thus, we might also be interested in studying how variables that are not given or manipulated during the study, even by other persons, schools, or clinics, predict various other variables that are of interest.

Other labels for the independent variable. SPSS uses a variety of terms, such as **factor** (Chapter 11) and **grouping variable** (Chapter 10), for the independent variables. In other cases, (Chapters 8 and 9) the program and statisticians do not make a distinction between the independent and dependent variable; they just label them **variables.** For example, technically there is no independent variable for a correlation or chi-square. Even for chi-square and correlation, we think it is sometimes conceptually useful to think of one variable as the predictor (independent variable) and the other as the outcome (dependent variable); however, it is important to realize that the statistical tests of correlation and chi-square treat both variables in the same way, rather than treating one as a predictor and one as an outcome variable, as is the case in regression.

Type of independent variable and inferences about cause and effect. When we analyze data from a research study, the statistical analysis does not differentiate whether the independent variable is an active independent variable or an attribute independent variable. However, even though most statistics books use the label independent variable for both active and attribute variables, there is a crucial difference in interpretation.

A major goal of scientific research is to be able to identify a causal relationship between two variables. For those in applied disciplines, the need to demonstrate that a given intervention or treatment causes a change in behavior or performance can be extremely important. Only the approaches that have an active independent variable (randomized experimental and, to a lesser extent, quasi-experimental) can provide data that allow one to infer that the independent variable caused the change or difference in the dependent variable.

In contrast, a significant difference between or among persons with different values of an attribute independent variable should *not* lead one to conclude that the attribute independent variable caused the dependent variable to change. Thus, this distinction between active and attribute independent variables is important because terms such as **main effect** and **effect size** used by the program and most statistics books might lead one to believe that if you find a significant difference, the independent variable *caused* the difference. These terms can be misleading when the independent variable is an attribute.

Although nonexperimental studies (those with attribute independent variables) are limited in what can be said about causation, they can lead to solid conclusions about the differences between groups and about associations between variables. Furthermore, if the focus of your research is on attribute independent variables, a nonexperimental study is the *only* available approach. For example, if you are interested in learning how boys and girls differ in learning mathematical concepts, you are interested in the attribute independent variable of gender.

Values of the independent variable. SPSS uses the term **values** to describe the several options or categories of a variable. These values are *not* necessarily ordered, and several other terms, **categories, levels, groups,** or **samples,** are sometimes used interchangeably with the term values, especially in statistics books. Suppose that an investigator is performing a study to investigate the effect of a treatment. One group of participants is assigned to the treatment group. A second group does not receive the treatment. The study could be conceptualized as having one independent variable (*treatment type)*, with two values or levels (*treatment* and *no treatment*). The independent variable in this example would be classified as an active independent variable. Now, suppose instead that the investigator was interested primarily in comparing two different treatments but decided to include a third no-treatment group as a control group in the study. The study would still be conceptualized as having one active independent variable (*treatment type*), but with three values or levels (the two treatment conditions and the control condition). This variable could be diagrammed as follows:

Variable Label	*Values*	*Value Labels*
	1	= Treatment 1
Treatment type	2	= Treatment 2
	0	= No treatment (control)

As an additional example, consider *gender*, which is an attribute independent variable with two values, *male* and *female*. It could be diagrammed as follows:

Variable Label	*Values*	*Value Labels*
	0	= Male
Gender		
	1	= Female

Note that in SPSS each variable is given a **variable label;** moreover, the values, which are often categories, have **value labels** (e.g., male and female). Each value or level is assigned a number used to compute statistics. It is especially important to know the value labels when the variable is **nominal**, that is, when the values of the variable are just names and thus are not ordered.

Dependent Variables

The **dependent variable** is assumed to <u>measure or assess the effect of the independent variable</u>. It is thought of as the <u>presumed outcome or criterion</u>. Dependent variables are often test scores, ratings on questionnaires, readings from instruments (e.g., electrocardiogram, galvanic skin response, etc.), or measures of physical performance. When we discuss measurement in Chapters 2 and 3, we are usually referring to the dependent variable. Dependent variables, like independent variables, must have at least two values; most of the dependent variables used in this book have <u>many values, varying from low to high</u> so they are not as easy to diagram as the independent variables shown earlier.

SPSS also uses a number of other terms for the dependent variable. **Dependent list** is used in cases where you can do the same statistic several times for a list of dependent variables (e.g., in Chapter 11 with one-way ANOVA). The term **test variable** is used in Chapter 10 for the dependent variable in a *t* test.

Extraneous Variables

These are variables (also called nuisance variables or, in some designs, covariates) that are <u>not of interest in a particular study but could influence the dependent variable</u>. Environmental factors (e.g., temperature or distractions), time of day, and characteristics of the experimenter, teacher, or therapist are some possible extraneous variables that need to be controlled. SPSS does not use the term extraneous variable. However, sometimes such variables are "controlled" using statistics that are available in this program.

Research Hypotheses and Questions

Research hypotheses are predictive statements about the relationship between variables. **Research questions** are similar to hypotheses, except that they do not entail specific predictions and are phrased in question format. For example, one might have the following research question: "Is there a difference in students' scores on a standardized test if they took two tests in one day versus taking only one test on each of two days?" A hypothesis regarding the same issue might be: "Students who take only one test per day will score *higher* on standardized tests than will students who take two tests in one day."

We divide research questions into three broad types: difference, associational, and descriptive, as shown in the middle of Fig. 1.1. The figure also shows the general and specific purposes and the general types of statistics for each of these three types of research question. We think it is educationally useful to divide inferential statistics into two types corresponding to difference and associational hypotheses or questions.[2] Difference inferential statistics (e.g., *t* test or analysis of variance) are <u>used for approaches that test for differences between groups</u>. Associational inferential statistics <u>test for associations or relationships between variables</u> and use, for example, correlation or multiple regression analysis. We utilize this contrast between difference and associational inferential statistics in Chapter 6 and later in this book.

Difference research questions. For these questions, we compare two or more different groups, each of which is composed of individuals with one of the values or levels of the independent variable. This type of question attempts to demonstrate that the <u>groups are not the same on the dependent variable</u>.

Associational research questions. Here we associate or relate two or more variables. This approach usually involves an attempt to see how two or more variables covary (For example, if a person has higher values on one variable, is he or she also likely to have higher, or perhaps lower, values on another variable). An associational question could instead ask how one or more variables enable one to predict another variable.

---

[2] We realize that all parametric inferential statistics are relational so this dichotomy of using one type of data analysis procedure to test for differences (when there are a few values or levels of the independent variables) and another type of data analysis procedure to test for associations (when there are continuous independent variables) is somewhat artificial. Both continuous and categorical independent variables can be used in a general linear model approach to data analysis. However, we think that the distinction is useful because most researchers utilize the dichotomy in selecting statistics for data analysis.

Descriptive research questions. These are not answered with inferential statistics. They merely describe or summarize data for the sample actually studied, without trying to generalize to a larger population of individuals.

Fig. 1.1 shows that <u>both difference and associational questions</u> or hypotheses <u>explore the relationships between variables</u>; however, they are conceptualized differently, as will be described shortly.[3] Note that difference and associational questions differ in specific purpose and the kinds of statistics they use to answer the question.

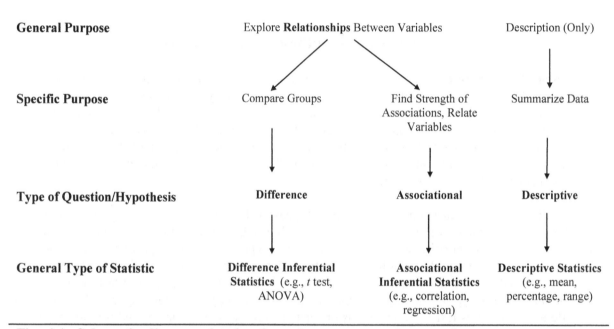

Fig. 1.1. Schematic diagram showing how the purpose and type of research question correspond to the general type of statistic used in a study.

Table 1.1 provides the general format and one example of a basic difference question, a basic associational question, and a basic descriptive question. Remember that research questions are similar to hypotheses, but they are stated in question format. We think it is advisable to use the question format for the descriptive approach or when one does not have a clear directional prediction. Use the hypothesis format when you have a specific prediction based on the literature or theory. More details and examples are given in Appendix B. As implied by Fig. 1.1, it is <u>acceptable to phrase any research question that involves two variables as whether or not there is a relationship between the variables</u> (e.g., is there a relationship between *gender* and *math achievement* or is there a relationship between *anxiety* and *GPA*?). However, we think that phrasing the question as a difference or association is preferable because it helps one identify an appropriate statistic and interpret the result.

---

[3] This similarity is in agreement with the statement by statisticians that all common parametric inferential statistics are relational. We use the term associational for the second type of research question rather than relational or correlational to distinguish it from the *general purpose* of both difference and associational questions/hypotheses, which is to study relationships. Also we want to distinguish between correlation, as a specific statistical technique, and the broader type of associational question and that group of statistics.

Complex Research Questions

Some research questions involve more than two variables at a time. We call such questions and the appropriate statistics **complex**. Some of these statistics are called **multivariate** in other texts, but there is not a consistent definition of multivariate in the literature. We provide examples of how to write certain complex research questions in Appendix B, and in Chapters 9 and 11, we introduce two complex statistics: multiple regression and factorial ANOVA. Complex statistics are discussed in more detail in our companion volume, Leech et al. (2011).

Table 1.1. *Examples of Three Kinds of Basic Research Questions/Hypotheses*

1. *Basic Difference (group comparison) Questions*
   - Usually used for randomized experimental, quasi-experimental, and comparative approaches.
   - For this type of question, the groups of individuals who share a level of an active independent variable (e.g., intervention group) or an attribute independent variable (e.g., male gender) are compared to individuals who share the other levels of that same independent variable (e.g., control group or female gender) to see if the groups differ with regard to the average scores on the dependent variable (e.g., aggression scores).
   - Example: Do persons who experienced an emotion regulation intervention differ from those who did not experience that intervention with respect to their average aggression scores? In other words, will the average aggression score of the intervention group be significantly different from the average aggression score for the control group following the intervention?

2. *Basic Associational (relational) Questions*
   - Used for the associational approach, in which the independent variable usually is continuous (i.e., has many ordered levels).
   - For this type of question, the scores on the independent variable (e.g., anxiety) are associated with or related to the dependent variable scores (e.g., GPA).
   - Example: Will students' degree of anxiety be associated with their overall GPA? In other words, will knowing students' level of anxiety tell us anything about their tendency to make higher versus lower grades? If there is a *negative* association (correlation) between anxiety scores and grade point average, those persons who have high levels of anxiety will tend to have low GPAs, those with low anxiety will tend to have high GPAs, and those in the middle on anxiety will tend to be in the middle on GPA.

3. *Basic Descriptive Questions*
   - Used for the descriptive approach.
   - For this type of question, scores on a single variable are described in terms of their central tendency, variability, or percentages in each category/level.
   - Example: What percentage of students make a B or above? What is the average level of anxiety found in 9th grade students? The average GPA was 2.73, or 30% had high anxiety.

A Sample Research Problem:
The Modified High School and Beyond (HSB) Study

The file name of the data set used throughout this book is hsbdata.sav; it stands for high school and beyond data, and can be found at http://www.psypress.com/ibm-spss-intro-stats. It is based on a national sample of data from more than 28,000 high school students. The current data set is a sample of 75 students drawn randomly from the larger sample. The data that we have for this sample include school outcomes such as grades and the mathematics achievement test scores of the students in high school. Also, there are several kinds of standardized test data and demographic data such as gender and mother's and father's education. To provide an example of rating scale questionnaire data, we have included 14 items about mathematics attitudes. These data were developed for this book and thus are not really the math attitudes of the 75 students in this sample; however, they are based on real data gathered by one of the authors to study motivation. Also, we made up data for religion, ethnic group, and SAT-math, which are somewhat realistic overall. These inclusions enable us to do some additional statistical analyses.

The Research Problem

Imagine that you are interested in the general problem of <u>what factors seem to influence mathematics achievement</u> at the end of high school. You might have some hunches or hypotheses about such factors based on your experience and your reading of the research and popular literature. Some factors that might influence *mathematics achievement* are commonly called demographics; they include *gender, ethnic group,* and *mother's* and *father's education.* A probable influence would be the math courses that the student has taken. We might speculate that *grades in math* and in other subjects could have an impact on *math achievement.*[4] However, other variables, such as *students' IQs* or *parents' encouragement,* could be the actual causes of both high grades and math achievement. Such variables could influence what courses one took and the grades one received, and they might be correlates of the demographic variables. We might wonder how spatial performance scores, such as pattern or *mosaic test scores* and *visualization scores,* might enable a more complete understanding of the problem, and whether these skills seem to be influenced by the same factors as is *math achievement.*

The HSB Variables[5]

Before we state the research problem and questions in more formal ways, we need to step back and discuss the types of variables and the approaches that might be used to study the previous problem. We need to identify the independent/antecedent (presumed causes) variables, the dependent/outcome variable(s), and any extraneous variables.

The primary dependent variable. Because the research problem focuses on achievement tests at the end of the senior year, the primary dependent variable (or **Target**) is *math achievement.*

Independent and extraneous variables. *Father's* and *mother's education* and participant's *gender, ethnicity* and *religion,* are best considered to be **input** (the SPSS term), antecedent, or independent variables in this study. These variables would usually be thought of as independent

---

[4] We have decided to use the short version of mathematics (i.e., math) throughout the book to save space and because it is used in common language.

[5] New to version 18 of the program was the **Role** column in the **Variable View.** SPSS 20 allows the user to assign the term **Target** to dependent variables, **Input** for independent variables, and **Both** for variables that are used as either or both independent and dependent variables.

rather than as dependent variables because they occurred before the math achievement test and don't vary during the study. However, some of these variables, such as ethnicity and religion, might be viewed as extraneous variables that need to be "controlled."

Many of the variables, including *visualization* and *mosaic pattern scores*, could be viewed *either* as independent or dependent variables depending on the specific research question because they were measured at approximately the same time as math achievement. We have labeled them **Both** under **Role**. Note that student's class is a constant and is not a variable in this study because all the participants are high school seniors (i.e., it does not vary; it is the population of interest).

Types of independent variables. As we previously discussed, independent variables can be **active** (given to the participant during the study or manipulated by the investigator) or **attributes** of the participants or their environments. Are there any **active** independent variables in this study? No! There is no intervention, new curriculum, or similar treatment. All the independent variables, then, are attribute variables because they are attributes or characteristics of these high school students. Given that all the independent variables are attributes, the research approach cannot be experimental. This means that we will *not* be able to draw definite conclusions about cause and effect (i.e., we will find out what is related to math achievement, but we will not know for sure what causes or influences math achievement).

Now we examine the *hsbdata.sav* file that you will use to study this complex research problem. We have provided on the Web site described in the Preface these data for each of the 75 participants on 38 variables. The variables in the *hsbdata.sav* file have already been labeled (see Fig. 1.2) and entered (see Fig. 1.3) to enable you to get started on analyses quickly. This file contains data files for you to use, but it does not include the actual SPSS Statistics program to which you will need access in order to do the problems.

The Variable View

Figure 1.2 is a piece of what is called the **Variable View** in the **Data Editor** for the *hsbdata.sav* file. Figure 1.2 shows information about each of the first 17 variables. When you open this file and click on **Variable View** at the bottom left corner of the screen, this is what you will see. We describe what is in the variable view screen in more detail in Chapter 2; for now, focus on the Name, Label, Values, and Missing columns. **Name** is a short name for each variable (e.g., *faed* or *alg1*).[6] **Label** is a longer label for the variable (e.g., *father's education* or *algebra 1 in h.s.*). The **Values** column contains the **value labels,** but you can see only the label for one value at a time (e.g., 0 = male). That is, you cannot see that 1 = female unless you click on the gray square in the value column. The **Missing** column indicates whether there are any special, user-identified missing values. **None** just means that there are no special missing values, just the usual **system missing** value, which is a blank. Appendix A shows how to get this data.

Variables in the Modified HSB Data Set

The 39 variables shown in Table 1.2 (with the values/levels or range of their values in parentheses) are found in the *hsbdata.sav* file. Also included in Table 1.2, for completeness, are seven variables (numbers 40–46) that are not yet in the *hsbdata.sav* data set because you will

---

[6] The variable **Name** must start with a letter and must not contain blank spaces or certain special characters (e.g., !, ?, ', or *). Certain reserved keywords cannot be used as variable names (e.g., ALL, AND, EQ, BY, TO, or WITH). The variable **label** can be up to 40 characters including spaces, but the outputs are neater if you keep labels to 20 characters or less.

compute them in Chapter 5. Note that variables 34–39 have been computed already from the math attitude variables (19–32) so that you would have fewer new variables to compute in Chapter 5.

The variables of *ethnic* and *religion* were added to the data set to provide true nominal (unordered) variables with a few (4 and 3) levels or values. In addition, for *ethnic* and *religion*, we have made two missing value codes to illustrate this possibility. All other variables use blanks, the system missing value, for missing data.

	Name	Type	Width	Decimals	Label	Values	Missing	Columns	Align	Measure	Role
File Edit View Data Transform Analyze Direct Marketing Graphs Utilities Add-ons Window Help
1	gender	Numeric	1	0	gender	{0, male}...	None	6	Right	Nominal	Input
2	faed	Numeric	2	0	father's education	{2, < h.s. gr...	None	6	Right	Ordinal	Input
3	maed	Numeric	2	0	mother's educa...	{2, < h.s.}...	None	6	Right	Ordinal	Input
4	alg1	Numeric	1	0	algebra 1 in h.s.	{0, not take...	None	6	Right	Nominal	Both
5	alg2	Numeric	1	0	algebra 2 in h.s.	{0, not take...	None	6	Right	Nominal	Both
6	geo	Numeric	1	0	geometry in h.s.	{0, not take...	None	6	Right	Nominal	Both
7	trig	Numeric	1	0	trigonometry in ...	{0, not take...	None	5	Right	Nominal	Both
8	calc	Numeric	1	0	calculus in h.s.	{0, not take...	None	5	Right	Nominal	Both
9	mathgr	Numeric	1	0	math grades	{0, less A-B...	None	6	Right	Nominal	Both
10	grades	Numeric	1	0	grades in h.s.	{1, less tha...	None	6	Right	Ordinal	Both
11	mathach	Numeric	4	2	math achievem...	{-8.33, low}...	None	6	Right	Scale	Target
12	mosaic	Numeric	3	1	mosaic, pattern...	{-4.0, Low}...	None	6	Right	Scale	Both
13	visual	Numeric	4	2	visualization test	{-4.00, low}...	None	6	Right	Scale	Both
14	visual2	Numeric	4	2	visualization 2	{.00, Lowest...	None	6	Right	Scale	Both
15	satm	Numeric	3	0	scholastic aptit...	{200, minm...	None	5	Right	Scale	Both
16	ethnic	Numeric	2	0	ethnicity	{1, Euro-Am...	98, 99	6	Right	Nominal	Input
17	religion	Numeric	2	0	religion	{1, protesta...	98, 99	6	Right	Nominal	Input

Fig. 1.2. Part of the hsbdata.sav variable view in the data editor.

For *ethnicity*, 98 indicates multiethnic and other. For *religion*, all the high school students who were not *protestant* or *catholic* or said they were *not religious* were coded 98 and considered to be missing because none of the other religious affiliations (e.g., Muslim) had enough members to make a reasonable size group. Those who left the ethnicity or religion questions blank were coded as 99, also missing.

Table 1.2. *HSB Variable Descriptions*

Name	Label (and Values)

Demographic School and Test Variables

1.	gender	*gender* (0 = male, 1 = female).
2.	faed	*father's education* (2 = less than h.s. grad to 10 = PhD/MD)
3.	maed	*mother's education* (2 = less than h.s. grad to 10 = PhD/MD)
4.	alg1	*algebra 1 in h.s.* (1 = taken, 0 = not taken)
5.	alg2	*algebra 2 in h.s.* (1 = taken, 0 = not taken)
6.	geo	*geometry in h.s.* (1 = taken, 0 = not taken)
7.	trig	*trigonometry in h.s.* (1 = taken, 0 = not taken)
8.	calc	*calculus in h.s.* (1 = taken, 0 = not taken)
9.	mathgr	*math grades* (0 = low, 1 = high)
10.	grades	*grades in h.s.* (1 = less than a D average to 8 = mostly an A average)

11.	mathach	*math achievement score* (-8.33 to 25).[7] This is a test something like the ACT math.
12.	mosaic	*mosaic, pattern test score* (-4 to 56). This is a test of pattern recognition ability involving the detection of relationships in patterns of tiles.
13.	visual	*visualization score* (-4 to 16). This is a 16-item test that assesses visualization in three dimensions (i.e., how a three-dimensional object would look if its spatial position were changed).
14.	visual2	*visualization 2* The visualization test rated by a second researcher who observed the same test.
15.	satm	*scholastic aptitude test – math* (200 = lowest, 800 = highest possible)
16.	ethnic	*ethnicity* (1 = Euro-American, 2 = African-American, 3 = Latino-American, 4 = Asian-American, 98 = other or multiethnic, 99 = missing, left blank)
17.	religion	*religion* (1 = protestant, 2 = catholic, 3 = not religious, 98 = chose one of several other religious affiliations, 99 = left blank)
18.	ethnic2	*ethnicity reported by student* (same as values for ethnic)

Math Attitude Questions 1 – 14 (Rated from 1 = very atypical to 4 = very typical)

19.	item01	*Motivation* "I practice math skills until I can do them well."
20.	item02	*Pleasure* "I feel happy after solving a hard problem."
21.	item03	*Competence* "I solve math problems quickly."
22.	item04	*(low) motiv* "I give up easily instead of persisting if a math problem is difficult."
23.	item05	*(low) comp* "I am a little slow catching on to new topics in math."
24.	item06	*(low) pleas* "I do not get much pleasure out of math problems."
25.	item07	*Motivation* "I prefer to figure out how to solve problems without asking for help."
26.	item08	*(low) motiv* "I do not keep at it very long when a math problem is challenging."
27.	item09	*Competence* "I am very competent at math."
28.	item10	*(low) pleas* "I smile only a little (or not at all) when I solve a math problem."
29.	item11	*(low) comp* "I have some difficulties doing math as well as other kids my age."
30.	item12	*Motivation* "I try to complete my math problems even if it takes a long time to finish."
31.	item13	*Motivation* "I explore all possible solutions of a complex problem before going on to another one."
32.	item14	*Pleasure* "I really enjoy doing math problems."
33.	mosaic2	*Mosaic pattern test 2.* The score rated by a second researcher who observed the same test.

New Variables Computed From the Previous Variables

34.	item04r	*item04 reversed* (4 now = high motivation)
35.	item05r	*item05 reversed* (4 now = high competence)
36.	item08r	*item08 reversed* (4 now = high motivation)
37.	item11r	*item11 reversed* (4 now = high competence)
38.	competence	*competence scale.* An average computed as follows: (item03 + item05r + item09 + item11r)/4
39.	motivation	*motivation scale* (item01 + item04r + item07 + item08r + item12 + item13)/6

---

[7] Negative test scores may result from a penalty for guessing.

Variables to be Computed in Chapter 5

40.	mathcrs	*math courses taken* (0 = none, 5 = all five)
41.	faedRevis	*father's educ revised* (1 = HS grad or less, 2 = some college, 3 = BS or more)
42.	maedRevis	*mother's educ revised* (1 = HS grad or less, 2 = some college, 3 = BS or more)
43.	item06r	*item06 reversed* (4 now = high pleasure)
44.	item10r	*item10 reversed* (4 now = high pleasure)
45.	pleasure	*pleasure scale* (item02 + item06r + item 10r + item14)/4
46.	parEduc	*parents' education* (average of the <u>unrevised</u> mother's and father's educations)

The Raw HSB Data and Data Editor

Figure 1.3 is a piece of the *hsbdata.sav* file showing raw data for the first 17 student participants for variables 1 through 17 (gender through religion). When you open this file and click on **Data View** at the bottom left corner of the screen, this is what you will see. Notice the short variable names (e.g., *gend, faed,* etc.) at the top of the hsbdata file. Be aware that the participants are listed down the left side of the page, and the variables are listed across the top. For all the statistics in this book, <u>you will always enter data this way</u>. If a variable is measured more than once, such as *visual* and *visual 2* (see Fig. 1.3), it will be entered as two variables with slightly different names.

NOTE.[8]

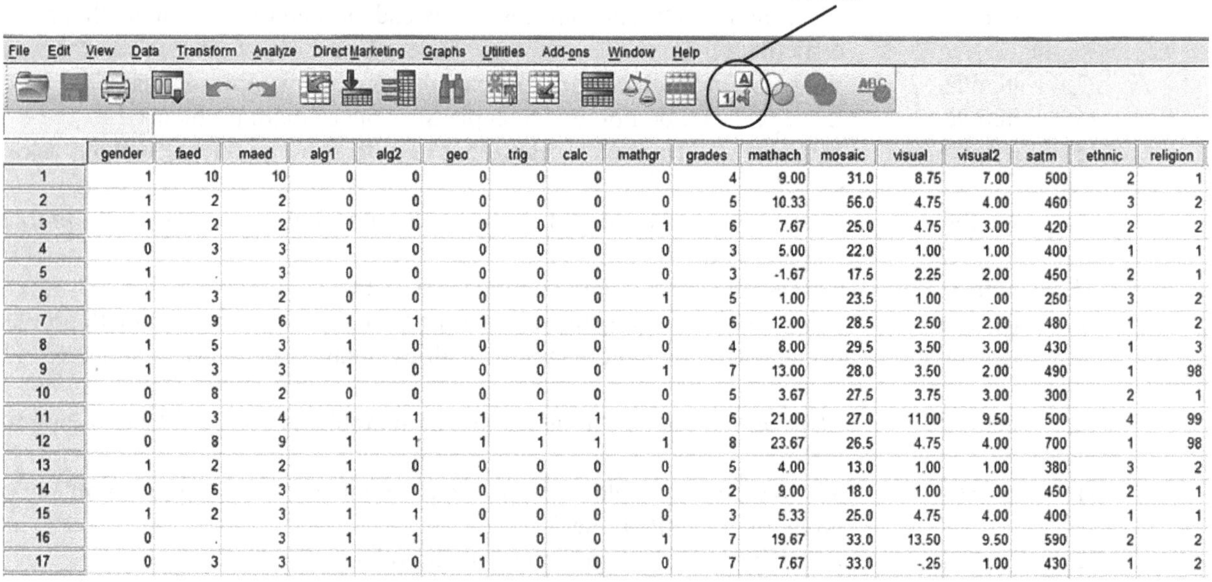

File   Edit   View   Data   Transform   Analyze   Direct Marketing   Graphs   Utilities   Add-ons   Window   Help

	gender	faed	maed	alg1	alg2	geo	trig	calc	mathgr	grades	mathach	mosaic	visual	visual2	satm	ethnic	religion
1	1	10	10	0	0	0	0	0	0	4	9.00	31.0	8.75	7.00	500	2	1
2	1	2	2	0	0	0	0	0	0	5	10.33	56.0	4.75	4.00	460	3	2
3	1	2	2	0	0	0	0	0	1	6	7.67	25.0	4.75	3.00	420	2	2
4	0	3	3	1	0	0	0	0	0	3	5.00	22.0	1.00	1.00	400	1	1
5	1		3	0	0	0	0	0	0	3	-1.67	17.5	2.25	2.00	450	2	1
6	1	3	2	0	0	0	0	0	1	5	1.00	23.5	1.00	.00	250	3	2
7	0	9	6	1	1	1	0	0	0	6	12.00	28.5	2.50	2.00	480	1	2
8	1	5	3	1	0	0	0	0	0	4	8.00	29.5	3.50	3.00	430	1	3
9	1	3	3	1	0	0	0	0	1	7	13.00	28.0	3.50	2.00	490	1	98
10	0	8	2	0	0	0	0	0	0	5	3.67	27.5	3.75	3.00	300	2	1
11	0	3	4	1	1	1	1	1	0	6	21.00	27.0	11.00	9.50	500	4	99
12	0	8	9	1	1	1	1	1	1	8	23.67	26.5	4.75	4.00	700	1	98
13	1	2	2	1	0	0	0	0	0	5	4.00	13.0	1.00	1.00	380	3	2
14	0	6	3	1	0	0	0	0	0	2	9.00	18.0	1.00	.00	450	2	1
15	1	2	3	1	1	0	0	0	0	3	5.33	25.0	4.75	4.00	400	1	1
16	0		3	1	1	1	0	0	1	7	19.67	33.0	13.50	9.50	590	2	2
17	0	3	3	1	0	1	0	0	0	7	7.67	33.0	-.25	1.00	430	1	2

Fig. 1.3. Part of the hsbdata data view in the data editor.

Note that in Fig. 1.3, most of the values are single digits, but *mathach, mosaic,* and *visual* include some decimals and even negative numbers. Notice also that some cells, like *father's education* for participant 5, are blank because a datum is missing. Perhaps Participant 5 did not know her father's education. Blank is the system missing value that can be used for any missing data in a SPSS data file. We suggest that you leave missing data blank unless there is some reason you need to distinguish among types of or reasons for missing data (see *religion* for subjects 9, 11, and 12 and the description of what 98 and 99 mean in Table 1.2).

---

[8] If the values for *gender* are shown as *female* or *male*, the **value labels** rather than the numerals are being displayed. In that case, click on the circled symbol to change the format to show only the numeric values for each variable.

Research Questions for the Modified HSB Study[9]

In this book, we generate a large number of research questions from the modified HSB data set. In this section, we list some research questions, which the HSB data will help answer, in order to give you an idea of the range of types of questions that one might have in a typical research project like a thesis or dissertation. In addition to the **difference** and **associational questions** that are commonly seen in a research article, we have asked **descriptive questions** and questions about assumptions in the early assignments. Templates for writing the research problem and research questions or hypotheses are given in Appendix B, which should help you write questions for your own research.

1. Often, we start with basic **descriptive questions** about the demographics of the sample. Thus, we could answer, with the results in Chapter 4, the following basic descriptive question: "What is the average educational level of the fathers of the students in this sample?" "What percentage of the students is male and what percentage is female?"

2. In the assignment for Chapter 4, we also examine whether the continuous variables (those that might be used to answer associational questions) are distributed normally, an **assumption** of many statistics. One question is "Are the frequency distributions of the math achievement scores markedly skewed, that is, different from the normal curve distribution?"

3. Chapter 7 presents several statistics that are frequently used to check the data for reliability and validity and to reduce a large number of variables, such as the math attitude questions, to a smaller, more manageable number of composite variables. One usually wouldn't formally state research questions about reliability and validity in a research article. However, this chapter could help you answer questions such as "Are the codes for ethnicity from the school records and the students similar; i.e., reliable?"

4. Tables cross-tabulating two categorical variables (ones with a few values or categories) are computed in Chapter 8. Cross-tabulation and the chi-square statistic can answer research questions such as "Is there a relationship between gender and math grades (high or low)?"

5. In Chapter 9, we answer **basic associational research questions** (using Pearson product-moment correlation coefficients) such as "Is there a positive association/relationship between grades in high school and math achievement?" This assignment also produces a correlation matrix of all the correlations among several key variables, including math achievement. Similar matrixes will provide the basis for computing multiple regression. In Chapter 7, correlation is also used to assess reliability.

6. Chapter 9 also poses a **complex associational question** such as "How well does a combination of variables predict math achievement?" in order to introduce you to multiple regression.

---

[9] The High School and Beyond (HSB) study was conducted by the National Opinion Research Center. The example discussed here and throughout the book is based on 13 variables obtained from a random sample of 75 out of 28,240 high school seniors. These variables include achievement scores, grades, and demographics. The raw data for the 13 variables were slightly modified from published HSB data. That file had no missing data, which is unusual in behavioral science research.

7. Several basic **difference questions**, utilizing an independent samples *t* test, are asked in Chapter 10. For example, "Do males and females differ on math achievement?" Basic difference questions in which the independent variable has three or more values are asked in Chapter 11. For example, "Are there differences among the three fathers' education groups in regard to average scores on math achievement?" An answer is based on a one-way or single factor analysis of variance (ANOVA).

8. **Complex difference questions** are also asked in Chapter 11. One *set* of three questions is as follows: (1) "Is there a difference between students who have fathers with no college, some college, or a BS or more with respect to the student's math achievement?" (2) "Is there a difference between students who had a B or better math grade average and those with less than a B average on a math achievement test at the end of high school?" and (3) "Is there an interaction between a father's education and math grades with respect to math achievement?" Answers to this set of three questions are based on factorial ANOVA, introduced briefly in Chapter 11.

This introduction to the research problem and questions raised by the HSB data set should help make the assignments meaningful, and it should provide a guide and some examples for your own research.

Interpretation Questions

1.1   Compare the terms *active independent variable* and *attribute independent variable*. What are the similarities and differences?

1.2   What kind of independent variable (active or attribute) is necessary to infer cause? Can one *always* infer cause from this type of independent variable? If so, why? If not, when can one infer cause and when might causal inferences be more questionable?

1.3   What is the difference between the independent variable and the dependent variable?

1.4   Compare and contrast associational, difference, and descriptive types of research questions.

1.5   Write a research question *and* a corresponding hypothesis regarding variables of interest to you but not in the HSB data set. Is it an associational, difference, or descriptive question?

1.6   Using one or more of the following HSB variables, *religion, mosaic pattern test,* and *visualization score:*
(a) Write an associational question.
(b) Write a difference question.
(c) Write a descriptive question.

CHAPTER 2
Data Coding, Entry, and Checking

This chapter begins with a very brief overview of the initial steps in a research project. After this introduction, the chapter focuses on: (a) getting your data ready to enter into the data editor or a spreadsheet, (b) defining and labeling variables, (c) entering the data appropriately, and (d) checking to be sure that data entry was done correctly without errors.

Plan the Study, Pilot Test, and Collect Data

Plan the study. As discussed in Chapter 1, the research starts with identification of a research problem and research questions or hypotheses. It is also necessary to plan the research design before you select the data collection instrument(s) and begin to collect data. Most research methods books discuss this part of the research process extensively (e.g., see Gliner, Morgan, & Leech, 2009).

Select or develop the instrument(s). If there is an appropriate, available instrument that provides reliable and valid data and it has been used with a population similar to yours, it is usually desirable to use it. However, sometimes it is necessary to modify an existing instrument or develop your own. For this chapter, we have developed a short questionnaire to be given to students at the end of a course. Remember that questionnaires or surveys are only one way to collect quantitative data. You could also use structured interviews, observations, tests, standardized inventories, or some other type of data collection method. Research methods and measurement books have one or more chapters devoted to the selection and development of data collection instruments. A useful book on the development of questionnaires is Fink (2009).

Pilot test and refine instruments. It is always desirable to try out your instrument and directions with, at the very least, a few colleagues or friends. When possible, you also should conduct a **pilot study** with a sample similar to the one you plan to use later. This is especially important if you developed the instrument or if it is going to be used with a population different from the one(s) for which it was developed and on which it was previously used.

Pilot participants should be asked about the clarity of the items and whether they think any items should be added or deleted. Then, use the feedback to make modifications in the instrument before beginning the actual data collection. If the instrument is changed, the pilot data should not be added to the data collected for the study. **Content validity** can also be checked by asking experts to judge whether your items cover all aspects of the domain you intended to measure and whether they are in appropriate proportions relative to that domain.

Collect the data. The next step in the research process is to collect the data. There are several ways to collect questionnaire or survey data (such as telephone, mail, or e-mail). We do not discuss them here because that is not the purpose of this book. The Fink (2009) book, *How to Conduct Surveys: A Step by Step Guide*, provides information on the various methods for collecting survey data.

You should <u>check your raw data</u> after you collect it even <u>before it is entered</u> into the computer. Make sure that the participants marked their score sheets or questionnaires appropriately; check to see if there are double answers to a question (when only one is expected) or answers that are marked between two rating points. If this happens, you need to have a rule (e.g., "use the average") that you can apply consistently. Thus, you should "clean up" your data, making sure they are clear, consistent, and readable, before entering them into a data file.

Let's assume that the completed questionnaires shown in Figs. 2.1 and 2.2 were given to a small class of 12 students and that they filled them out and turned them in at the end of the class. The researcher numbered the forms from 1 to 12, as shown opposite ID.

After the questionnaires were turned in and numbered (i.e., given an ID number in the top right corner), the researcher was ready to begin the coding process, which we describe in the next section.

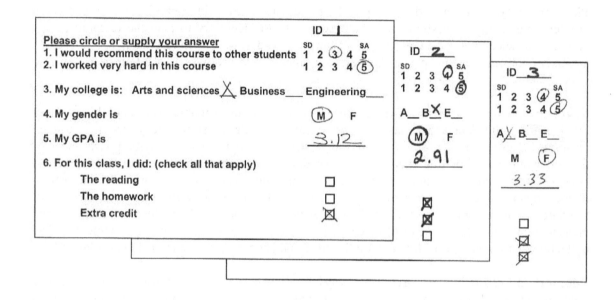

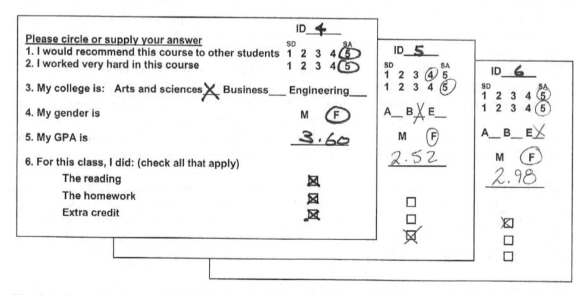

Fig. 2.1. Completed questionnaires for participants 1 through 6.

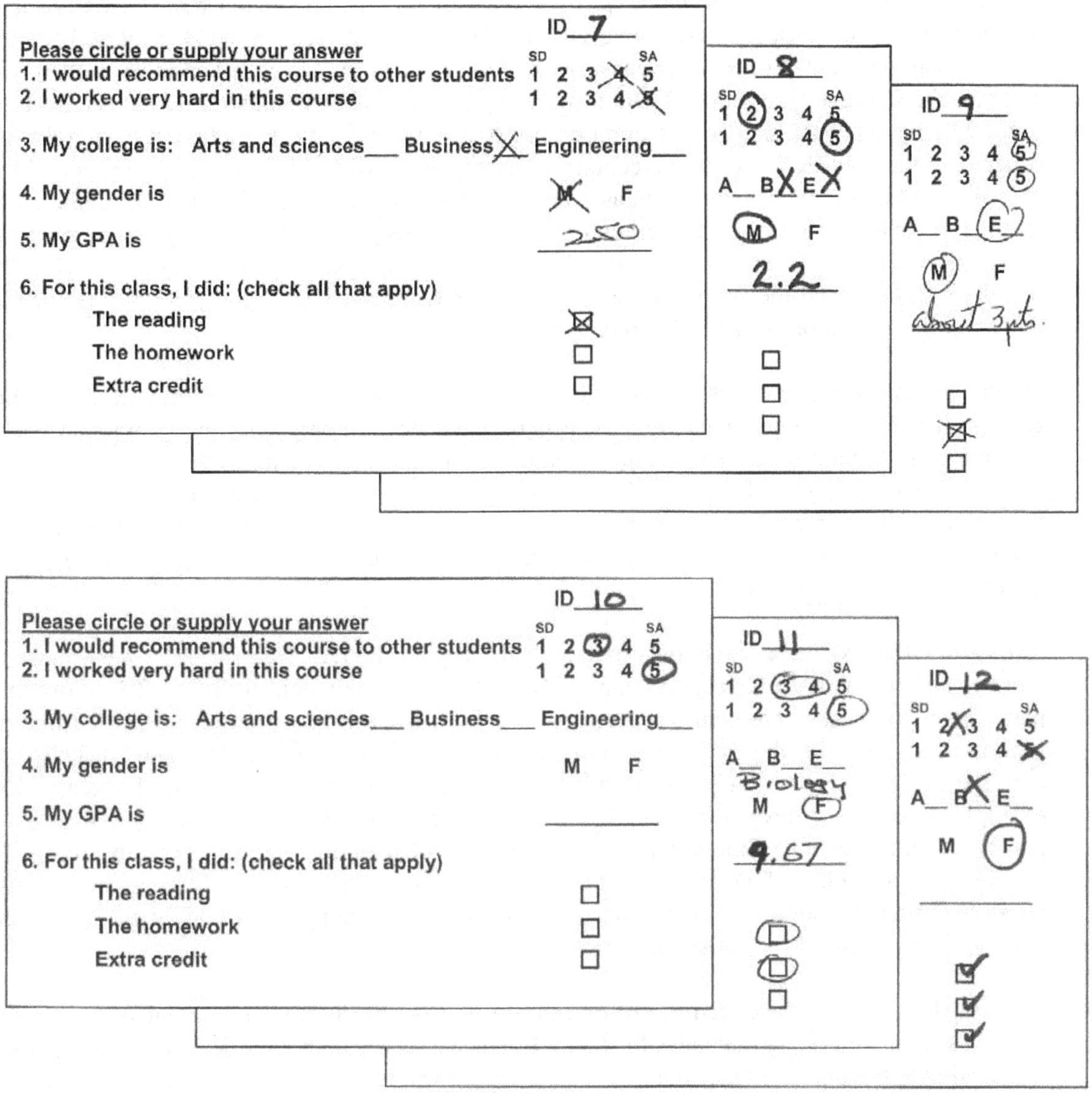

Fig. 2.2. Completed questionnaires for participants 7 through 12.

Code Data for Data Entry

Guidelines for Data Coding

Coding is the process of assigning numbers to the values or levels of each variable. Before starting the coding process, we want to present some broad suggestions or rules to keep in mind as you proceed. These suggestions are adapted from rules proposed in Newton and Rudestam's (1999) useful book entitled *Your Statistical Consultant*. We believe that our suggestions are appropriate, but some researchers might propose alternatives, especially for guidelines 1, 2, 4, 5, and 7.

1. **All data should be numeric.** Even though it is possible to use letters or words (string variables) as data, it is not desirable when using SPSS to do so. For example, we could code gender as M for male and F for female, but in order to do most statistics you would have to

convert the letters or words to numbers. It is easier to do this conversion before entering the data into the computer as we have done with the HSB data set (see Fig. 1.3). You will see in Fig. 2.3 that we decided to code females as 1 and males as 0. This is called **dummy coding**. In essence, the 0 means "not female." Dummy coding is useful if you will want to use the data in some types of analyses and for obtaining descriptive statistics. For example, the mean of data coded this way will tell you the percentage of participants who fall in the category coded as "1." We could, of course, code males as 1 and females as 0, or we could code one gender as 1 and the other as 2. However, it is crucial that you <u>be consistent in your coding</u> (e.g., for this study, all males are coded 0 and females 1) and that you have a way to remind yourself and others of how you did the coding. Later in this chapter, we show how you can provide such a record, called a **codebook** or **dictionary**.

2. **Each variable for each case or participant must occupy the same column in the Data Editor.** It is important that data from <u>each participant occupy only one line (row)</u>, and each column must contain data on the same variable for all the participants. The data editor, into which you will enter data, facilitates this by putting the short variable names that you choose at the top of each column, as you saw in Chapter 1, Fig. 1.3. If a variable is measured more than once (e.g., pretest and posttest), it will be entered in two columns with somewhat different names, such as *mathpre* and *mathpost*.[1]

3. **All values (codes) for a variable must be mutually exclusive.** That is, only one value or number can be recorded for each variable. Some items, like our item 6 in Fig. 2.3, allow for participants to check more than one response. In that case, the item should be divided into a separate variable for each possible response choice, with one value of each variable (usually 1) corresponding to yes (i.e., checked) and the other to no (usually 0, for not checked). For example, item 6 becomes variables 6, 7, and 8 (see Fig. 2.3). Items should be phrased so that persons would logically choose only one of the provided options, and all possible options should be provided. A final category labeled "other" may be provided in cases where all possible options cannot be listed, but these "other" responses are usually quite diverse and thus may not be very useful for statistical purposes.

4. **Each variable should be coded to obtain maximum information.** Do not collapse categories or values when you set up the codes for them. If needed, let the computer do it later. In general, it is desirable to code and enter data in as detailed a form as available. Thus, enter actual test scores, ages, GPAs, and so forth, if you know them. It is good practice to ask participants to provide information that is quite specific. However, you should be careful not to ask questions that are so specific that the respondent may not know the answer or may not feel comfortable providing it. For example, you will obtain more information by asking participants to state their GPA to two decimals (as in Figs. 2.1 and 2.2) than if you asked them to select from a few broad categories (e.g., less than 2.0, 2.0–2.49, 2.50–2.99, etc). However, if students don't know their GPA or don't want to reveal it precisely, they may leave the question blank or write in a difficult to interpret answer, as discussed later.

These issues might lead you to provide a number of categories, each with a relatively narrow range of values, for variables such as age, weight, and income. Never collapse such categories before you enter the data into the data editor. For example, if you have age categories for university undergraduates 15–17, 18–20, 21–23, and so forth, and you realize that there are

---

[1] For some advanced statistics (e.g., multileveled linear modeling), the data for a subject are organized differently, so that each participant has data on more than one line. All of the statistics in this book and most intermediate statistics are entered as shown here and in Chapter 1.

only a few students younger than 18, keep the codes as is for now. <u>Later</u> you can make a new category of 20 or younger by using a function, **Transform => Recode**. If you collapse categories before you enter the data, the extra information will no longer be available.

5. **For each participant, there must be a code or value for each variable**. These codes should be numbers, except for variables for which the data are missing. We recommend using blanks when data are missing or unusable because <u>SPSS is designed to handle blanks as missing values</u>. However, sometimes you may have more than one type of missing data, such as items left blank *and* those that had an answer that was not appropriate or usable. In this case you may assign numeric codes such as 98 and 99 to them, but you <u>must tell the program that these codes are for missing values,</u> or it will treat them as actual data. (See Fig. 1.2 and Table 1.2.)

6. **Apply any coding rules consistently for all participants.** This means that if you decide to treat a certain type of response as, say, missing for one person, you must do the same for all other participants.

7. **Use high numbers (values or codes) for the "agree," "good," or "positive" end of a variable that is ordered.** Sometimes you will see questionnaires that use 1 for "strongly agree," and 5 for "strongly disagree." This is not wrong as long as you are clear and consistent. However, you are less likely to get confused when interpreting your results if high values have a positive meaning.

Make a Coding Form

Now you need to make some decisions about how to code the data provided in Figs. 2.1 and 2.2, especially data that are not already in numerical form. When the responses provided by participants are numbers, the variable is said to be "self-coding." You can just enter the number that was circled or checked. On the other hand, variables such as *gender* or *college* have no intrinsic value associated with them. See Fig. 2.3 for the decisions we made about how to number the variables, code the values, and name the eight variables. Don't forget to number each of the questionnaires so that you can later check the entered data against the questionnaires.

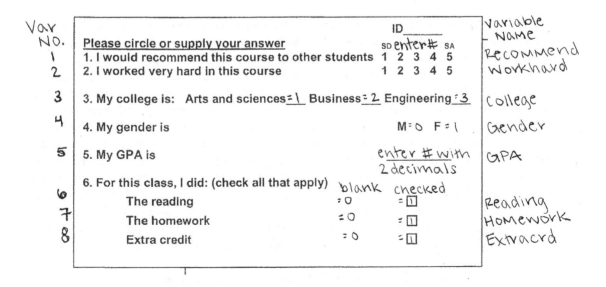

Fig. 2.3. A blank survey showing how to code the data.

Problem 2.1: Check the Completed Questionnaires

Now, examine Figs. 2.1 and 2.2 for incomplete, unclear, or double answers. **Stop** and do this now, before proceeding. What issues did you see? The researcher needs to make rules about how to handle these problems and note them on the questionnaires or on a master "coding instructions" sheet so that the same rules are used for all cases.

We have identified at least 11 responses on 6 of the 12 questionnaires that need to be clarified. Can you find them all? How would you resolve them? <u>Write on Figs. 2.1 and 2.2 how you would handle each issue</u> that you see.

Make Rules About How to Handle These Problems

For each type of incomplete, blank, unclear, or double answer, you need to make a rule for what to do. As much as possible, you should make these rules before data collection, but there may well be some unanticipated issues. It is important that you apply the rules consistently for all similar problems so as not to bias your results.

Interpretation of Problem 2.1 and Fig. 2.4

Now, we will discuss each of the issues and how we decided to handle them. Of course, some reasonable choices could have been different from ours. We think that the data for Participants 1–6 are quite clear and ready to enter with the help of Fig. 2.3. However, the questionnaires for participants 7–12 pose a number of minor and more serious problems for the person entering the data. We discuss next and have written our decisions in numbered callout boxes on Fig. 2.4, which are the surveys and responses for Subjects 7–12.

1. For Participant 7, the *GPA* appears to be written as 250. It seems reasonable to assume that he meant to include a decimal after the 2, and so we would enter 2.50. We could instead have said that this was an invalid response and coded it as missing. However, missing data create problems in later data analysis, especially for complex statistics. Thus, we want to use as much of the data provided as is reasonable. The important thing here is that you *must* treat all other similar problems the same way.

2. For Subject 8, two colleges were checked. We could have developed a new legitimate response value (4 = other). Because this fictitious university requires that students be identified with one and only one of its three colleges, we have developed two missing value codes (as we did for ethnic group and religion in the HSB data set). Thus, for this variable only, we used **98** for multiple checked colleges or other written-in responses that did not fit clearly into one of the colleges (e.g., business engineering or history and business). We treated such responses as missing because they seemed to be invalid and/or because we would not have had enough of any given response to form a reasonable size group for analysis. We used **99** as the code for cases where nothing was checked or written on the form. Having two codes enabled us to distinguish between these two types of missing data, if we ever wanted to later. Other researchers (e.g., Newton & Rudestam, 1999) recommend using 8 and 9 in this case, but we think that it is best to use a code that is very different from the "valid" codes so that they stand out visually in the **Data View** and will lead to noticeable differences in the **Descriptives** if you forget to code them as missing values.

3. Also, Subject 8 wrote 2.2 for his *GPA*. It seems reasonable to enter 2.20 as the *GPA*. Actually, in this case, if we enter 2.2, the program will treat it as 2.20 because we will tell it to use two decimal places for this variable.

4. We decided to enter 3.00 for Participant 9's *GPA*. Of course, the actual *GPA* could be higher or, more likely, lower, but 3.00 seems to be the best choice given the information provided by the student (i.e., "about 3 pt").

5. Participant 10 only answered the first two questions, so there were lots of missing data. It appears that he or she decided not to complete the questionnaire. We made a rule that if three out of the first five items were blank or invalid, we would throw out that whole questionnaire as invalid. In your research report, you should state how many questionnaires were thrown out and for what reason(s). Usually you would not enter any data from that questionnaire, so you would only have 11 subjects or cases to enter. To show you how you would code someone's *college* if they left it blank, we did not delete this subject at this time.

6. For Subject 11, there are several problems. First, she circled both 3 and 4 for the first item; a reasonable decision is to enter the average or midpoint, 3.50.

7. Participant 11 has written in "biology" for *college*. Although there is no biology college at this university, it seems reasonable to enter 1 = arts and sciences in this case and in other cases (e.g., history = 1, marketing = 2, civil = 3) where the actual college is clear. See the discussion of Issue 2 for how to handle unclear examples.

8. Participant 11 also entered 9.67 for the *GPA*, which is an invalid response because this university has a 4-point grading system (4.00 is the maximum possible *GPA*). To show you one method of checking the entered data for errors, we will go ahead and enter 9.67. If you examine the completed questionnaires carefully, you should be able to spot errors like this in the data and enter a blank for missing/invalid data.

9. Enter 1 for reading and homework for Participant 11 (even though they were circled rather than checked). Also enter 0 for extra credit (not checked) as you would for all the boxes left unchecked by other participants (except Subject 10, who, as stated in number 5 above, did not complete the questionnaire). Even though this person circled the boxes rather than putting X's or checks in them, her intent is clear.

10. As in Point 6, we decided to enter 2.5 for Participant 12's X between 2 and 3.

11. Participant 12 also left *GPA* blank so, using the general (system) missing value code, we left it blank.

Clean up Completed Questionnaires

Now that you have made your rules and decided how to handle each problem, you need to make these rules clear to whoever will enter the data. As mentioned earlier, we put our decisions in callout boxes on Fig. 2.4; a common procedure would be to write your decisions on the questionnaires, perhaps in a different color.

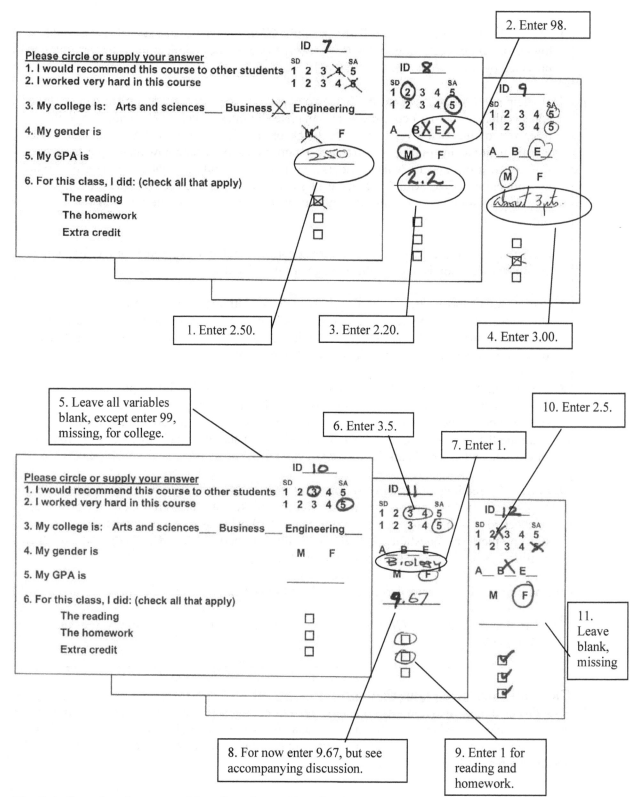

Fig. 2.4. Completed survey with callout boxes showing how we handled problem responses.

Problem 2.2: Define and Label the Variables

The next step is to create a data file into which you will enter the data. If you do not have the program open, you need to log on. When you see the startup window, click the **Type in data** button; then you should see a blank **Data Editor** that will look something like Fig. 2.5. Also be sure that **Display Commands in the Log** is checked (see Appendix A). You should also examine Appendix A if you need more help getting started.

This section helps you name and label the variables. In the next section, we show you how to enter data. First, let's define and label the first two variables, which are two 5-point Likert ratings. To do this we need to use the **Variable View** screen. Look at the bottom left corner of the **Data Editor** to see whether you are in the **Data View** or **Variable View** screen by noting which tab is white. If you are in **Data View,** to get to **Variable View** do the following:

- Click on the **Variable View** tab at the bottom left of your screen. This will bring up a screen similar to Fig. 2.5. (Or, *double* click on **var** above the blank column to the far left side of the **Data View.**)

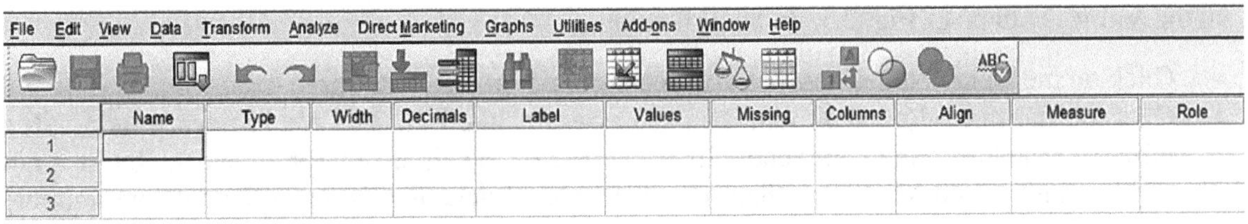

	Name	Type	Width	Decimals	Label	Values	Missing	Columns	Align	Measure	Role
1											
2											
3											

Fig. 2.5. Blank variable view screen in the data editor.

In this window, you will see 11 columns that will allow you to input the variable **name**, **type** of variable, **width**, number of **decimals**, variable **label**, **value** labels, **missing** values other than blanks, **columns**, **align** data left or right, **measurement** type, and variable **role**.

Define and Label Two Likert-Type Variables
We now begin to enter information to name, label, and define the characteristics of the variables used in this chapter.
- Click in the blank box directly under **Name** in Fig. 2.5.
- Type *recommend* in this box. Notice the number 1 to the left of this box. This indicates that you are entering your first variable.[2]
- Press enter. This will insert the program's default values for variables. You need to check to be sure these are correct for each of your variables and make changes if needed.

Note that the **Type** is numeric, **Width** = 8, **Decimals** = 2, **Label** = (blank), **Values** = None, **Missing** = None, **Columns** = 8, **Align** = right, **Measure** = scale, **Role** = input.

---

[2] It is no longer necessary to keep variable names to eight characters or less, although short names are desirable. Other rules about variable names still apply (see footnote 6 in Chapter 1). Note also that in this book we use bullets to indicate instructions about SPSS actions (e.g., click, highlight), and we use bold for key terms displayed in SPSS windows (e.g., **Name**).

For this assignment, we will keep the default values for **Type**, **Width**, **Columns**, and **Align**. On the **Variable View** screen, you will notice that the default for **Type** is **Numeric**. This refers to the type of variable you are entering. Usually, you will only use the **Numeric** option. Numeric means the data are numbers. **String** would be used if you input words or letters such as "M" for males and "F" for females. However, it is best not to enter words or letters because you wouldn't be able to do many statistics without recoding them as numbers. In this book, we will always keep the Type as Numeric.

We recommend keeping the **Width** at eight, and keeping the **Columns** at eight. We will always **Align** the numbers to the right. Sometimes, we will change the settings for the other columns.

Now let's continue with defining and labeling the *recommend* variable.
- For this variable, leave the decimals at 2.
- Click on the box under "Label" and type *I recommend course* in the **Label** box. This longer label will show in appropriate windows and on your printouts. The labels can be up to 40 characters but it is best to keep them about 20 or less or your outputs may be difficult to read.

In the **Values** column of Fig. 2.5, do the following:

- Click on the word "None" and you will see a small blue box with three dots.
- Click on the three dots. You will then see a screen like Fig. 2.6. We decided to add **value labels** for the lower and upper end of the Likert scale to help us interpret the data, but it is not as important to add labels for Likert or other ordered data as it is when the data are nominal or unordered.

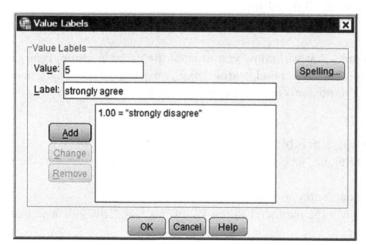

Fig. 2.6. Value labels window.

- Type 1 in the **Value** box in Fig. 2.6.
- Type *strongly disagree* in the **Value Label** box. Press **Add**.
- Type *5* and *strongly agree* in the **Values** and **Value Labels** boxes. Your window should look like Fig. 2.6 just before you click on **Add** for the second time.
- Click on **Add.**
- Then click **OK**.
- Leave the cells for the **Missing** to **Measure** columns in Fig. 2.5 as they currently appear.

- Change **Role** to **Target** because *recommend* could be used as a **Target** (dependent or outcome) variable. See Figure 2.7. Different researchers might code these variables differently. For example, if they planned to use *recommend* only as an independent variable in their study, they would code **Role** as **Input**.

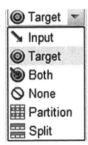

Fig. 2.7. Role selection.

Now let's define and label the next variable.

- Click on the next blank box under **Name** (in Row 2) to enter the name of the next variable. Note spaces are not allowed in variable names. Spaces are allowed in labels.
- Type *workhard* in the **Name** column and press Enter.
- Click on the box in Row 2 under Label and type *I worked hard* in the **Label** column.
- Insert the highest and lowest **Values** for this variable the same way you did for *recommend* (1 = *strongly disagree* and 5 = *strongly agree*).
- Change **Role** to **Both** because it could be used as either an **Input** (independent) or **Target** (dependent) variable.

Define and Label College and Gender

- Now, select the cell under **Name** in Row 3.
- Call this third variable *college* by typing that in the box.
- Click on the third box under **Decimals**. For this variable, there is no reason to have any decimal places because people were asked to choose only one of the three colleges. You will notice that when you select the box under **Decimals**, up and down arrows appear on the right side of the box. You can either click the arrows to raise or lower the number of decimals, or you can double click on the box and manually type in the desired number.
- For the purposes of this variable, select or type 0 as the number of **decimals.**
- Next, click the box under **Label** to type in the variable label *college*.
- Under **Values**, click on None and then click on the small blue box with three dots.
- In the **Value Labels** window, type 1 in the **Value** box, type *arts and sciences* in the **Value Label** box.
- Then click **Add**. Do the same for 2 = *business*, 3 = *engineering*, 98 = *other, multiple ans.*, 99 = *blank*.

The **Value Labels** window should resemble Fig. 2.8 just before you click **Add** for the last time.

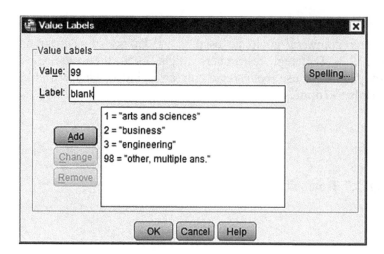

Fig. 2.8. Value labels window.

- Then click **OK**.
- Under **Measure,** click the box that reads **Scale.**
- Click the down arrow and choose **Nominal** because for this variable the categories are unordered or nominal.

Your screen should look like Fig. 2.9 just after you click on nominal.

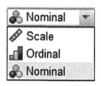

Fig. 2.9. Measurement selection.

- Change **Role** to **Input** because college will only be used as an independent variable.
- Under **Missing,** click on None and then on the three dots. Click on **Discrete Missing Values** and enter 98 and 99 in the first two boxes. (See Fig. 2.10.) <u>This step is essential if you have one or more specific values that you want to use as missing value code(s)</u>. If you leave the **Missing** cell at **None**, the program will not know that 98 and 99 should be considered missing. **None** in this column is somewhat misleading. <u>None means no special missing values</u> (i.e., only blanks are considered missing).

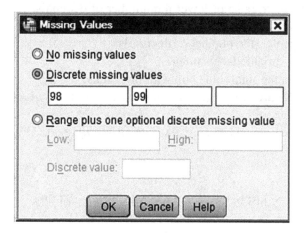

Fig. 2.10. Missing values.

- Then click on **OK**.

Your **Data Editor** should now look like Fig. 2.11.

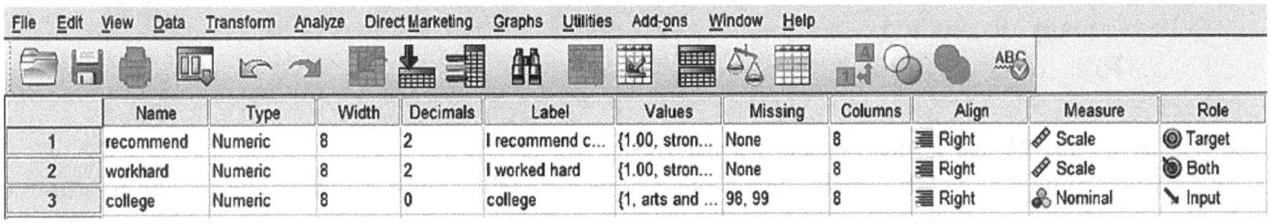

	Name	Type	Width	Decimals	Label	Values	Missing	Columns	Align	Measure	Role
1	recommend	Numeric	8	2	I recommend c...	{1.00, stron...	None	8	Right	Scale	Target
2	workhard	Numeric	8	2	I worked hard	{1.00, stron...	None	8	Right	Scale	Both
3	college	Numeric	8	0	college	{1, arts and ...	98, 99	8	Right	Nominal	Input

Fig. 2.11. Completed variable view for the first three variables.

Now define and label *gender* similarly to how you did this for *college*.
- First, type the variable **Name** *gender* in the next blank row in Fig. 2.11.
- Click on **Decimals** to change the decimal places to 0 (zero).
- Now click on **Labels** and label the variable *gender*.
- Next you <u>must label</u> the values or levels of the *gender* variable. You need to be sure your coding matches your labels. We arbitrarily decided to code *male* as zero and *female* as 1. We could have coded *female* as zero and *male* as 1. There are some advantages to using 0 and 1 for the codes ("dummy coding"), as indicated below.
- Click on the **Values** cell.
- Then, click on the blue three-dot box to get a window like Fig. 2.6 again. Remember, this is the same process you conducted when entering the labels for the values of the first three variables.
- Now, type 0 to the right of **Value**.
- To the right of **Label** type *male*. Click on **Add.**
- Repeat this process for 1 = *female*. Click on **Add.**
- Click **OK.**
- Click on **Scale** under **Measure** to change the level of measurement to **Nominal** because this is an unordered, dichotomous variable.
- Finally, click on **Input** under **Role** because *gender* will be an independent variable.

Once again, realize that the researcher has made a series of decisions that another researcher could have done differently, as we noted earlier with the **Role** of the *recommend* variable. For example, you could have used 1 and 2 as the values for gender, and you might have given males the higher number. We have chosen, in this case, to do what is called dummy coding. In essence, 1 is female and 0 is not female. This type of coding is useful for interpreting gender when used in statistical analysis. Similarly, we could have decided to consider the level of measurement ordinal, since dummy coded dichotomous variables can be used in analyses that require ordered data, as we will discuss in later chapters.

Define and Label Grade Point Average
You should now have enough practice to define and label the *gpa* variable. After naming the variable *gpa,* do the following:
- For **Decimals** leave the decimals at 2.
- Now click on **Label** and label it *grade point average*.
- Click on **Values.** Type 0 = *All Fs* and 4 = *All As*. (Note that for this variable, we have used actual GPA to 2 decimals, rather than dividing it into ordered groups such as a C average, B average, A average.)

- Under **Measure**, leave it as **Scale** because this variable has many ordered values and is likely to be normally distributed.
- Under **Role**, click on **Both.**

Define and Label the Last Three Variables

Now you should define the three variables related to the parts of the class that a student completed. Remember we said the **Names** of these variables would be: *reading, homework*, and *extracrd.* The variable **Labels** will be *I did the reading, I did the homework, I did extra credit.* The **Value** labels are: 0 = not checked/blank and 1 = checked. These variables should have no decimals, and the **Measure** should be changed to **Nominal. Role** should be changed to **Both** because these could be used as other independent or dependent variables. Your complete **Variable View** should look like Fig. 2.12.

File Edit View Data Transform Analyze Direct Marketing Graphs Utilities Add-ons Window Help

	Name	Type	Width	Decimals	Label	Values	Missing	Columns	Align	Measure	Role
1	recommend	Numeric	8	2	I recommend c...	{1.00, stron...	None	8	Right	Scale	Target
2	workhard	Numeric	8	2	I worked hard	{1.00, stron...	None	8	Right	Scale	Both
3	college	Numeric	8	0	college	{1, arts and ...	98, 99	8	Right	Nominal	Input
4	gender	Numeric	8	0	gender	{0, male}...	None	8	Right	Nominal	Input
5	gpa	Numeric	8	2	grade point aver...	{.00, All Fs}...	None	8	Right	Scale	Both
6	reading	Numeric	8	0	I did the reading	{0, not chec...	None	8	Right	Nominal	Both
7	homework	Numeric	8	0	I did the homew...	{0, not chec...	None	8	Right	Nominal	Both
8	extracrd	Numeric	8	0	I did extra credit	{0, not chec...	None	8	Right	Nominal	Both

Fig. 2.12. Completed variable view.

Problem 2.3: Display Your Dictionary or Codebook

Now that you have defined and labeled your variables, you can print a codebook or dictionary of your variables. It is a very useful record of what you have done. Notice that the information in the codebook is essentially the same as that in the variable view (Fig. 2.12) so you do not really have to have both, but the codebook makes a more complete printed record of your labels and values.

- Select **File → Display Data File Information → Working File.** Your codebook should look like Output 2.1, without the callout boxes. The codebook is divided into parts: the **Variable Information** (which is very similar to the **Variable View** in Fig. 2.12) and the **Variable Values** (which are partially hidden in the **Variable View**).

To rescale (shrink) the wide **Variable Information** table and print the whole codebook, see the Appendix A section about **Resize/Rescale to Print**. You may not be able to see all of the file information/codebook on your computer screen. However, you should be able to print the entire codebook.

Output 2.1: Codebook

DISPLAY *DICTIONARY*.

File Information

Short variable name.

Most variables use blanks, the system missing value, but *college* has two missing value codes, 98 and 99.

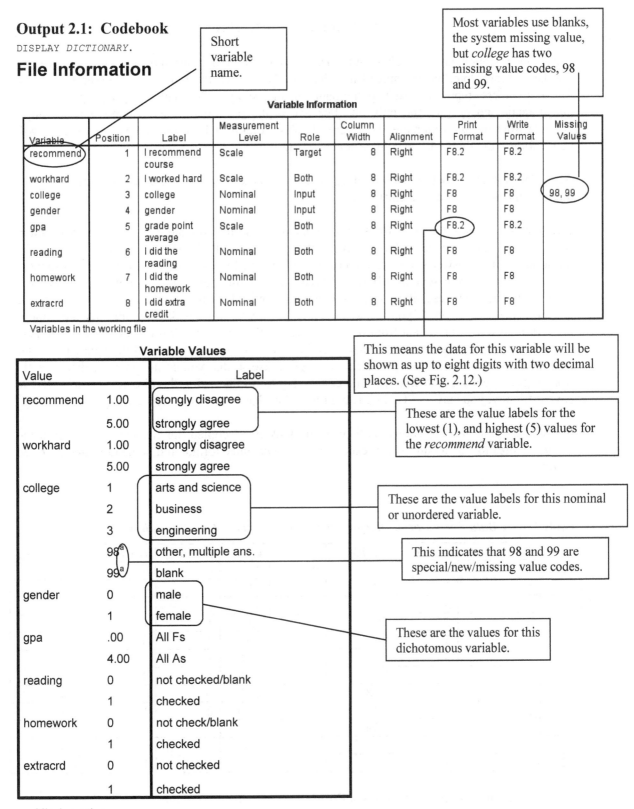

Variable Information

Variable	Position	Label	Measurement Level	Role	Column Width	Alignment	Print Format	Write Format	Missing Values
recommend	1	I recommend course	Scale	Target	8	Right	F8.2	F8.2	
workhard	2	I worked hard	Scale	Both	8	Right	F8.2	F8.2	
college	3	college	Nominal	Input	8	Right	F8	F8	98, 99
gender	4	gender	Nominal	Input	8	Right	F8	F8	
gpa	5	grade point average	Scale	Both	8	Right	F8.2	F8.2	
reading	6	I did the reading	Nominal	Both	8	Right	F8	F8	
homework	7	I did the homework	Nominal	Both	8	Right	F8	F8	
extracrd	8	I did extra credit	Nominal	Both	8	Right	F8	F8	

Variables in the working file

This means the data for this variable will be shown as up to eight digits with two decimal places. (See Fig. 2.12.)

Variable Values

Value		Label
recommend	1.00	stongly disagree
	5.00	strongly agree
workhard	1.00	strongly disagree
	5.00	strongly agree
college	1	arts and science
	2	business
	3	engineering
	98 [a]	other, multiple ans.
	99 [a]	blank
gender	0	male
	1	female
gpa	.00	All Fs
	4.00	All As
reading	0	not checked/blank
	1	checked
homework	0	not check/blank
	1	checked
extracrd	0	not checked
	1	checked

These are the value labels for the lowest (1), and highest (5) values for the *recommend* variable.

These are the value labels for this nominal or unordered variable.

This indicates that 98 and 99 are special/new/missing value codes.

These are the values for this dichotomous variable.

a. Missing value

Problem 2.4: Enter Data

Close the codebook, and then click on the **Data View** tab on the bottom of the screen to give you the data editor. Note that the spreadsheet has numbers down the left-hand side (see Fig. 2.13). These numbers represent each participant in the study. The data for each participant's questionnaire go on one and only one line across the page with each column representing a variable from our questionnaire. Therefore, the first column will be *recommend*, the second will be *workhard*, the third will be *college*, and so forth.

After defining and labeling the variables, your next task is to enter the data directly from the questionnaires or from a data entry form.

Occasionally a researcher will transfer the data from the questionnaires to a **data entry form** (like Table 2.1) by hand before entering the data into SPSS. This may be helpful if the questionnaires or answer sheet are not easily readable by the data entry person, if the responses are to be entered from several different sources, or if additional coding or recoding is required before data entry. In these situations, you could make mistakes entering the data directly from the questionnaires. However, if you use a data entry form, you could make copying mistakes, and it takes time to transfer the data from questionnaires to the data entry form. Thus, few researchers use a data entry form as an intermediate step between the questionnaire and the data editor. Our cleaned up questionnaires should be easy enough to use so that you could enter the data directly from Fig. 2.1 and Fig. 2.4 into the data editor. Try to do that using the directions below. If you have difficulty, you may use Table 2.1, but remember that it took an extra step to produce.

In Table 2.1, the data are shown as they would look if we copied the cleaned up data from the questionnaires to a data entry sheet, except that the data entry form could be handwritten on ruled paper.

Table 2.1. *A Data Entry Form: Responses Copied From the Questionnaires*

	Recommend	Workhard	College	Gender	Gpa	Reading	Homework	Extracrd
1	3	5	1	0	3.12	0	0	1
2	4	5	2	0	2.91	1	1	0
3	4	5	1	1	3.33	0	1	1
4	5	5	1	1	3.60	1	1	1
5	4	5	2	1	2.52	0	0	1
6	5	5	3	1	2.98	1	0	0
7	4	5	2	0	2.50	1	0	0
8	2	5	98	0	2.20	0	0	0
9	5	5	3	0	3.00	0	1	0
10			99					
11	3.5	5	1	1	9.67	1	1	0
12	2.5	5	2	1		1	1	1

To enter the data, ensure that your **Data Editor** is showing.
- If it is not already highlighted, click on the far left column, which should say *recommend*.
- To enter the data into this highlighted column, simply type the number and press the **right arrow**. For example, first type 3 (the number will show up in the blank space above the row

of variable names) and then press the **right arrow**; the number will be entered into the highlighted box. Next, type 5 in the *workhard* column and so forth.

In Fig. 2.13, all the data for the participants have been entered.

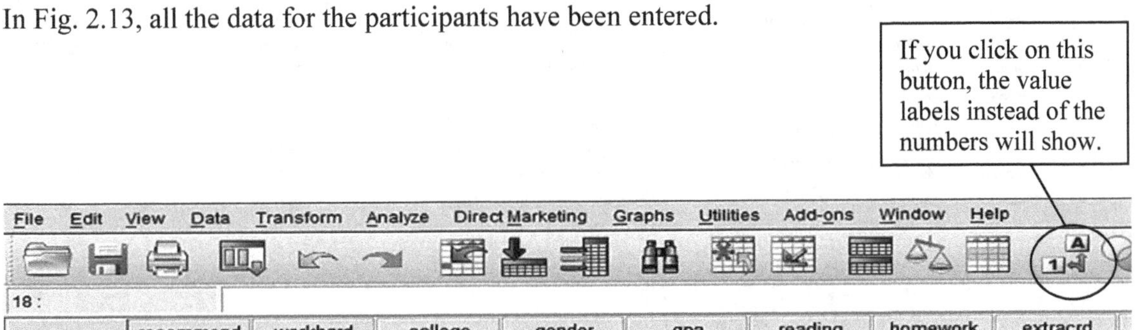

If you click on this button, the value labels instead of the numbers will show.

	recommend	workhard	college	gender	gpa	reading	homework	extracrd
1	3.00	5.00	1	0	3.12	0	0	1
2	4.00	5.00	2	0	2.91	1	1	0
3	4.00	5.00	1	1	3.33	0	1	1
4	5.00	5.00	1	1	3.60	1	1	1
5	4.00	5.00	2	1	2.52	0	0	1
6	5.00	5.00	3	1	2.98	1	0	0
7	4.00	5.00	2	0	2.50	1	0	0
8	2.00	5.00	98	0	2.20	0	0	0
9	5.00	5.00	3	0	3.00	0	1	0
10	.	5.00	99		.	.	.	.
11	3.50	5.00	1	1	9.67	1	1	0
12	2.50	5.00	2	1	.	1	1	1
13								

Fig. 2.13. Data Editor participants entered.

- Now enter from your cleaned up questionnaires the rest of the data in Fig. 2.1 and Fig. 2.4. If you make a mistake when entering data, correct it by clicking on the cell (the cell will be highlighted), type the correct score, and press enter or the arrow key.

Before you do any analysis, <u>compare the data on your questionnaires with the data in the **Data Editor**.</u> If you have lots of data, a sample can be checked, but it is preferable to check all of the data. If you find errors in your sample, you should check all the entries.

Problem 2.5: Run Descriptives and Check the Data

In order to get a better "feel" for the data and to check for other types of errors or problems on the questionnaires, we recommend that you run the statistics program called **Descriptives.** To compute basic descriptive statistics for all your subjects, you will need to do these steps:

- Select **Analyze → Descriptive Statistics → Descriptives...** (see Fig. 2.14).[3]

After selecting **Descriptives**, you will be ready to compute the mean, minimum, and maximum values for all participants or cases on all variables in order to examine the data.

---

[3] This is how we indicate, in this and the following chapters, that you first pull down the **Analyze** menu, then select **Descriptive Statistics** from the first flyout menu, and finally select **Descriptives** from the last flyout menu.

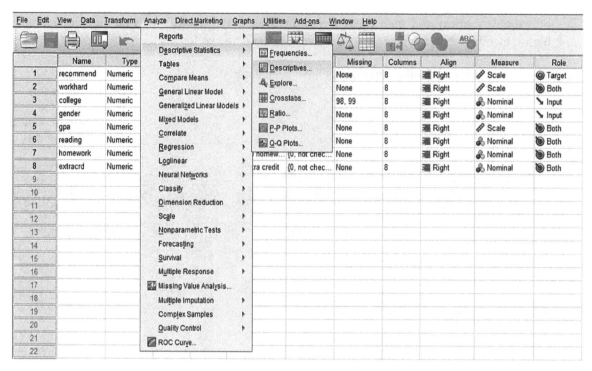

Fig. 2.14 Analyze menu.

- Now highlight all of the variables. To highlight, click on the first variable, then hold down the "shift" key and click on the last variable so that *all* of the variables listed are highlighted (see Fig. 2.15a). Note that in SPSS 14 and later versions, there is a symbol to the left of each variable name; it indicates whether you have labeled the measurement level as nominal , ordinal , or scale . Measurement levels are discussed in detail in Chapter 3 of this book.

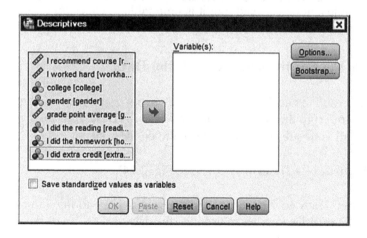

Fig. 2.15a. Descriptives—before moving variables.

- Click on the **arrow** button pointing right. The **Descriptives** dialog box should now look like Fig. 2.15b.

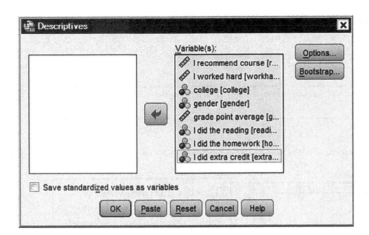

Fig. 2.15b. Descriptives—after moving variables.

- Be sure that *all* of the variables have moved out of the left window. If your screen looks like Fig. 2.15b, then click on **Options.** You will get Fig. 2.16.

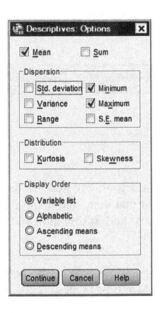

Fig. 2.16. Descriptives: options.

Follow these steps:

- Notice that the **Mean, Std. deviation, Minimum**, and **Maximum** were already checked. Click off **Std. deviation**. At this time, we will not request more descriptive statistics. We will do them in Chapter 4.
- Ensure that the **Variable list** bubble is checked in the **Display Order** section. Note: You can also click on **Ascending or Descending means** if you want your variables listed in order of the means. If you wanted the variables listed alphabetically, you would check **Alphabetic**, but we won't check any of these alternatives so the variables will be printed in the same order as on the **Variable View**.
- Click on **Continue**, which will bring you back to the main **Descriptives** dialog box (Fig. 2.15b).
- Then click on **OK** to run the program.

You should get an output like Fig. 2.17. If it looks similar, you have done the steps correctly.

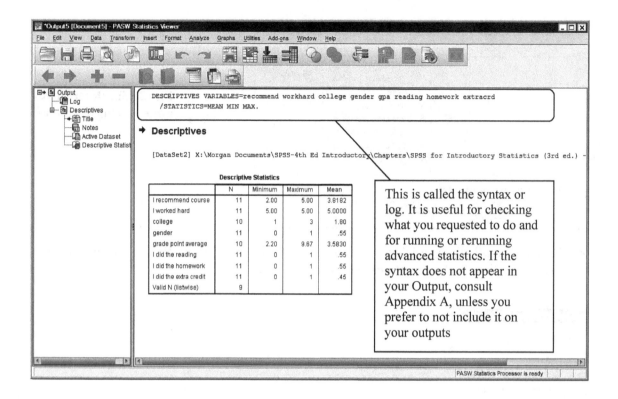

Fig. 2.17. Output viewer for descriptives.

The left side of Fig. 2.17 lists the various parts of your output. You can click on any item on the left (e.g., **Title, Notes,** or **Descriptive Statistics**) to activate the output for that item, and then you can edit it. For example, you can click on **Title** and then expand the title or add information such as your name and the date. (See Appendix A for more on editing outputs.)

● Double click on the large, bold word **Descriptives** in Fig. 2.17. Type your name in the box that appears so it will appear on your output when you print it later. Also type "Output 2.2" at the top so you and/or your instructor will know what it is later.

For each variable, compare the minimum and maximum scores in Fig. 2.17 with the highest and lowest appropriate values in the codebook (Output 2.1). This checking of data before doing any more statistics is important to further ensure that data entry errors have not been made and that the missing data codes are being used properly.

Note that after each output we have provided a brief interpretation in a box. On the output itself, we have pointed out some of the key things by circling them and making some comments in boxes, which are known as **callout boxes**. Of course, these circles and information boxes will not show up on your printout.

Output 2.2: Descriptives

```
DESCRIPTIVES VARIABLES=recommend workhard college gender gpa reading homework extracrd
  /STATISTICS=MEAN STDDEV MIN MAX .
```

Descriptives

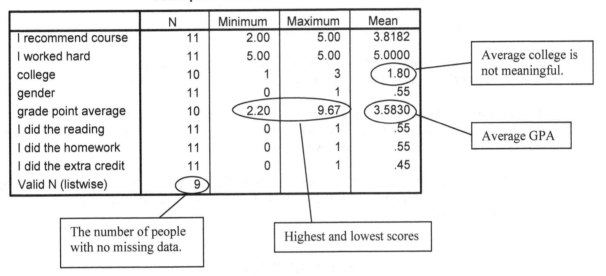

Descriptive Statistics

	N	Minimum	Maximum	Mean
I recommend course	11	2.00	5.00	3.8182
I worked hard	11	5.00	5.00	5.0000
college	10	1	3	1.80
gender	11	0	1	.55
grade point average	10	2.20	9.67	3.5830
I did the reading	11	0	1	.55
I did the homework	11	0	1	.55
I did the extra credit	11	0	1	.45
Valid N (listwise)	9			

Average college is not meaningful.

Average GPA

The number of people with no missing data.

Highest and lowest scores

Interpretation of Output 2.2

This output shows, for each of the eight variables, the number (*N*) of participants with no missing data on that variable. The **Valid N (listwise)** is the number (9) who have no missing data on any variable. The table also shows the **Minimum** and **Maximum** score that any participants had on that variable. For example, no one circled a 1, but one or more persons circled a 2 for the *I recommend course* variable, and at least one person circled 5. Notice that for *I worked hard*, 5 is both the minimum and maximum, everyone said they worked hard. This item is, therefore, really a constant and not a variable; it will not be useful in statistical analyses.

The table also provides the **Mean** or average score for each variable. Notice the mean for *I worked hard* is 5 because everyone circled 5. The mean of 1.80 for *college*, a nominal (unordered) variable with 3 or more categories, is nonsense, so ignore it. However, the means of .55 for the dichotomous variables *gender, I did the reading,* and *I did the homework* indicate that in each case 55% chose the answers that corresponded to 1 (female gender and "yes" for doing the reading and homework). The mean *grade point average* was 3.58, which is probably an error because it is too high for the overall *GPA* for most groups of undergrads. Note also that there has to be an error in *GPA* because the maximum *GPA* of 9.67 is not possible at this university, which has a 4.00 maximum (see codebook). Thus the 9.67 for participant 11 is an invalid response. The questionnaires should be checked again to be sure there wasn't a data entry error. If, as in this case, the survey says 9.67, it should be changed to blank, the missing value code.

Interpretation Questions

2.1. What steps or actions should be taken after you collect data and before you run the analyses aimed at answering your research questions or testing your research hypotheses?

2.2. Are there any other rules about data coding of questionnaires that you think should be added? Are there any of our "rules" that you think should be modified? Which ones? How and why?

2.3. Why would you print a codebook or dictionary?

2.4. If you identified other problems with the completed questionnaires, what were they? How did you decide to handle the problems and why?

2.5. If the university in the example allowed for double majors in different colleges (such that it would actually be possible for a student to be in two colleges), how would you handle cases in which 2 colleges are checked? Why?

2.6 (a) Why is it important to check your raw (questionnaire) data before and after entering them into the data editor? (b) What are ways to check the data before entering them? After entering them?

Extra SPSS Problems

Using the college student data.sav file, from http://www.psypress.com/ibm-spss-intro-stats/ ("Data Sets (ZIPS)" button) or the Moodle Web site for this book, do the following problems. Print your outputs and circle the key parts for discussion.

2.1 Compute the N, minimum, maximum, and mean for all the variables in the college student data file. How many students have complete data? Identify any statistics on the output that are not meaningful. Explain.

2.2 What is the mean height of the students? What about the average height of the same sex parent? What percentage of students are males? What percentage have children?

CHAPTER 3

Measurement and Descriptive Statistics

Frequency Distributions

Frequency distributions are critical to understanding our use of measurement terms. We begin this chapter with a discussion of frequency distributions and two examples. Frequency tables and distributions can be used whether the variable involved has ordered or unordered levels or **values**. In this section, we only consider variables with many ordered values.

A **frequency distribution** is a tally or count of the <u>number of times each score on a single variable occurs</u>. For example, the frequency distribution of final grades in a class of 50 students might be 7 As, 20 Bs, 18 Cs, and 5 Ds. Note that in this frequency distribution most students have Bs or Cs (grades in the middle) and similar smaller numbers have As and Ds (high and low grades). When there are a small number of scores for the low and high values and most scores are for the middle values, the distribution is said to be **approximately normally distributed.** We discuss this distribution and the normal curve later in this chapter.

When the variable is continuous or has many ordered levels (or values), the frequency distribution usually is based on ranges of values for the variable. For example, the frequencies (number of students), shown by the bars in Fig. 3.1, are for a range of points. (In this case the SPSS program selected a range of 50: 250–299, 300–349, 350–399, etc.) Notice that the largest number of students (about 20) had scores in the middle two bars of the range (450–499 and 500–549). Similar small numbers of students have very low and very high scores. The bars in the histogram form a distribution (pattern or curve) that is similar to the normal, bell-shaped curve. Thus, the frequency distribution of the *SAT math* scores is said to be **approximately normal**.

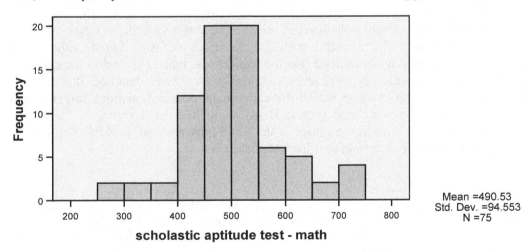

Fig. 3.1. A grouped frequency distribution for SAT math scores.

Figure 3.2 shows the frequency distribution for the *competence scale*. Notice that the bars form a pattern very different from the normal curve in Figure 3.1. This distribution can be said to be **not normally distributed**. As we see later in the chapter, the distribution is **negatively skewed**. That is, extreme scores or the tail of the curve are on the low end or left side. As you will see in the Levels of Measurement section, we call the *competence scale* variable **ordinal**.

You can create these figures yourself using the **hsbdata.sav** file.[1] Select:

- **Graphs → Legacy Dialogs → Histogram…**
- Then move *scholastic aptitude test – math* (or *competence scale*) into the **Variable** box.
- Click **OK.** The program can superimpose a normal curve on the histogram if you request it, but we have found this curve more confusing than helpful to our students.

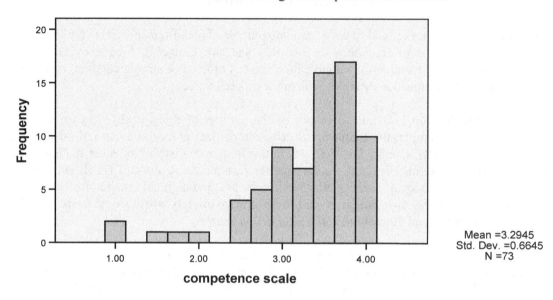

Mean =3.2945
Std. Dev. =0.6645
N =73

Fig 3.2. A grouped frequency distribution for the competence scale.

Levels of Measurement

Measurement is the assignment of numbers or symbols to the different characteristics (values) of variables according to rules. In order to understand your variables, it is important to know their level of measurement. Depending on the level of measurement of a variable, the data can mean different things. For example, the number 2 might indicate a score of two; it might indicate that the subject was a male; or it might indicate that the subject was ranked second in the class. To help understand these differences, types or levels of variables have been identified. It is common and traditional to discuss four levels or scales of measurement, **nominal, ordinal, interval, and ratio,** which vary from the unordered (nominal) to the highest level (ratio).[2]   These four traditional terms are not the same as those used in the SPSS program, and we think that they are not always the most useful for determining what statistics to use.

---

[1] In this chapter, we do not phrase the creation of the outputs as "problems" for you to answer. However, we describe with bullets and arrows (as we did in Chapter 2) how to create the figures shown in this chapter. You may want to use the SPSS program to see how to create these figures and tables. See Appendix A, Getting Started , for how to download the hsbdata.sav file to your computer.

[2] Unfortunately, the terms "level" and "scale" are used several ways in research. Levels refer to the categories or values of a variable (e.g., male or female or 1, 2, or 3); level can also refer to the three or four different types of measurement (nominal, ordinal, etc.). These several types of measurement have also been called "scales of measurement," but SPSS uses scale specifically for the highest type or level of measurement. Other researchers use scale to describe questionnaire items that are rated from strongly disagree to strongly agree (Likert scale) and for the sum of such items (summated scale). We wish there weren't so many uses of these terms; the best we can do is try to be clear about our usage.

SPSS uses three terms (**nominal, ordinal, and scale**) for the levels or types of measurement. How these correspond to the traditional terms is shown in Table 3.1. When you name and label variables with the SPSS program, you have the opportunity to select one of these three types of measurement, as was demonstrated in Chapter 2 (see Fig. 2.9). An appropriate choice indicates that you understand your data and may help guide your selection of statistics.

Table 3.1. *Comparison of Traditional, SPSS, and Our Measurement Terms*

Traditional Term	*Traditional Definition*	*SPSS Term*	*Our Term*	*Our Definitions*
Nominal	Two or more <u>unordered</u> categories	Nominal	Nominal	Three or more <u>unordered</u> categories.
NA	NA	NA	Dichotomous	Two categories, either ordered or unordered.
Ordinal	<u>Ordered</u> levels, in which the difference in magnitude between levels is not equal	Ordinal	Ordinal	Three or more <u>ordered</u> levels, in which the difference in magnitude between pairs of adjacent levels (e.g., scores such as 1 and 2, or 2 and 3) is unequal and distorts the meaning of the data. And/or the frequency distribution of the scores is <u>not</u> normally distributed (often it is skewed).
Interval & Ratio	**Interval:** <u>ordered</u> levels, in which the difference between levels is equal, but no true zero. **Ratio:** <u>ordered</u> levels; the difference between levels is equal, and there is a true zero.	Scale	Approximately Normal (or Normal)	Many (at least five) <u>ordered</u> levels or scores, with the frequency distribution of the scores being approximately normal.

We believe that the terms **nominal, dichotomous, ordinal**, and **approximately normal** (for normally distributed) are usually more useful than the traditional or SPSS measurement terms for the selection and interpretation of statistics. In part, this is because statisticians disagree about the usefulness of the traditional levels of measurement in determining the appropriate selection of statistics. Furthermore, our experience is that the traditional terms are frequently misunderstood and applied inappropriately by students. The main problem with the SPSS terms is that the term scale is not commonly used as a measurement level, and it has other meanings (see footnote 2) that make its use here confusing. Hopefully, our terms are clear and useful.

Table 3.1 compares the three sets of terms and provides a summary description of our definitions of them. Professors differ in the terminology they prefer and on how much importance to place on levels or scales of measurement. Unfortunately, you will see all of these terms and others mentioned in textbooks and articles.

Nominal Variables

This is the most basic or lowest level of measurement, in which the numerals assigned to each category stand for the name of the category, but they have no implied order or value. For example, in the HSB study, the values for the *religion* variable are 1= *protestant*, 2 =*catholic*, 3 = *not religious*. This does not mean that two protestants equal one catholic or any of the typical mathematical uses of the numerals. The same reasoning applies to many other true nominal variables, such as ethnic group, type of disability, or section number in a class schedule. In each of these cases, the categories are distinct and nonoverlapping, but not ordered. Each category or group in the modified HSB variable *ethnicity* is different from every other but there is no order to the categories. Thus, the categories could have been numbered 1 for *Asian American*, 2 for *Latino American*, 3 for *African American*, and 4 for *European American* or the reverse or any combination of assigning one number to each category.

What this implies is that you must *not* treat the numbers used for identifying nominal categories as if they were numbers that could be used in a formula, added together, subtracted from one another, or used to compute an average. Average ethnic group makes no sense. However, if you ask SPSS to compute the average ethnic group, it will do so and give you meaningless information. The important aspect of nominal measurement is to have clearly defined, nonoverlapping, or mutually exclusive categories that can be coded reliably by observers or by self-report.

Using only nominal variables does dramatically reduce the statistics that can be used with your data, but it does not altogether eliminate the possible use of statistics to summarize your data and make inferences. Therefore, even when the data are unordered or nominal categories, your research may benefit from the use of appropriate statistics. Later we discuss the types of statistics, both descriptive and inferential, that are appropriate for nominal data.

Other terms for nominal variables. Unfortunately, the literature is full of similar but not identical terms to describe the measurement aspects of variables. **Categorical, qualitative,** and **discrete** are terms sometimes used interchangeably with nominal, but we think that nominal is better because it is possible to have ordered, discrete categories (e.g., low, medium, and high IQ, which we and other researchers would consider an ordinal variable). "Qualitative" is also used to discuss a different approach to doing research, with important differences in philosophy, assumptions, and methods of conducting research.

Dichotomous Variables

Dichotomous variables always have only two levels or categories. In some cases, they may have an implied order (e.g., *math grades* in high school are coded 0 for *less than an A or B* average and 1 for *mostly A or B*). Other dichotomous variables do not have any order to the categories (e.g., *male* or *female*). For many purposes, it is best to use the same statistics for dichotomous and nominal variables. However, a statistic such as the mean or average, which would be meaningless for a three or more category nominal variable (e.g., *ethnicity*), does have meaning when there are only two categories, and when coded as dummy variables (0, 1) is especially easily interpretable. For example, in the HSB data, the average *gender* is .55 (with *males* = 0 and *females* = 1). This means that 55% of the participants were *females*, the higher code. Furthermore, we see with multiple regression that dichotomous variables, usually coded as *dummy variables*, can be used as independent variables along with other variables that are normally distributed.

Other terms for dichotomous variables. In the **Variable View** (e.g., see Fig. 2.11), we label dichotomous variables "nominal," and this is common in textbooks. However, please <u>remember that dichotomous variables are really a special case</u> and for some purposes they can be treated <u>as if</u> they were normal or scale. Dichotomous data have two discrete categories and are sometimes called **discrete variables** or **categorical variables** or **dummy variables**.

Ordinal Variables

In ordinal measurement, there are not only mutually exclusive categories as in nominal scales, but the categories are <u>ordered</u> from low to high, such that ranks could be assigned (e.g., 1st, 2nd, 3rd). Thus in an ordinal scale one knows which participant is highest or most preferred on a dimension, but the intervals between the various categories are not equal. Our definition of ordinal focuses on whether the frequency counts for each category or value are distributed like the bell-shaped, normal curve with more responses in the middle categories and fewer in the lowest and highest categories. If not approximately normal, we would call the variable ordinal. Ordered variables with only a few categories (say 2–4) would also be called ordinal. As indicated in Table 3.1, however, the traditional definition of ordinal focuses on whether the differences between pairs of levels are equal. This can be important, for example, if one will be creating summed or averaged scores (as in subscales of a questionnaire that involve aggregating a set of questionnaire items). If differences between levels are *meaningfully* unequal, then averaging a score of 5 (e.g., indicating the participants' age is 65+) and a score of 2 (e.g., indicating that the participants' age is 20-25) may not make sense. Averaging the *ranks* of the scores may be more meaningful if it is clear that they are ordered but that the differences between adjacent scores differ across levels of the variable. However, sometimes even if the differences between levels are not literally equal (e.g., the difference between a level indicating infancy and a level indicating preschool is not equal in years to the difference between a level of "young adulthood" and "older adulthood"), it may be reasonable to treat the levels as interval level data if the levels comprise the most meaningful distinctions and data are <u>normally distributed</u>.

Other terms for ordinal variables. Some authors use the term **ranks** interchangeably with ordinal. However, most analyses that are designed for use with ordinal data (nonparametric tests) rank the data as a part of the procedure, assuming that the data you are entering are not already ranked. Moreover, the process of ranking changes the distribution of data such that it can be used in many analyses usually requiring normally distributed data. Ordinal data are often **categorical** (e.g., good, better, best are three ordered *categories*) so ordinal is sometimes used to include both nominal and ordinal data. The categories may be **discrete** (e.g., number of children in a family is a discrete number; e.g., 1 or 2, etc.; it does not make sense for one family to have a number of children in between 1 and 2).

Approximately Normal (or Scale) Variables

Approximately normally distributed variables not only have levels or scores that are *ordered* from low to high, but also, as stated in Table 3.1, the frequencies of the scores are approximately normally distributed. That is, most scores are somewhere in the middle with similar smaller numbers of low and high scores. Thus a Likert scale, such as strongly agree to strongly disagree, would be considered normal if the frequency distribution was approximately normal. We think normality, because it is an assumption of many statistics, should be the focus of this highest level of measurement. Many normal variables are continuous (i.e., they have an infinite number of possible values within some range). If not continuous, we suggest that there be at least five ordered values or levels and that they have an implicit, underlying continuous nature. For example, a 5-point Likert scale has only five response categories but, in theory, a person's rating could fall anywhere between 1 and 5 (e.g., halfway between 3 and 4).

Other terms for approximately normal variables. Continuous, dimensional, and **quantitative** are some terms that you will see in the literature for variables that vary from low to high, and are assumed to be normally distributed. SPSS Statistics uses **scale,** as previously noted. Traditional measurement terminology uses the terms intervkurtosisal and ratio. Because they are common in the literature and overlapping with the SPSS term scale, we describe them briefly. **Interval** variables have ordered categories that are equally spaced (i.e., have equal intervals between them). Most physical measurements (e.g., *length, weight, temperature,* etc.) have equal intervals between them. Many physical measurements (e.g., *length* and *weight*) in fact not only have equal intervals between the levels or scores, but also a true zero, which means, in the previous examples, no length or no weight. Such variables are called **ratio** variables. Almost all psychological scales do *not* have a true zero and thus even if they are very well constructed equal interval scales, it is not possible to say that zero means that one has no intelligence or no extroversion or no attitude of a certain type. However, the differences between interval and ratio scales are not important for us because we can do all of the types of statistics that we have available with interval data. SPSS Statistics terminology supports this nondistinction by using the term **scale** for both interval and ratio data. An assumption of most parametric statistics is that the variables be approximately normally distributed, not whether they have equal intervals between levels.

Labeling Levels of Measurement in SPSS Statistics

When you label variables with this program, the **Measure** column (see Fig. 2.12) provides only three choices: nominal, ordinal, or scale. How do you decide which one to use?

Labeling variables as nominal. If the variable has only two levels (e.g., Yes or No, Pass or Fail), most researchers and we would label it **nominal** in the SPSS Statistics **Variable View** because that is traditional and it is often best to use the same statistics with dichotomous variables that you would with a nominal variable. As mentioned earlier, there are times when dichotomous variables can be treated as if they were ordinal; however, as long as you use numbers to code them, SPSS will still allow you to use them in such analyses. If there are three or more categories or values, you need to determine whether the categories are ordered (vary from low to high) or not. If the categories are just different names and not ordered, label the variable as **nominal** in the Variable View. Especially if there are more than two categories, this distinction between nominal and ordered variables makes a lot of difference in choosing and interpreting appropriate statistics.

Labeling variables as ordinal. If the categories or values of a variable vary from low to high (i.e., are ordered), and there are only three or four such values (e.g., good, better, best, or strongly disagree, disagree, agree, strongly agree), we recommend that you initially label the variable **ordinal**. Also, even if there are five or more ordered levels or values of a variable, if you suspect that the frequency distribution of the variable is substantially non-normal, label the variable **ordinal**. That is, if you do not think that the distribution is approximately symmetrical and that most of the participants had scores somewhere in the middle of the distribution, call the variable ordinal. If most of the participants are thought to be either quite high or low or you suspect that the distribution will be some shape other than bell-shaped, label the variable ordinal.

Labeling variables as scale. If the variable has five or more ordered categories or values and you have no reason to suspect that the distribution is non-normal, label the variable **scale** in the variable view **measure** column. If the variable is essentially continuous (e.g., is measured to one or more decimal places or is the average of several items), it is likely to be at least approximately normally distributed, so call it **scale**. As you will see in Chapter 4, we recommend that you check the skewness of your variables with five or more ordered levels and then adjust what you initially called a variable's measurement, if necessary. That is, you might want to change it from ordinal to scale if it turns out to be approximately normal or change from scale to ordinal if it turns out to be too skewed.[3]

Why We Prefer Our Four Levels of Measurement: A Review

As shown in Table 3.1 and Table 3.2, we distinguish between four levels of measurement: nominal, dichotomous, ordinal, and normal. Even though you can't label variables as dichotomous or normal in the SPSS Statistics variable view, we think that these four levels are conceptually and practically useful. Remember that because dichotomous variables form a special case, they can be used and interpreted much like normally distributed variables, which is why we think it is good to distinguish between nominal and dichotomous even though the SPSS program does not.

Likewise, we think that normally distributed or normal is a better label than the term scale because the latter could easily be confused with other uses of the term scale (see footnote 2) and because whether or not the variable is approximately normally distributed is, for us, what distinguishes it from an ordinal variable. Furthermore, what is important for most of the inferential statistics (e.g., *t* test) that you will compute with SPSS is the assumption that the dependent variable must be at least approximately normally distributed.

Table 3.2. *Characteristics and Examples of Our Four Levels of Measurement*

	Nominal	*Dichotomous*	*Ordinal*	*Normal (scale)*
Characteristics	3+ levels Not ordered True categories Names, labels	2 levels Ordered or not	3+ levels Ordered levels Unequal intervals between levels Not normally distributed, often skewed	5+ levels Ordered levels Approximately normally distributed Equal intervals between levels
Examples	Ethnicity Religion Curriculum type Hair color	Gender Math grades (high vs. low)	Competence scale Mother's education	SAT math Math achievement Height

Remember that in SPSS, there are only three measurement types or levels, and you are the one who determines if the variable is called nominal, ordinal, or scale (see Fig. 2.9 again). We called dichotomous variables nominal and we have labeled approximately normal variables as scale in our hsbdata file.

---

[3] Another alternative would be to transform the variable to normalize the distribution.

Descriptive Statistics and Plots

Frequency Tables

Now we expand our discussion of frequency distributions to include frequency tables, which are constructed in very similar ways for all four types of measurement. A difference is that with **nominal** data, the order in which the categories are listed is arbitrary. In Fig. 3.3, the frequency table listed *protestant, catholic,* and then *not religious*. However, *protestant* could be put after or between *catholic* and *not religious* because the categories are not ordered. In ordinal and approximately normal data, the order cannot vary (e.g., medium always should be between low and high).

religion

		Frequency	Percent	Valid Percent	Cumulative Percent
Valid	protestant	30	40.0	44.8	44.8
	catholic	23	30.7	34.3	79.1
	not religious	14	18.7	20.9	100.0
	Total	67	89.3	100.0	
Missing	other religion	4	5.3		
	blank	4	5.3		
	Total	8	10.7		
Total		75	100.0		

Fig. 3.3. A frequency table for *religion,* a nominal variable.

Fig. 3.3 is a table that shows religious affiliation from the hsbdata that we are using in this book. In this example, there is a **Frequency** column that shows the numbers of students who checked each type of religion (e.g., 30 said *protestant* and 4 left it *blank*). Notice that there is a *total* (67) for the three responses considered **Valid** and a *total* (8) for the two types of responses considered to be **Missing** as well as an overall *total* (75). The **Percent** column indicates that 40.0% are *protestant*, 30.7% are *catholic*, 18.7% are *not religious*, 5.3% had one of several *other religions*, and 5.3% left the question *blank*. The **Valid Percent** column excludes the eight missing cases and is often the column that you would use. Given this data set, it would be accurate to say that <u>of those not coded as missing</u>, 44.8% were *protestant,* 34.3%, *catholic,* and 20.9% were *not religious.*

To get Fig. 3.3, select:
- **Analyze → Descriptive Statistics → Frequencies** → move *religion* to the **Variable(s):** box → **OK** (make sure that the **Display frequency tables** box is checked.

When the variable has ordered levels (i.e., is **ordinal** or **approximately normal**), the procedure is the same and the frequency table has the same structure. However, when the variable is ordinal or approximately normal, the **Cumulative Percent** column is useful. With a nominal variable, the cumulative percent column usually is not useful. From Fig. 3.4, we can say that 22.7% of the students had grades that were *mostly Cs* <u>or less</u> and that 64% had *mostly Bs* <u>or less</u>.

To create Fig. 3.4, select:
- **Analyze → Descriptive Statistics → Frequencies** → move *grades in h.s.* to the **Variable(s):** box → **OK**.

grades in h.s.

		Frequency	Percent	Valid Percent	Cumulative Percent
Valid	mostly D	1	1.3	1.3	1.3
	half CD	8	10.7	10.7	12.0
	mostly C	8	10.7	10.7	22.7
	half BC	16	21.3	21.3	44.0
	mostly B	15	20.0	20.0	64.0
	half AB	18	24.0	24.0	88.0
	mostly A	9	12.0	12.0	100.0
	Total	75	100.0	100.0	

Fig. 3.4. A frequency table for an ordered variable: *grades* in h.s.

As mentioned earlier, frequency distributions indicate how many participants are in each category, giving you a feel for the distribution of scores. If one wants to make a diagram of a frequency distribution, there are several choices, four of which are bar charts, frequency polygons, histograms, and box and whisker plots.

Bar Charts

With **nominal** data, you should not use a graphic that connects adjacent categories because with nominal data there is no necessary ordering of the categories or levels. Thus, it is better to make a bar graph or chart of the frequency distribution of variables like *religion, ethnic group,* or other nominal variables; the points that happen to be adjacent in your frequency distribution are not by necessity adjacent.

Fig. 3.5 is a bar chart created by selecting:
- **Analyze → Descriptive Statistics → Frequencies →** move *religion* **→ Charts → Bar charts → Continue → OK.**

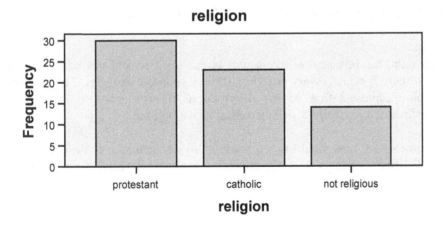

Fig. 3.5. Sample frequency distribution bar chart for the nominal variable of *religion*.

Histograms

As we can see if we compare Fig. 3.5 to the histograms in Fig. 3.1 and 3.2, histograms look much like bar charts except in histograms there is no space between the boxes, indicating that there is theoretically a continuous variable underlying the scores (i.e., scores could theoretically be any point on a continuum from the lowest to highest score). Histograms can be used even if data, as measured, are not continuous, if the underlying variable is conceptualized as continuous. For example, the *competence scale* items were rated on a 4-point scale, but one could, theoretically, have any amount of competence.

Frequency Polygons

Figure 3.6 is a frequency polygon; it connects the points between the categories and is best used with **approximately normal** data, but it can be used with ordinal data.

To create Fig. 3.6, select:
*   **Graphs →Legacy Dialogs →Line...** (be sure that **Simple** and **Summaries for groups of cases** are checked) → **Define** → *motivation scale* to **Category Axis** box → **OK.**

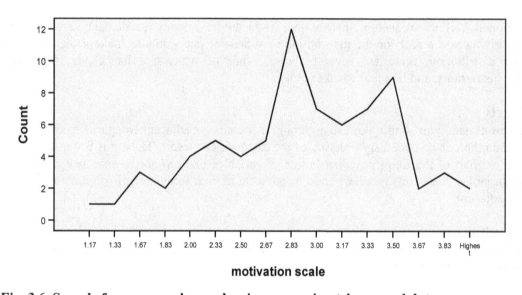

Fig. 3.6. Sample frequency polygon showing approximately normal data.

Box and Whiskers Plot

For **ordinal** and **normal** data, the box and whiskers plot is useful; it should not be used with nominal data because then there is no necessary ordering of the response categories. The box and whiskers plot is a graphic representation of the distribution of scores and is helpful in distinguishing between ordinal and normally distributed data, as we will see.

Using our hsbdata set, you can see how useful this graphic analysis technique is for comparing frequency distributions of different groups. Fig. 3.7 compares genders on scores from the math section of the SAT.

This box and whiskers plot was created by selecting:
*   **Analyze → Descriptive Statistics → Explore →** *scholastic aptitude test – math* to **Dependent List** box → *gender* to **Factor List** → under **Display** select **Plots** → **OK.**

Fig. 3.7 shows two box plots, one for males and one for females. The box represents the middle 50% of the cases (i.e., those between the 25th and 75th percentiles). The whiskers indicate the <u>expected range of scores</u>. Scores outside of this range are considered unusually high or low. Such scores, called **outliers**, are shown above and/or below the whiskers with circles or asterisks (for very extreme scores) and with the **Data View** line number for that participant. Note there are no outliers for the 34 males, but there is a low (#6) and a high (#54) female outlier. (Note this number will not be the participant's ID unless you specify that the program should report this by ID number or the ID numbers correspond exactly to the line numbers.)

We will come back to Fig. 3.7 in several later sections of this chapter.

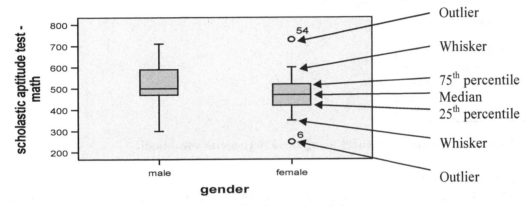

Fig. 3.7. A box and whiskers plot for ordinal or normal data.

Measures of Central Tendency

Three measures of the center of a distribution are commonly used: **mean, median,** and **mode**. Any of them can be used with normally distributed data. With ordinal data, the mean of the raw scores is *not* appropriate, but the mean of the *ranked* scores provides useful information. With nominal data, the mode is the only appropriate measure.

Mean. The arithmetic average or mean takes into account all of the available information in computing the central tendency of a frequency distribution. Thus, it is usually the statistic of choice, assuming that the data are normally distributed data. The mean is computed by adding up all the raw scores and dividing by the number of scores ($M = \Sigma X/N$).

Median. The middle score or median is the appropriate measure of central tendency for ordinal level raw data. The median is a better measure of central tendency than the mean when the frequency distribution is skewed. For example, the median income of 100 mid-level workers and one millionaire reflects the central tendency of the group better (and is substantially lower) than the mean income. The average or mean would be inflated in this example by the income of the one millionaire. For normally distributed data, the median is in the center of the **box and whiskers plot**. Notice that in Fig. 3.7 the median for males is not in the center of the box.

Mode. The most common category, or mode, can be used with any kind of data but generally provides the least precise information about central tendency. Moreover, if one's data are continuous, there often are multiple modes, none of which truly represents the "typical" score. In fact, if there are multiple modes, this program provides only the lowest one. One would use the mode as the measure of central tendency if the variable is nominal or you want a quick noncalculated measure. The mode is the tallest bar in a bar graph or histogram (e.g., in Fig. 3.5, *protestant,* category 1, is the mode).

You also can compute the **Mean, Median,** and **Mode,** plus other descriptive statistics, with this program by using the **Frequencies** command.

To get Fig 3.8, select:

- **Analyze** → **Descriptive Statistics** → **Frequencies** → move *scholastic aptitude test – math* → **Statistics** → **Mean, Median, and Mode** → **Continue** → **OK**.

Note in Fig. 3.8 that the mean and median are very similar, which is in agreement with our conclusion from Fig. 3.1 that *SATM* is approximately normally distributed. Note that the mode is 500, as shown in Fig. 3.1 by the highest bars.

Statistics

scholastic aptitude test - math

N	Valid	75
	Missing	0
Mean		490.53
Median		490.00
Mode		500

Fig. 3.8. Central tendency measures using the Frequencies command.

Measures of Variability

Variability tells us about the spread or dispersion of the scores. If all of the scores in a distribution are the same, there is no variability. If the scores are all different and widely spaced apart, the variability will be high. The **range** (highest minus lowest score) is the crudest measure of variability but does give an indication of the spread in scores if they are ordered.

Standard deviation. This common measure of variability is most appropriate when one has normally distributed data, although the standard deviation of ranked ordinal data may also be useful in some cases. The standard deviation is based on the deviation (x) of each score from the mean of all the scores. Those deviation scores are squared and then summed (Σx^2). This sum is divided by $N - 1$, and, finally, the square root is taken ($SD = \sqrt{\sum x^2 / N - 1}$).

We can use the **Descriptives** command to get measures of central tendency and variability. Figure 3.9 is a printout from the hsbdata set for the *scholastic aptitude test – math* scores. We can easily see that of the 75 people in the data set, the **Minimum** (low) score was 250 and the **Maximum (**high) score was 730. The **Range** is 480 (730−250). (Remember the two female outliers in Fig. 3.7, the box and whiskers plot.) The **mean** score was 490.53 and **std** (standard deviation) 94.55. A rough estimate of the standard deviation is the range divided by 5 (e.g., 480/5 = 96).

To get Fig. 3.9, select:

- **Analyze** → **Descriptives Statistics** → **Descriptive** → move *scholastic aptitude test – math* → **Options** → **Mean, Std Deviation, Range, Minimum, Maximum,** and **Skewness** → **Continue** → **OK**.

We discuss **Skewness** later in the chapter.

Descriptive Statistics

	N	Range	Minimum	Maximum	Mean	Std.	Skewness	
	Statistic	Statistic	Statistic	Statistic	Statistic	Statistic	Statistic	Std. Error
scholastic aptitude test - math	75	480	250	730	490.53	94.553	.128	.277
Valid N (listwise)	75							

Fig. 3.9. Descriptive statistics for the scholastic aptitude test – math (SATM).

Interquartile range. For ordinal data, the interquartile range, seen in the **box plot** (Fig. 3.7) as the distance between the top and bottom of the box, is a useful measure of variability. Note that the whiskers indicate the expected range, and scores outside that range are shown as outliers.

With nominal data, none of the previous variability measures (range, standard deviation, or interquartile range) is appropriate. Instead, for nominal data, one would need to ask how many different categories there are and what the percentages or frequency counts are in each category to get some idea of variability. Minimum and maximum frequency may provide some indication of distribution as well.

Measurement and Descriptive Statistics

Table 3.3 summarizes much of the previous information about the appropriate use of various kinds of descriptive statistics given nominal, dichotomous, ordinal, or normal data.

Table 3.3. *Selection of Appropriate Descriptive Statistics and Plots*

	Nominal	*Dichotomous*	*Ordinal*	*Normal*
Frequency Distribution	Yes[a]	Yes	Yes	OK[b]
Bar Chart	Yes	Yes	Yes	OK
Histogram	No[c]	No	OK	Yes
Frequency Polygon	No	No	OK	Yes
Box and Whiskers Plot	No	No	Yes	Yes
Central Tendency				
Mean	No	OK	Of ranks, OK	Yes
Median	No	OK = Mode	Yes	OK
Mode	Yes	Yes	OK	OK
Variability				
Range	No	Always 1	Yes	Yes
Standard Deviation	No	No	Of ranks, OK	Yes
Interquartile range	No	No	OK	OK
How many categories	Yes	Always 2	OK	Not if truly continuous
Shape				
Skewness	No	No	Yes	Yes

[a]Yes means a good choice with this level of measurement.
[b]OK means OK to use, but not the best choice at this level of measurement.
[c]No means not appropriate at this level of measurement.

Conclusions about Measurement and the Use of Statistics

Statistics based on means and standard deviation are valid for normally distributed or **normal** data. Typically, these data are used in the most powerful tests called **parametric** statistics. However, if the data are ordered but grossly non-normal (i.e., **ordinal**), means and standard deviations of the raw data may not provide accurate information about central tendency and variability. Then the median and a **nonparametric** test would be preferred. Nonparametric tests typically have somewhat less **power** than parametric tests (they are less able to demonstrate significant effects even if a real effect exists), but the sacrifice in power for nonparametric tests based on ranks usually is relatively minor. If the data are **nominal**, one would have to use the mode or counts.

The Normal Curve

Figure 3.10 is an example of a normal curve. The frequency distributions of many of the variables used in the behavioral sciences are distributed approximately as a normal curve when N is large. Examples of such variables that approximately fit a normal curve are height, weight, intelligence, and many personality variables. Notice that for each of these examples, most people would fall toward the middle of the curve, with fewer people at the extremes. If the average height of men in the United States was 5'10", then this height would be in the middle of the curve. The heights of men who are taller than 5'10" would be to the right of the middle on the curve, and those of men who are shorter than 5'10" would be to the left of the middle on the curve, with only a few men 7 feet or 5 feet tall.

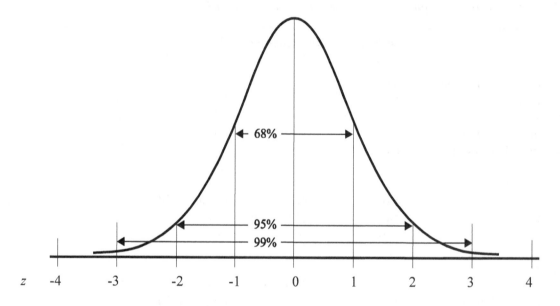

Fig. 3.10. Frequency distribution and areas under the normal curve.

The normal curve can be thought of as derived from a frequency distribution. It is theoretically formed from counting an "infinite" number of occurrences of a variable. Usually, when the normal curve is depicted, only the X axis (horizontal) is shown. To determine how a frequency distribution is obtained, you could take a fair coin, flip it 10 times, and record the number of heads on this first set or trial. Then flip it another 10 times and record the number of heads. If you had nothing better to do, you could do 100 trials. After performing this task, you could plot the number of times that the coin turned up heads out of each trial of 10. What would you expect? Of course, the largest number of trials probably would show 5 heads out of 10. There would be very few, if any, trials where 0, 1, 9, or 10 heads occurred. It could happen, but the probability is quite low, which brings us to a probability distribution. If we performed this experiment 100 times, or 1,000 times, or 1,000,000 times, the frequency distribution would "fill in" and look more and more like a normal curve.

Properties of the Normal Curve

The normal curve has five properties that are always present.

1. The normal curve is unimodal. It has one "hump," and this hump is in the middle of the distribution. The most frequent value is in the middle.
2. The mean, median, and mode are equal.
3. The curve is symmetric. If you fold the normal curve in half, the right side would fit perfectly with the left side; that is, it is not **skewed**.
4. The range is infinite. This means that the extremes approach but never touch the X axis.
5. The curve is neither too peaked nor too flat and its tails are neither too short nor too long; it has no **kurtosis**. Its proportions are like those in Fig. 3.10.

Non-Normally Shaped Distributions

Skewness. If one tail of a frequency distribution is longer than the other, and if the mean and median are different, the curve is skewed. Because most common inferential statistics (e.g., t test) assume that the dependent variable is normally distributed (the data are normal), it is important that we know whether our variables are highly skewed.

Figure 3.2 showed a frequency distribution that is skewed to the left. This is called a negative skew. A perfectly normal curve has a skewness of zero (0.0). The curve in Fig. 3.2, for the *competence* scale, has a skewness statistic of –1.63, which indicates that the curve is quite different from a normal curve. We use a somewhat arbitrary guideline that if the skewness is more than +1.0 or less than –1.0, the distribution is markedly skewed and it would be prudent to use a nonparametric (ordinal type) statistic (or to transform the variable). However, some parametric statistics, such as the two-tailed t test and ANOVA, are quite robust, so even a skewness of more than +/–1 may not change the results much. We provide more examples and discuss this more in Chapter 4.

Kurtosis. If a frequency distribution is more peaked than the normal curve shown in Fig. 3.10, it is said to have positive kurtosis and is called leptokurtic. Note in Fig. 3.1 that the *scholastic aptitude test – math* histogram is peaked (i.e., the bar for 500 would extend above the theoretical normal curve line), and thus there is some positive kurtosis. If a frequency distribution is relatively flat with heavy tails, it has negative kurtosis and is called platykurtic. Although the program can easily compute a kurtosis value for any variable using an option in the **Frequencies** command, usually we do not do so because kurtosis does not seem to affect the results of most statistical analyses very much.

Areas under the Normal Curve

The normal curve is also a probability distribution. Visualize that the area under the normal curve is equal to 1.0. Therefore, portions of this curve could be expressed as fractions of 1.0. For example, if we assume that 5'10" is the average height of men in the United States, then the probability of a man being 5'10" or taller is .5. The probability of a man being over 6'3" or less than 5'5" is considerably smaller. It is important to be able to conceptualize the normal curve as a probability distribution because statistical convention sets acceptable probability levels for rejecting the null hypothesis at .05 or .01. As we shall see, when events or outcomes happen very infrequently, that is, only 5 times in 100 or 1 time in 100 (way out in the left or right tail of the curve), we wonder if they belong to that distribution or perhaps to a different distribution. We come back to this point later in the book.

All normal curves, regardless of whether they are narrow or spread out, can be divided into areas or units in terms of the standard deviation. Approximately 34% of the area under the normal curve is between the mean and one standard deviation above or below the mean (see Fig. 3.10 again). If we include both the area to the right *and* to the left of the mean, 68% of the area under the normal curve is within one standard deviation from the mean. Another approximately 13.5% of the area under the normal curve is accounted for by adding a second standard deviation to the first standard deviation. In other words, two standard deviations to the right of the mean account for an area of approximately 47.5%, and two standard deviations to the left *and* right of the mean make up an area of approximately 95% of the normal curve. If we were to subtract 95% from 100%, the remaining 5% relates to that ever-present probability or *p* value of 0.05 needed for statistical significance. Values not falling within two standard deviations of the mean are seen as relatively rare events.

The Standard Normal Curve

All normal curves can be converted into standard normal curves by setting the mean equal to zero and the standard deviation equal to one. Because all normal curves have the same proportion of the curve within one standard deviation, two standard deviations, and so forth of the mean, this conversion allows comparisons among normal curves with different means and standard deviations. Figure 3.10, the normal distribution, has the standard normal distribution units underneath. These units are referred to as **z scores.** If you examine the normal curve table in any statistics book, you can find the areas under the curve for one standard deviation ($z = 1$), two standard deviations ($z = 2$), and so on. As described in Appendix A, it is easy to convert raw scores into *standard scores*. This is often done when one wants to aggregate or add together several scores that have quite different means and standard deviations.

Interpretation Questions

3.1   If you have categorical, ordered data (such as low income, middle income, high income) what type of measurement would you have? Why?

3.2   (a) Compare and contrast nominal, dichotomous, ordinal, and normal variables. (b) In social science research, why isn't it important to distinguish between interval and ratio variables?

3.3   What percent of the area under the standard normal curve is within one standard deviation of (above or below) the mean? What does this tell you about scores that are more than one standard deviation away from the mean?

3.4   (a) How do *z* scores relate to the normal curve? (b) How would you interpret a *z* score of −3.0? (c) What percentage of scores is between a *z* of −2 and a *z* of +2? Why is this important?

3.5   Why should you not use a frequency polygon if you have nominal data? What would be better to use to display nominal data?

Extra SPSS Problems

Use the hsbdata.sav file from http://www.psypress.com/ibm-spss-intro-stats/ ("Data Sets (ZIPS)" button) to do these problems with one or more of these variables: *math achievement, mother's education, ethnicity, and gender*. Use Tables 3.2, 3.3, and the instructions in the text to produce the appropriate plots or descriptive statistics. Be sure that the plots and/or descriptive statistics make sense (i.e. that they are a "good choice" or "OK") for the variable.

3.1   Create bar charts. Discuss why you did or didn't create a bar chart for each variable.

3.2   Create histograms. Discuss why you did or didn't create a histogram for each variable.

3.3   Create frequency polygons. Discuss why you did or didn't create a frequency polygon for each variable. Compare the plots in Extra SPSS Problems 3.1, 3.2, and 3.3.

3.4   Compute the range, standard deviation, and skewness. Discuss which measures of variability are meaningful for each of the four variables.

3.5   Compute the mean, median, and mode. Discuss which measures of central tendency are meaningful for each of the four variables.

CHAPTER 4

Understanding Your Data and Checking Assumptions

Before computing any inferential statistics, it is important to do exploratory data analysis (EDA), as outlined below. This chapter helps you understand your data, helps you to see if there are any errors, and helps you to know if your data meet basic assumptions for the statistics that you will compute.

To enable you to understand your data, you will undertake different types of analyses and create different types of plots depending on the level of measurement of the variables. As discussed in Chapter 3, this program labels the levels of measurement **nominal**, **ordinal**, and **scale**. Remember that we think it is useful to distinguish between **nominal** and **dichotomous**, and we think that **normal** is more descriptive than the term **scale**. Keep in mind that there are times when whether you call a variable ordinal or scale might change based on your EDA. For example, a variable that you initially considered to be ordinal may be normally distributed and thus may be better thought of as normal. Recall from Chapters 2 and 3 that making the appropriate choice requires that you understand your data; thus EDA should help guide your selection of a statistic.

Exploratory Data Analysis (EDA)

What Is EDA?
After the data are entered into this program, the first step to complete (before running any inferential statistics) is EDA, which involves computing various descriptive statistics and graphs. **Exploratory data analysis** is used to <u>examine and get to know your data</u>. Chapters 2, 3, and especially this chapter, focus on ways to do exploratory data analysis. EDA is important to do for several reasons:

1. To see if there are problems in the data such as outliers, non-normal distributions, problems with coding, missing values, and/or errors from inputting the data.

2. To examine the extent to which the assumptions of the statistics that you plan to use are met.

In addition to these two reasons, which are discussed in this chapter, one could also do EDA for other purposes, such as:

3. To get basic information regarding the demographics of subjects to report in the Method or Results section.

4. To examine relationships between variables to determine how to conduct the hypothesis-testing analyses. For example, correlations can be used to see if two or more variables are so highly related that they should be combined for further analyses and/or if only one of them should be included in the central analyses. We create *parents' education*, in Chapter 5, by combining *father's education* and *mother's education*, because they are quite highly correlated.

How to Do EDA
There are two general methods used for EDA: generating plots of the data and generating numbers from your data. Both are important and can be very helpful methods of investigating the

data. Descriptive statistics (including the minimum, maximum, mean, standard deviation, and skewness), frequency distribution tables, boxplots, histograms, and stem and leaf plots are a few procedures used in EDA.

After collecting data and inputting them, many students jump immediately to doing inferential statistics (e.g., *t* tests and ANOVAs). Don't do this! Many times there are errors or problems with the data that need to be located and either fixed or at least noted before doing any inferential statistics.

At this point, you are probably asking "Why?" or "I'll do that boring descriptive stuff later while I am writing the methods section." Wait! Being patient can alleviate many problems down the road.

In the next two sections, we discuss checking for errors and checking assumptions. Some of this discussion reviews material presented in Chapters 2 and 3, but it is so important that it is worth repeating.

Check for Errors

There are many ways to check for errors. For example:

1. Look over the raw data (questionnaires, interviews, or observation forms) to see if there are inconsistencies, double coding, obvious errors, and so forth. Do this before entering the data into the computer.
2. Check some, or preferably all, of the raw data (e.g., questionnaires) against the data in your **Data Editor** file to be sure that errors were not made in the data entry.
3. Compare the minimum and maximum values for each variable in your **Descriptives** output with the allowable range of values in your codebook.
4. Examine the means and standard deviations to see if they look reasonable, given what you know about the variables.
5. Examine the *N* column to see if any variables have a lot of missing data, which can be a problem when you do statistics with two or more variables. Missing data could also indicate that there was a problem in data entry.
6. Look for outliers (i.e., extreme scores) in the data.

Statistical Assumptions

Every inferential statistical test has assumptions. Statistical assumptions are much like the directions for appropriate use of a product found in an owner's manual. **Assumptions** explain when it is and isn't reasonable to perform a specific statistical test. When the *t* test was developed, for example, the person who developed it needed to make certain assumptions about the distribution of scores in order to be able to calculate the statistic accurately. If the assumptions are not met, the value that the program calculates, which tells the researcher whether or not the results are statistically significant, will not be completely accurate and may even lead the researcher to draw the wrong conclusion about the results. In Chapters 7–10, inferential statistics and their assumptions are described.

Parametric tests. These include most of the familiar ones (e.g., *t* test, ANOVA, correlation). They usually have more assumptions than do nonparametric tests. Parametric tests were designed for data that have certain characteristics, including approximately normal distributions.

Some parametric statistics have been found to be "robust" with regard to one or more of their assumptions. **Robust** means that the assumption can be violated quite a lot without damaging the validity of the statistic. For example, one assumption of the *t* test and ANOVA is that the dependent variable is normally distributed for each group. Statisticians who have studied these statistics have found that even when data are not normally distributed (e.g., are skewed) they can still be used under many circumstances.

Nonparametric tests. These tests (e.g., chi-square, Mann–Whitney U, Spearman rho) have fewer assumptions and often can be used when the assumptions of a parametric test are violated. For example, they do not require normal distributions of variables or homogeneity of variances.

Check Assumptions

Homogeneity of variances. Both the *t* test and ANOVA may be affected if the variances (standard deviation squared) of the groups to be compared are substantially different. Thus, this is a critical assumption to meet or correct for. Fortunately, the program provides the Levene's test to check this assumption, and it provides ways to adjust the results if the variances are significantly different.

Normality. As mentioned previously, many parametric statistics assume that certain variables are distributed approximately normally. That is, the frequency distribution would look like a symmetrical bell-shaped or normal curve, with most subjects having values in the mid range and with similar small numbers of participants with both high and low scores. A distribution that is asymmetrical with more high than low scores (or vice versa) is **skewed**. Thus, it is important to check skewness. There are also several other ways to check for normality, some of which are presented in Chapter 3. In this chapter, we look in detail at one graphic method, boxplots. However, remember that *t* (if two-tailed) and ANOVA are quite robust to violations of normality.

Check other assumptions of the specific statistic. In later chapters, we discuss other assumptions as they are relevant to the problem posed.

The type of variable you are exploring (whether it is nominal, ordinal, dichotomous, or normal/ scale) influences the type of exploratory data analysis (EDA) you will want to do. Thus, we have divided the problems in this chapter by the measurement levels of the variable because, for some types of variables, certain descriptive statistics or plots will not make sense (e.g., a mean for a nominal variable, or a boxplot for a dichotomous variable). Remember that the researcher has labeled the type of measurement as either nominal, ordinal, or scale when completing the **Data Editor Variable View.** Because the researcher is the one making these decisions, the label can and should change if the results of the EDA determine the variables are not labeled correctly. Remember also that <u>we decided to label dichotomous variables as **nominal,**</u> and <u>variables that we assumed were normally distributed were labeled as **scale**</u>.

For <u>all the problems in Chapter 4, you will be using the HSB data file.</u>

- Retrieve **hsbdata.sav** from the Web site if you haven't already. It is desirable to make a working copy of this file. See Appendix A for instructions if you need help with this or getting started. Appendix A also shows how to set your computer to print the syntax.

Problem 4.1: Descriptive Statistics for the Ordinal and Scale Variables

In this problem, we use all of the HSB variables that we initially labeled as ordinal or scale in the **Variable View.** With those types of variables, it is important to see if the means make sense (are they close to what you expected?), to examine the dispersion/spread of the data, and to check the shape of the distribution (i.e., skewness value).

4.1. Examine the data to get a good understanding of the central tendency, variability, range of scores, and the shape of the distribution for each of the ordinal and scale variables. Which variables are normally distributed?

This problem includes descriptive statistics and ways to examine your data to see if the variables are approximately normally distributed, an assumption of most of the parametric inferential statistics that we use. Remember that **skewness** is an important statistic for understanding whether a variable is normally distributed; it is an index that helps determine how much a variable's distribution deviates from the distribution of the normal curve. Skewness refers to the lack of symmetry in a frequency distribution. Distributions with a long "tail" to the right have a **positive skew** and those with a long tail on the left have a **negative skew**. If a frequency distribution of a variable has a large (plus or minus) skewness, that variable is said to deviate from normality. In this assignment, we examine this assumption for several key variables. However, some of the parametric inferential statistics that we use later in the book are robust or quite insensitive to violations of normality. Thus, we assume that it is okay to use parametric statistics to answer most of our research questions as long as the variables are not extremely skewed.

We answer Problem 4.1 by using the **Descriptives** command, which makes a compact, space-efficient output. You could instead run **Frequencies** because you can get the same statistics with that command. We use the Frequencies command later in the chapter. We use the Descriptives command to compute the basic descriptive statistics for all of the variables that we initially labeled ordinal or scale. We will <u>not</u> include the nominal variables (*ethnicity* and *religion*) or *gender, algebra1, algebra2, geometry, trigonometry, calculus,* and *math grades,* which are dichotomous variables but are labeled nominal here. We use them in a later problem.

4.1a. First, we will compute **Descriptives** for the **ordinal** variables. Use these steps:

- Select **Analyze → Descriptive Statistics → Descriptives…**

After selecting **Descriptives**, you will be ready to compute the mean, standard deviation, skewness, minimum, and maximum for all participants or cases on all the variables that we initially called ordinal under **Measure** in the **Variable View** of the **Data Editor.**

- While holding down the control key (i.e., the key marked "Ctrl"), click on all of the variables in the left box that we called **ordinal** so that they are highlighted.. These include *father's education, mother's education, grades in h.s.,* and all the "item" variables (*item 01* through *item 11 reversed)*. Note that each of these variables has the symbol ![icon], which indicates that it was called **ordinal** in the variable view.
- Click on the **arrow** button pointing right to produce Fig. 4.1.
- Be sure that all of the requested variables have moved out of the left window.

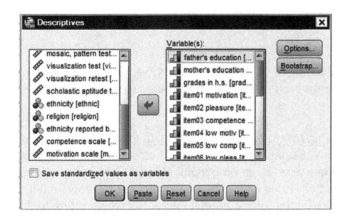

Fig. 4.1. Descriptives.

- Click on **Options.** The Descriptives: Options window (Fig. 4.2) will open.
- Be sure that **Mean** has a check next to it.
- Under **Dispersion,** select **Std. Deviation, Variance, Range, Minimum,** and **Maximum** so that each has a check.
- Under **Distribution,** check **Skewness.** Your window should look like Fig. 4.2

Fig. 4.2. Descriptives: Options.

- Click on **Continue** to get back to Fig. 4.1.
- Click on **OK** to produce Output 4.1a.

4.1b. Next, we compute **Descriptives** for the variables that were labeled **scale** in the **Data Editor.** Note that these variables have the symbol ![symbol] next to them.

- Click on **Reset** in Fig. 4.1 to move the ordinal variables back to the left. This also deletes what we chose under Options.
- Highlight *math achievement, mosaic pattern test, visualization test, visualization retest, scholastic aptitude test – math, competence scale,* and *motivation scale* and move them to the **Variables** box.
- Click on **Options** and check the same descriptive statistics as you did in Fig. 4.2.

Compare your syntax and output to Outputs 4.1a and 4.1b. If they look the same, you have done the steps correctly. If the syntax is not showing in your output, consult Appendix A to see how to set your computer so that the syntax is displayed.

Output 4.1a: Descriptives for the Variables Initially Labeled Ordinal

```
DESCRIPTIVES VARIABLES=faed maed grades item01 item02 item03 item04 item05 item06
item07 item08 item09 item10 item11 item12 item13 item14 item04r item05r item08r item11r
  /STATISTICS=MEAN STDDEV VARIANCE RANGE MIN MAX SKEWNESS.
```

> Syntax or log file shows the variables and statistics that you requested.

Descriptives

Descriptive Statistics

	N	Range	Minimum	Maximum	Mean	Std.	Variance	Skewness	
	Statistic	Statistic	Statistic	Statistic	Statistic	Statistic	Statistic	Statistic	Std. Error
father's education	73	8	2	10	4.73	2.830	8.007	.684	.281
mother's education	75	8	2	10	4.11	2.240	5.015	1.124	.277
grades in h.s.	75	6	2	8	5.68	1.570	2.464	-.332	.277
item01 motivation	74	3	1	4	2.96	.928	.861	-.763	.279
item02 pleasure	75	3	1	4	3.52	.906	.821	-1.910	.277
item03 competence	74	3	1	4	2.82	.897	.804	-.579	.279
item04 low motiv	74	3	1	4	2.16	.922	.850	.422	.279
item05 low comp	75	3	1	4	1.61	.971	.943	1.581	.277
item06 low pleas	75	3	1	4	2.43	.975	.951	-.058	.277
item07 motivation	75	3	1	4	2.76	1.051	1.104	-.433	.277
item08 low motiv	75	3	1	4	1.95	.914	.835	.653	.277
item09 competence	74	3	1	4	3.32	.760	.578	-1.204	.279
item10 low pleas	75	3	1	4	1.41	.737	.543	1.869	.277
item11 low comp	75	3	1	4	1.36	.747	.558	2.497	.277
item12 motivation	75	3	1	4	3.00	.822	.676	-.600	.277
item13 motivation	75	3	1	4	2.67	.794	.631	-.320	.277
item14 pleasure	75	3	1	4	2.84	.717	.515	-.429	.277
item04 reversed	74	3	1	4	2.84	.922	.850	-.422	.279
item05 reversed	75	3	1	4	3.39	.971	.943	-1.581	.277
item08 reversed	75	3	1	4	3.05	.914	.835	-.653	.277
item11 reversed	75	3	1	4	3.64	.747	.558	-2.497	.277
Valid N (listwise)	69								

Output 4.1b Descriptives for Variables Initially Labeled as Scale

```
DESCRIPTIVES
  VARIABLES=mathach mosaic visual visual2 satm competence motivation
  /STATISTICS=MEAN STDDEV VARIANCE RANGE MIN MAX SKEWNESS .
```

Descriptives

Descriptive Statistics

	N	Range	Minimum	Maximum	Mean	Std.	Variance	Skewness	
	Statistic	Statistic	Statistic	Statistic	Statistic	Statistic	Statistic	Statistic	Std. Error
math achievement te	75	25.33	-1.67	23.67	12.5645	6.67031	44.493	.044	.277
mosaic, pattern test	75	60.0	-4.0	56.0	27.413	9.5738	91.658	.529	.277
visualization test	75	15.00	-.25	14.75	5.2433	3.91203	15.304	.536	.277
visualization retest	75	9.50	.00	9.50	4.5467	3.01816	9.109	.235	.277
scholastic aptitude test - math	75	480	250	730	490.53	94.553	8940.252	.128	.277
Competence scale	73	3.00	1.00	4.00	3.2945	.66450	.442	-1.634	.281
Motivation scale	73	2.83	1.17	4.00	2.8744	.63815	.407	-.570	.281
Valid N (listwise)	71								

Interpretation of Outputs 4.1a and 4.1b

These outputs provide descriptive statistics for all of the variables labeled as **ordinal** (4.1a) and **scale** (4.1b). Notice that the variables are listed down the left column of the outputs and the requested descriptive statistics are listed across the top row. The descriptive statistics included in the output are the number of subjects (*N*), the **Range, Minimum** (lowest) and **Maximum** (highest) scores, the **Mean** (or average) for each variable, the **Std.** (the standard deviation), the **Variance**, the **Skewness** statistic, and the **Std. error** of the skewness. Note, from the bottom line of the outputs, that the **Valid N (listwise)** is 69 for Output 4.1a and 71 for 4.1b rather than 75, which is the number of participants in the data file. This is because the **listwise** *N* only includes the persons with *no* missing data on any variable requested in the output. Notice that several variables (e.g., *father's education, item01, motivation,* and *competence*) each have a few participants missing.

Using your output to check your data for errors. For both the ordinal and scale variables, check to make sure that all **Means** seem reasonable. That is, you should check your means to see if they are within the ranges you expected (given the information in your codebook) and if the means are close to what you might expect (given your understanding of the variable). Next, check the output to see that the **Minimum** and **Maximum** are within the appropriate (codebook) range for each variable. If the minimum is smaller or the maximum is bigger than you expected (e.g., 0 or 100 for a variable that has 1–50 for possible values), then there was an error somewhere. Finally, you should check the *N* column to see if the *N*s are what you were expecting. If it happens that you have more participants missing than you expected, check the original data to see if you forgot to enter some data, or data were entered incorrectly. Notice that the *competence scale* and the *motivation scale* each have two participants missing.

Using the output to check assumptions. The main assumption that we can check from this output is normality. We won't pay much attention to the skewness for *item 01* to *item 11 reversed*, which have only four levels (1–4). These ordinal variables have fewer than five levels, so they will not be considered to be scale even though some of the "item" variables are not very skewed. We do not use them as individual variables because we are combining them to create summated variables (the *motivation, competence,* and *pleasure* scales) before using inferential statistics. Most statistics books do not provide advice about how to decide whether a variable is at least approximately normal. SPSS recommends that you divide the skewness by its standard error. If the result is less than 2.5 (which is approximately the $p = .01$ level) then skewness is *not* significantly different from normal. A problem with this method, aside from having to use a calculator, is that the standard error depends on the sample size, so with large samples most variables would be found to be non-normal, yet, actually, data for large samples are more likely to be approximately normal. A simpler guideline is that if the absolute value (value without considering whether or not there is a negative sign) of the skewness is less than one, the variable is at least approximately normal. From Output 4.1a, we can see that two of the variables that we initially called **ordinal** (*father's education* and *grades in h.s.*) are approximately normally distributed. These ordinal variables, with five or more levels, have skewness values between –1 and 1. Thus, we can assume that they are more like scale variables, and we can use inferential statistics that have the assumption of normality. To better understand these variables, it may be helpful to change the **Measure** column in the **Variable View** so that these two variables are labeled as **scale**; we call them **normal**.

We expect the variables that we initially labeled as scale to be normally distributed. Look at the **Skewness Statistic** in Output 4.1b to see if it is between –1 and 1. From the output we see that most of these variables have skewness values between –1 and 1, but one (*competence*) does not, so it may be helpful to change it to **ordinal** in the **Measure** column.

There are several ways to check this assumption in addition to checking the skewness value. If the mean, median, and mode, which can be obtained with the Frequencies command, are approximately equal, then you can assume that the distribution is approximately normally distributed. For example, remember from Chapter 3 (Fig. 3.8) that the mean (490.53), median (490.00), and mode (500) for *scholastic aptitude test – math* were very similar values, and the skewness value was .128 (see Output 4.1). Thus, we can assume that *SAT-math* is approximately normally distributed.

Problem 4.2: Boxplots for One Variable and for Multiple Variables

In addition to numerical methods for understanding your data, there are several graphic methods. In Chapter 3, we demonstrated the use of histograms and also frequency polygons (line graphs) to roughly assess normality. The trouble is that visual inspection of histograms can be deceiving because some approximately normal distributions don't look very much like a normal curve. Thus, we don't find the superimposed normal curve line on histograms very useful.

In this problem, we use **Boxplots** to examine some HSB variables. Boxplots are a method of graphically representing ordinal and scale data. They can be made with many different combinations of variables and groups. Using boxplots for one, two, or more variables or groups in the same plot can be useful in helping you understand your data.

4.2a. Create a boxplot for *math achievement test.*

There are several commands that will compute boxplots; we show one way here. To create a boxplot, follow these steps:

- Select **Graphs** → **Legacy Dialogs** → **Boxplot …** The **Boxplot** window should appear.
- Select **Simple** and **Summaries of separate variables**. Your window should look like Fig. 4.3.
- Click on **Define.** The **Define Simple Boxplot: Summaries of Separate Variables** window (Fig. 4.4) will appear.

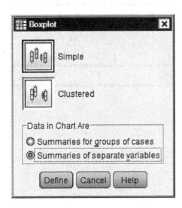

Fig. 4.3. Boxplot.

- Highlight the variable that you are interested in (in this case, it is *math achievement test*). Click on the arrow to move it into the **Boxes Represent** box. When you finish, the dialog box should look like Fig. 4.4.
- Click on **OK.**

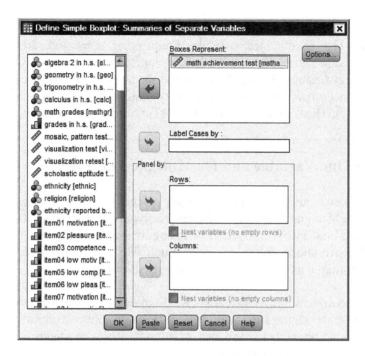

Fig. 4.4. Define simple boxplot: Summaries of separate variables.

Output 4.2a: Boxplot of Math Achievement Test

```
EXAMINE VARIABLES=mathach /COMPARE VARIABLE/PLOT=BOXPLOT/STATISTICS=NONE/NOTOTAL
  /MISSING=LISTWISE .
```

Explore

Case Processing Summary

	Cases					
	Valid		Missing		Total	
	N	Percent	N	Percent	N	Percent
math achievement test	75	100.0%	0	.0%	75	100.0%

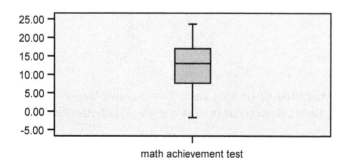

4.2b. Compare the boxplots of *competence* and *motivation* to each other.

To create more than one boxplot on the same graph, follow these commands:
- Select **Graphs** → **Legacy Dialogs** → **Boxplot** … The **Boxplot** window should appear (see Fig. 4.3).
- Select **Simple** and **Summaries of separate variables**. Your window should again look like Fig. 4.3.
- Click on **Define**. The **Define Simple Boxplot**: **Summaries of Separate Variables** window (Fig. 4.4) will appear again.
- Click on **Reset**.
- While holding down the control key (i.e., "Ctrl") highlight both of the variables that you are interested in (in this case they would be *competence* and *motivation*). Click on the arrow to move them into the **Boxes Represent** box.
- Click on **OK**.

Output 4.2b: Boxplots of Competence and Motivation Scales

```
EXAMINE VARIABLES=competence motivation /COMPARE VARIABLE/PLOT=BOXPLOT
 /STATISTICS=NONE/NOTOTAL
  /MISSING=LISTWISE .
```

Explore

Case Processing Summary

	Cases					
	Valid		Missing		Total	
	N	Percent	N	Percent	N	Percent
Competence scale	71	94.7%	4	5.3%	75	100.0%
Motivation scale	71	94.7%	4	5.3%	75	100.0%

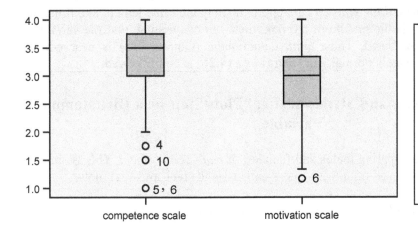

Notice that there are four outliers for *competence* and one for *motivation* in these boxplots. The numbers refer to which participant (line number) they represent, and the location of the dot indicates the score. So, participants 5 and 6 both scored 1 on the competence scale.

Interpretation of Outputs 4.2a and 4.2b

Outputs 4.2a and 4.2b include a **Case Processing Summary** table and boxplots. The **Valid** *N*, **Missing** cases, and **Total** cases are shown in the case processing summary table. In Output 4.2a, for *math achievement*, the valid *N* is 75, and there are no missing cases. The plot in Output 4.2a includes only one boxplot for our requested variable of *math achievement*. Each "box" represents the middle 50% of the cases and the "whiskers" at the top and bottom of the box indicate the "expected" top and bottom 25%. If there were **outliers** there would be "O"s and if there were really extreme scores they would be shown with asterisks, above or below the end of the whiskers. Notice that there are not any Os or *s in the boxplot in Output 4.2a.

The **Case Processing** table for Output 4.2b indicates that there are 71 valid cases, with 4 cases having missing data on at least one variable. The syntax indicated that this analysis involves "listwise" deletion, meaning that if a case is missing either variable, it will be omitted from boxplots for both variables. Each of the requested variables is listed separately in the case processing summary table. You can see there are two separate boxplots. As indicated by the Os at the bottom of the whiskers, the boxplot for *competence* shows there are three outliers, and the boxplot for *motivation* indicates there is one outlier; all are very low scores.

Using your output to check your data for errors. If there are Os or asterisks, then you need to check the raw data or score sheet to be sure there was not an error. The numbers next to the Os indicate the line number in the data editor next to the data of participants who have these scores. This can be helpful when you want to check to see if these are errors or if they are the actual scores of the subject. We decided not to create an identification variable because we could just use the numbers automatically assigned to each case. You can, however, make a variable that numbers each subject in some way that you find useful. Having such a variable may be helpful if you want to indicate some characteristics about participants using subject number, if you want to keep track of missing participants by skipping their ID numbers, or if you want to select certain cases by ID number for some analyses. If you wish to label outliers using such an ID number, which you have entered as a variable, you must indicate that variable in the dialog box in Fig. 4.4 where it says **Label Cases by.**

Using the output to check your data for assumptions. Boxplots can be useful for identifying variables with extreme scores, which can make the distribution skewed (i.e., non-normal). Also, if there are only a few outliers, if the whiskers are approximately the same length, and if the line in the box is approximately in the middle of the box, then you can assume that the variable is approximately normally distributed. Thus, *math achievement* (Output 4.2a) is near normal, *motivation* (4.2b) is approximately normal, but *competence* (4.2b) is quite skewed.

Problem 4.3: Boxplots and Stem-and-Leaf Plots Split by a Dichotomous Variable

Now let's make a boxplot comparing males and females on *math achievement*. This is similar to what we did in Chapter 3, but in addition we request statistics and **stem-and-leaf** plots.

4.3.   Create plots and statistics for *math achievement* split by *gender.*

Use these commands:
- **Analyze → Descriptive Statistics → Explore.**
- The **Explore** window (Fig. 4.5) will appear.
- Click on *math achievement* and move it to the **Dependent List**.

- Next, click on *gender* and move it to the **Factor** (or independent variable) **List.**
- Click on **Both** under **Display.** This will produce both a table of descriptive statistics and two kinds of plots: **stem-and-leaf** and **box-and-whiskers.**

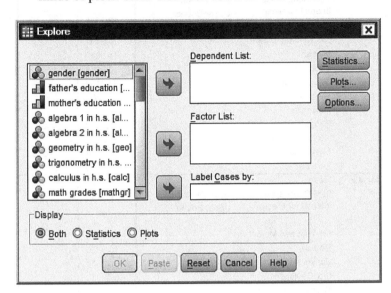

Fig. 4.5. Explore.

- Click on **OK.**

You will get an output file complete with syntax, statistics, stem-and-leaf plots, and boxplots. See Output 4.3 and compare it to your own output and syntax. As with most SPSS procedures, we could have requested a wide variety of other statistics if we had clicked on Statistics and/or Plots in Fig. 4.5.

Output 4.3: Boxplots Split by Gender With Statistics and Stem-and-Leaf Plots

```
EXAMINE VARIABLES=mathach BY gender
  /PLOT BOXPLOT STEMLEAF
  /COMPARE GROUP
  /STATISTICS DESCRIPTIVES
  /CINTERVAL 95
  /MISSING LISTWISE
  /NOTOTAL.
```

Explore

Gender

Case Processing Summary

		Cases					
		Valid		Missing		Total	
	gender	N	Percent	N	Percent	N	Percent
math achievement test	male	34	100.0%	0	.0%	34	100.0%
	female	41	100.0%	0	.0%	41	100.0%

Descriptives

	gender			Statistic	Std. Error
math achievement test	male	Mean		14.7550	1.03440
		95% Confidence Interval for Mean	Lower Bound	12.6505	
			Upper Bound	16.8595	
		5% Trimmed Mean		14.8454	
		Median		14.3330	
		Variance		36.379	
		Std. Deviation		6.03154	
		Minimum		3.67	
		Maximum		23.7	
		Range		20.00	
		Interquartile Range		10.00	
		Skewness		-.156	.403
		Kurtosis		-.963	.788
	female	Mean		10.7479	1.04576
		95% Confidence Interval for Mean	Lower Bound	8.6344	
			Upper Bound	12.8615	
		5% Trimmed Mean		10.6454	
		Median		10.3330	
		Variance		44.838	
		Std. Deviation		6.69612	
		Minimum		-1.7	
		Maximum		23.7	
		Range		25.33	
		Interquartile Range		10.50	
		Skewness		.331	.369
		Kurtosis		-.698	.724

Note that we have circled, for males and for females, three key statistics: mean, variance, and skewness.

math achievement test

Stem-and-Leaf Plots

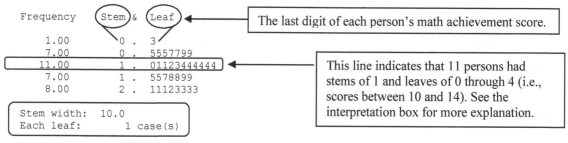

```
math achievement test Stem-and-Leaf Plot for
gender= male

 Frequency    Stem &  Leaf

     1.00       0 .  3
     7.00       0 .  5557799
    11.00       1 .  01123444444
     7.00       1 .  5578899
     8.00       2 .  11123333

 Stem width:   10.0
 Each leaf:      1 case(s)
```

The last digit of each person's math achievement score.

This line indicates that 11 persons had stems of 1 and leaves of 0 through 4 (i.e., scores between 10 and 14). See the interpretation box for more explanation.

```
math achievement test Stem-and-Leaf Plot for
gender= female

 Frequency    Stem &  Leaf

     1.00      -0 .  1
     7.00       0 .  1123344
    12.00       0 .  555666778999
    11.00       1 .  00002334444
     5.00       1 .  77779
     5.00       2 .  02233

 Stem width:   10.0
 Each leaf:      1 case(s)
```

1 person had a negative score (stem – 0) of -1.

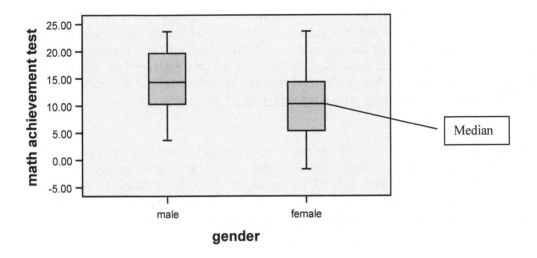

Interpretation of Output 4.3

The first table **(Case Processing Summary)** under **Explore** provides descriptive statistics about the number of males and females with **Valid** and **Missing** data. Note that we have 34 males and 41 females with valid *math achievement test* scores.

The **Descriptives** table contains many different statistics for males and females separately. Several of them are beyond what we cover in this book. Note that the average *math achievement test* score is 14.76 for males and 10.75 for females. We discuss the variances and skewness below under assumptions.

The **Stem-and-Leaf Plot**s for each gender separately are next. These plots are like a histogram or frequency distribution turned on the side. They give a visual impression of the distribution, and they show *each* person's score on the dependent variable (*math achievement*). Note that the legend indicates that **Stem width** equals 10 and **Each leaf** equals one case. This means that entries that have 0 for the stem are less than 10, those with 1 as the stem range from 10 to 19, and so forth. Each number in the **Leaf** column represents the last digit of one person's *math achievement* score. The numbers in the **Frequency** column indicate how many participants had scores in the range represented by that stem and range of leaves. Thus, in the male plot, one student had a **Stem** of 0 and a **Leaf** of 3, that is, a score of 03 (or 3). The Frequency of students with leaves between 05 and 09 is 7, and there were three scores of 5, two of 7, and two of 9. One had a **Stem** of 1 and a **Leaf** of 0 (a score of 10); two had scores of 11, and so forth.

Boxplots are the last part of the output. This figure has two boxplots (one for males and one for females). By inspecting the plots, we can see that the median score for males is quite a bit higher than that for females, although there is substantial overlap of the boxplots, with the highest female score equaling the highest male score. We therefore need to be careful in concluding that males score higher than females, especially based on a small sample of students. In Chapter 10, we show how an inferential statistic (the *t* test) can help us know how likely it is that this apparent difference could have occurred by chance, and will also see that other factors, such as the number of math courses taken, could influence these results.

Using the output to check your data for errors. Checking the box and stem-and-leaf plots can help identify outliers that might be data entry errors. In this case there aren't any.

Using the output to check your data for assumptions. As noted in the interpretation of Outputs 4.2a and 4.2b, you can tell if a variable is grossly non-normal by looking at the boxplots. The stem-and-leaf plots provide similar information. You can also examine the skewness values for each gender separately in the table of **Descriptives** (see the circled skewness values). Note that for both males and females, the skewness values are less than one, which indicates that math achievement is approximately normal for both genders. This is an assumption of the *t* test.

The **Descriptives** table also provides the variances for males and females. A key assumption of the *t* test is that the variances are approximately equal (i.e., the assumption of homogeneity of variances). Note that the variance is 36.38 for males and 44.84 for females. These do not seem grossly different, and we find out in Chapter 9 that they are, in fact, not significantly different. Thus, the important assumption of homogeneous variances is *not* violated.

Problem 4.4: Descriptives for Dichotomous Variables

Now let's explore the dichotomous variables. To do this, we do the **Descriptives** command for each of the dichotomous variables. Once again, we could have done **Frequencies,** with or without frequency tables, but we chose **Descriptives**. This time we select fewer statistics because the standard deviation, variance, and skewness values are not very meaningful with dichotomous variables.

4.4.   Examine the data to get a good understanding of each of the dichotomous variables.

When using the **Descriptives** command to compute basic descriptive statistics for the dichotomous variables, you need to do these steps:

- Select **Analyze → Descriptive Statistics → Descriptives**.

After selecting **Descriptives**, you will be ready to compute the *N*, minimum, maximum, and mean for all participants or cases on all selected dichotomous variables in order to examine the data.

- Before starting this problem, press Reset (see Fig. 4.1) to clear the **Variable** box.
- While holding down the control key (i.e., "Ctrl") *highlight all* of the **dichotomous** variables in the left box. These variables have only two levels. They are: *gender, algebra 1, algebra 2, geometry, trigonometry, calculus, and math grades.*
- Click on the **arrow** button pointing right.
- Be sure that all of these variables have moved out of the left window and into the Variable(s) window.
- Click on **Options**. The **Descriptives: Options** window will open.
- Select **Mean, Minimum, and Maximum**.
- Unclick **Std. Deviation**.
- Click on **Continue**.
- Click on **OK**.

Compare your output to Output 4.4. If it looks the same, you have done the steps correctly.

Output 4.4: Descriptives for Dichotomous Variables

```
DESCRIPTIVES VARIABLES=gender alg1 alg2 geo trig calc mathgr
/STATISTICS= MEAN MIN MAX .
```

Descriptives

Descriptive Statistics

	N	Minimum	Maximum	Mean
gender	75	0	1	.55
algebra 1 in h.s.	75	0	1	.79
algebra 2 in h.s.	75	0	1	.47
geometry in h.s.	75	0	1	.48
trigonometry in h.s.	75	0	1	.27
calculus in h.s.	75	0	1	.11
math grades	75	0	1	.41
Valid N (listwise)	75			

Interpretation of Output 4.4

Output 4.4 includes only one table of **Descriptive Statistics**. Across the top row are the requested statistics of *N*, **Minimum, Maximum,** and **Mean.** We could have requested other statistics, but they would not be very meaningful for dichotomous variables. Down the left column are the variable labels. The *N* column indicates that all the variables have complete data. The **Valid *N* (listwise)** is 75, which also indicates that all the participants had data for each of our requested variables.

The most helpful column is the **Mean** column. Although the mean is not meaningful for nominal variables with more than two categories, you can use the mean of dichotomous variables to understand what percentage of participants fall into each of the two groups. For example, the mean of *gender* is .55, which indicates that that 55% of the participants were coded as 1 (female); thus 45% were coded 0 (male). Because the mean is greater than .50, there are more females than males. If the mean is close to 1 or 0 (see algebra 1 and calculus), then splitting the data on that dichotomous variable might not be useful because there will be many participants in one group and very few participants in the other.

Checking for errors. The **Minimum** column shows that all the dichotomous variables had "0" for a minimum and the **Maximum** column indicates that all the variables have "1" for a maximum. This is good because it agrees with the codebook.

Problem 4.5: Frequency Tables for a Few Variables

Displaying Frequency tables for variables can help you understand how many participants are in each level of a variable and how much missing data of various types you have. For nominal variables, most descriptive statistics are meaningless. Thus, having a frequency table is usually the best way to understand your nominal variables. We created a frequency table for the nominal variable *religion* in Chapter 3 so we will not redo it here. However, you may want to create frequency distributions for all the nominal and ordinal variables in your own research to have a better understanding of your data.

4.5.   Examine the data to get a good understanding of the frequencies of scores for one nominal variable plus one scale/normal, one ordinal, and one dichotomous variable.

Use the following commands:

- Select **Analyze → Descriptive Statistics → Frequencies**.
- Click on **Reset** if any variables are in the **Variable(s)** box.
- Now *highlight* the **nominal** variable *ethnicity* in the left box.
- Click on the **arrow** button pointing right.
- Highlight and move over one **scale** variable (we chose *visualization retest*), one **ordinal** variable (we chose *father's education*), and one **dichotomous** variable (we used *gender*).
- Be sure the **Display frequency tables box** is checked.
- Do not click on **Statistics** because we do not want to select any this time.
- Click on **OK.**

Compare your output to Output 4.5. If it looks the same, you have done the steps correctly.

Output 4.5 Frequency Tables for Four Variables

```
FREQUENCIES VARIABLES=ethnic visual2 faed gend
  /ORDER=  ANALYSIS .
```

Frequencies

Statistics

		ethnicity	visualization retest	father's education	gender
N	Valid	73	75	73	75
	Missing	2	0	2	0

Frequency Table

See the Interpretation section for how to discuss these numbers.

ethnicity

		Frequency	Percent	Valid Percent	Cumulative Percent
Valid	Euro-Amer	41	54.7	56.2	56.2
	African-Amer	15	20.0	20.5	76.7
	Latino-Amer	10	13.3	13.7	90.4
	Asian-Amer	7	9.3	9.6	100.0
	Total	73	97.3	100.0	
Missing	multi ethnic	1	1.3		
	blank	1	1.3		
	Total	2	2.7		
Total		75	100.0		

visualization retest

		Frequency	Percent	Valid Percent	Cumulative Percent
Valid	Lowest	7	9.3	9.3	9.3
	1.00	7	9.3	9.3	18.7
	2.00	7	9.3	9.3	28.0
	3.00	10	13.3	13.3	41.3
	4.00	10	13.3	13.3	54.7
	5.00	8	10.7	10.7	65.3
	6.00	4	5.3	5.3	70.7
	7.00	5	6.7	6.7	77.3
	8.00	7	9.3	9.3	86.7
	highest	10	13.3	13.3	100.0
	Total	75	100.0	100.0	

father's education

		Frequency	Percent	Valid Percent	Cumulative Percent
Valid	< h.s. grad	22	29.3	30.1	30.1
	h.s. grad	16	21.3	21.9	52.1
	< 2 yrs voc	3	4.0	4.1	56.2
	2 yrs voc	8	10.7	11.0	67.1
	< 2 yrs coll	4	5.3	5.5	72.6
	> 2 yrs coll	1	1.3	1.4	(74.0)
	coll grad	7	9.3	9.6	83.6
	master's	6	8.0	8.2	91.8
	MD/PhD	6	8.0	8.2	100.0
	Total	73	97.3	100.0	
Missing	System	2	2.7		
Total		75	100.0		

74% of fathers have 2 years or less of college.

gender

		Frequency	Percent	Valid Percent	Cumulative Percent
Valid	male	34	45.3	45.3	45.3
	female	41	54.7	54.7	100.0
	Total	75	100.0	100.0	

Interpretation of Output 4.5
The first table, entitled **Statistics**, provides, in this case, only the number of participants for whom we have **Valid** data and the number with **Missing** data for each requested variable. We did not request any other statistics because almost all of them (e.g., skewness, standard deviation) are not appropriate to use with the nominal and dichotomous data, and we already have such statistics for the ordinal and normal/scale variables.

The other four tables are labeled **Frequency Table**; there is one for *ethnicity*, one for *visualization test*, one for *father's education*, and one for *gender*. The left-hand column shows the **Valid** categories (or levels or values), **Missing** values, and **Total** number of participants. The **Frequency** column gives the number of participants who had each value. The **Percent** column is the percent who had each value, including missing values. For example, in the ethnicity table, 54.7% of all participants were *Euro-American*, 20.0% were *African American*, 13.3% were *Latino-American*, and 9.3% were *Asian American*. There was also a total of 2.7% missing; 1.3% were *multiethnic*, and 1.3% were left *blank*. The **valid percent** shows the percent of those with *nonmissing* data at each value; for example, 56.2% of the 73 students with a single listed ethnic group were *Euro-Americans*. Finally, **Cumulative Percent** is the percent of subjects in a category *plus* the categories listed above it; however, this is not meaningful for ethnicity unless you want to know the percent of participants who are not in the last category (i.e., not *Asian American*, which is 90.4%).

As mentioned in Chapter 3, this last column usually is not very useful with nominal data, but can be quite informative for frequency distributions with several ordered categories. For example, in the distribution of *father's education*, 74% of the fathers had less than a bachelor's degree (i.e., they had not graduated from college).

Interpretation Questions

4.1.   Using Output 4.1a and 4.1b: (a) What is the mean *visualization test* score? (b) What is the skewness statistic for *math achievement?* What does this tell us? (c) What is the minimum score for *mosaic pattern test?* How can that be?

4.2.   Using Output 4.1b: (a) For which variables that we called scale, is the skewness statistic more than 1.00 or less than −1.00? (b) Why is the answer important? (c) Does this agree with the boxplot for Output 4.2? Explain.

4.3.   Using Output 4.2b: (a) How many participants have missing data? (b) What percent of students have a valid (nonmissing) *motivation* or *competence* score? (c) Can you tell from Outputs 4.1 and 4.2b how many are missing both *motivation* and *competence* scores? Explain.

4.4.   Using Output 4.4: (a) Can you interpret the means? Explain. (b) How many participants are there altogether? (c) How many have complete data (nothing missing)? (d) What percent are *male*? (e) What percent took *algebra 1*?

4.5.   Using Output 4.5: (a) 9.6% of what group are *Asian Americans?* (b) What percent of students have *visualization retest* scores of 6? (c) What percent had such scores of 6 or less?

Extra SPSS Problems

Using the college student data file, do the following problems. Print your outputs and circle the key parts of the output that you discuss.

4.1   For the variables with five or more ordered levels, compute the skewness. Describe the results. Which variables in the data set are approximately normally distributed/scale? Which ones are ordered but not normal?

4.2   Do a stem-and-leaf plot for the same sex parent's height split by gender. Discuss the plots.

4.3   Which variables are nominal? Run Frequencies for the nominal variables and other variables with fewer than five levels. Comment on the results.

4.4. Do boxplots for student height and for hours of study. Compare the two plots.

CHAPTER 5

Data File Management and Writing about Descriptive Statistics

In this assignment, you will do several data transformations to get your data into the form needed to answer the research questions. This aspect of data analysis is sometimes called file management and can be quite time consuming. That is especially true if you have many questions/items that you combine to compute the summated or composite variables that you want to use in later analyses. For example, in this chapter you will recode two of the math pleasure items and then compute the average of the four pleasure items to make the pleasure scale score. This is a somewhat mundane and tedious aspect of research, but it is important to do it carefully so you do not introduce errors into your data.

You will learn four useful data transformation techniques: **Count, Recode,** and two ways to **Compute** a new variable that is the sum or average of several variables. From these operations we will produce seven new variables. In the last problem, you will conduct, for five of the new variables, several of the descriptive statistics that we presented in the last chapter, and we will use them to check for errors and assumptions. Finally, at the end of the chapter, we discuss how you might write about some of the descriptive results that we produced in Chapters 4 and 5.

- Open the **hsbdata** file. See the **Get Data** step in Appendix A for reference.

Problem 5.1: Count Math Courses Taken

Sometimes you want to know how many items the participants have taken, bought, done, agreed with, etc. One time this happens is when the subject is asked to "check all that apply." In Chapter 2, we could have counted how many aspects of the class assignments (reading, homework, and extra credit) the students checked by counting the number of items checked. In this problem, we will **count** the number of *math courses* coded as 1, which means "taken."

5.1. How many math courses (*algebra 1, algebra 2, geometry, trigonometry,* and *calculus*) did each of the 75 participants take in high school? **Label** your new variable.

If the hsbdata file is not showing, click on the hsbdata bar at the bottom of your screen until you see your data showing. Now let's count the number of math courses (*mathcrs*) that each of the 75 participants took in high school. First, remember to set your computer to obtain a listing of the syntax (see Appendix A, **Print Syntax**) if it is not already set to do so.

- Select **Transform → Count Values within Cases….** You will see a window like Fig. 5.1 below.
- Now, type *mathcrs* in the **Target Variable** box. This is the program's name for your new variable.
- Next, type *math courses taken* in the **Target Label** box.
- Then, while holding down the shift key, highlight *algebra 1, algebra 2, geometry, trigonometry, and calculus* and click on the **arrow** button to move them over to the **Numeric Variables** box. Your **Count** window should look like Fig. 5.1.

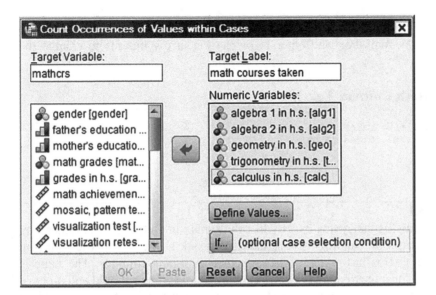

Fig. 5.1. Count.

- Click on **Define Values.**
- Type **1** in the **Value** box and click on **Add**. This sets up the computer to count how many 1s (or courses taken) each participant had. The window will now look like Fig. 5.2.
- Now click on **Continue** to return to the dialog box in Fig. 5.1.
- Click on **OK**. The first 10 numbers of your new variable, under *mathcrs*, should look like Fig. 5.3. It is the last variable, way over to the right side of your **Data View**, and the last variable way on the bottom of your **Variable View**.

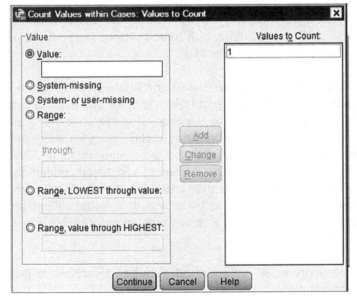

Fig. 5.2. Count values within cases.

mathcrs
.00
.00
.00
1.00
.00
.00
3.00
1.00
1.00
.00

Fig. 5.3. Data column.

Your output should look like the syntax in Output 5.1. There will not be any tables or plots.

If you want to delete the decimal places for your new data:

- Go to the **Variable View**.
- Scroll down to the last (new) variable, *mathcrs*.

- Click on the cell under **Decimals.**
- Highlight the 2 in the Decimals box and enter 0, or use the arrow buttons to change the number to zero.

Output 5.1: Counting Math Courses Taken

```
COUNT mathcrs=alg1 alg2 geo trig calc(1).
VARIABLE LABELS  mathcrs 'math courses taken'.
EXECUTE.
```

Interpretation of Output 5.1

Check your syntax and counts. Is the syntax exactly like the syntax in Output 5.1? Another way to check your count statement is by examining your data file. Look at the first participant (top row) and notice that there are zeros in the *alg1, alg2, geo, trig,* and *calc* columns. The same is true for participants 2 and 3. Thus, they have taken no (0) math courses. They should and do have zeros in the new *mathcrs* column, which is now the last column on the right. Also, it would be good to check a few participants who took several math courses just to be sure the count worked correctly.

Notice that there are no tables or figures for this output, just syntax. If you did not get any output, check to make sure that you set your computer to obtain a listing of the syntax (see Appendix A, **Print Syntax**).

Problem 5.2: Recode and Relabel Mother's and Father's Education

Now we will **Recode** *mother's education* and *father's education* so that those with no postsecondary education (2s and 3s) have a value of **1**, those with some postsecondary will have **2**, and those with a bachelor's degree or more will have a value of **3**.

It is usually *not* desirable to dichotomize (divide into two categories) or trichotomize (divide into three categories) an ordinal or, especially, a normal/scale variable in which all of the levels are ordered correctly and are meaningfully different from one another. However, we need an independent variable with a few levels or categories to demonstrate certain analyses later, and these variables seem to have a logical problem with the ordering of the categories/values. The problem can be seen in the codebook. A value of 5 is given for 2 years of vocational/community college (and presumably an associate's degree), but a 6 is given to a parent with less than 2 years of (a 4-year) college. Thus, we could have a case where a parent who went to a 4-year college for a short time would be rated as having more education than a parent with an associate's degree. This would make the variable not fully ordered.

Recodes also are used to combine two or more small groups or categories of a variable so that group size will be large enough to perform statistical analyses. For example, we have only a few fathers or mothers who have a master's or doctorate so we will combine them with bachelor's degrees and call them "B.S. or more."

5.2. **Recode** *mother's* and *father's education* so that those with no postsecondary education have a value of 1, those with some postsecondary education have a value of 2, and those with a bachelor's degree or more have a value of 3. **Label** the new variables and values. Also print the frequency distributions for *maed* and *faed*.

Follow these steps:

- Click on **Transform → Recode Into Different Variables** and you should get a window similar to Fig. 5.4.
- Now click on *mother's education* and then the **arrow** button.
- Click on *father's education* and the **arrow. This will** move both variables to the **Numeric Variables → Output Variable** box.
- Now highlight *faed* in the **Numeric Variable** box so that it changes color.
- Click on the **Name** box under **Output Variable**; and type *faedRevis*.
- Click on the **Label** box and type *father's educ revised*.
- Click on **Change**. Did you get *faed → faedRevis* in the **Numeric Variable → Output Variable** box as in Fig. 5.4?

Now repeat these procedures with *maed* in the **Numeric Variable → Output Variable** box.

- Highlight *maed*.
- Click on **Name** under **Output Variable**; type *maedRevis*.
- Click **Label**; type *mother's educ revised*.
- Click **Change**.
- Then click on **Old and New Values** to get a window similar to Fig. 5.5.

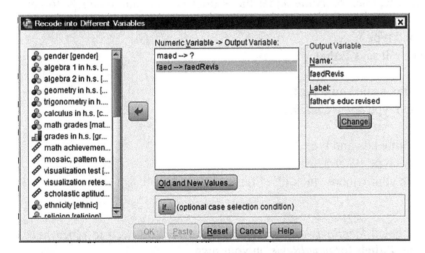

Fig. 5.4. Recode into different variables.

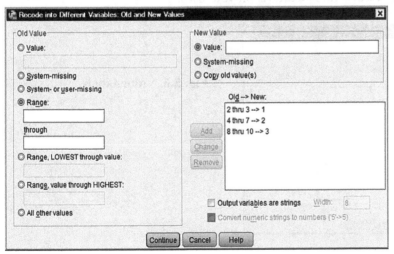

Fig. 5.5. Recode.

- Click on **Range** and type **2** in the first box and **3** in the second box.
- Click on **Value** (under **New Value** on the right) and type **1**.
- Then click on **Add**.
- Repeat these steps to change old values **4** through **7** to a new **Value** of **2**.
- Then **Range: 8** through **10** to **Value: 3**. Does it look like Fig. 5.5?
- If it does, click on **Continue**.
- Finally, click on **OK**.

Check your **Data View** to see if *faedRevis* and *maedRevis,* with numbers ranging from 1 to 3, have been added on the far right side. These are **ordinal** variables and will be used as **input** or independent variables so you should adjust the **Variable View** accordingly.

To be extra careful, check the data file for a few participants to be sure the recodes were done correctly. For example, the first participant had 10 for *faed*, which should be 3 for *faedRevis*. Is it? Check a few more to be sure or compare your syntax file with the one in Output 5.2 below.

- Now, we will **label** the new (1, 2, 3) values.
- Go to your hsbdata file and click on **Variable View** (it is in the bottom left corner).
- In the *faedRevis* variable row, click on **None** under the **Values** column and then [···] to get a window similar to Fig. 5.6.
- Click on the **Value** box and type **1**.
- Type *HS grad or less* where it says **Label**.
- Click on **Add**.
- Then click on the **Value** box again and type **2**.
- Click on the **Label** box and type *Some College*.
- Click on **Add**.
- Click once more on the **Value** box and type **3**.
- Click on the **Label** box and type *BS or More*.
- Again, click on **Add**. Does your window look like Fig. 5.6? If so,
- Click on **OK**.

__Important__: You have only labeled *faedRevis* (*father's educ revised*). You need to repeat these steps for *maedRevis*. Do **Value Labels** for *maedRevis* on your own.

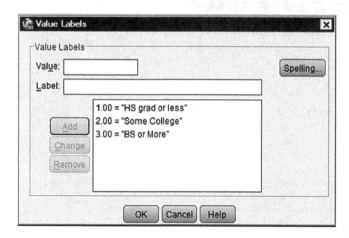

Fig. 5.6. Value labels.

Now that you have recoded and labeled both *faedRevis* and *maedRevis*, you are ready to run a frequency distribution for them as you did for other variables in Problem 4.5. (See that problem for commands.)

Output 5.2: Recoding Mother's and Father's Education and Computing Frequencies

```
RECODE maed faed (2 thru 3=1) (4 thru 7=2) (8 thru 10=3) INTO maedRevis faedRevis.
VARIABLE LABELS  maedRevis "mother's educ revised" /faedRevis "father's educ revised".
EXECUTE.
FREQUENCIES VARIABLES=maedRevis faedRevis
  /ORDER=ANALYSIS.
```

Frequencies

Statistics

		mother's educ revised	father's educ revised
N	Valid	75	73
	Missing	0	2

Frequency Table

mother's educ revised

		Frequency	Percent	Valid Percent	Cumulative Percent
Valid	HS grad or less	48	64.0	64.0	64.0
	Some College	19	25.3	25.3	89.3
	BS or More	8	10.7	10.7	100.0
	Total	75	100.0	100.0	

father's educ revised

		Frequency	Percent	Valid Percent	Cumulative Percent
Valid	HS grad or less	38	50.7	52.1	52.1
	Some College	16	21.3	21.9	74.0
	BS or More	19	25.3	26.0	100.0
	Total	73	97.3	100.0	
Missing	System	2	2.7		
Total		75	100.0		

Interpretation of Output 5.2

The syntax shows that you have recoded *father's* and *mother's education* so that 2 and 3 become 1, 4 through 7 become 2, and 8 through 10 become 3. The new variable names are *faedRevis* and *maedRevis*, and the labels are *father's educ revised* and *mother's educ revised*. Remember, it is crucial to check some of your recoded data to be sure that it worked the way you intended. The first **Frequencies** table shows the number of students who had valid data for each variable and the number who had missing data. Note that father's education was unknown/missing for two students. The second table shows the frequency distribution for the revised mother's education variable. Note that most (64%) of the mothers had only a high school education or less. The third table shows the distribution of father's education. Note that two are missing so the **Percent** is different from the **Valid Percent**, which is the percentage of those with valid data.

Problem 5.3: Recode and Compute Pleasure Scale Score

Now let's **Compute** the average "pleasure from math" scale score (*pleasure scale*) from *item02*, *item06*, *item10*, and *item14* <u>after</u> reversing (**Recoding**) *item06* and *item10*, which are negatively worded or low pleasure items (see the codebook in Chapter 1). We will keep both the new *item06r* and *item10r* and old (*item06* and *item10*) variables to check the recodes and to play it safe. Then we will **Label** the new computed variable as *pleasure scale*.

5.3.   **Compute** the average *pleasure scale* from *item02*, *item06*, *item10*, and *item14* <u>after</u> reversing (use the **Recode** function) *item06* and *item10*. Name the new computed variable *pleasure* and label its highest and lowest values.

- Click on **Transform** → **Recode Into Different Variables**.
- Click on **Reset** to clear the window of old information as a precaution.
- Click on *item06*.
- Click on the **arrow** button.
- Click on **Name** under **Output Variable** and type *item06r*.
- Click on **Label** and type *item06 reversed*.
- Finally click on **Change**.
- Now repeat these steps for *item10*. Does it look like Fig. 5.7?

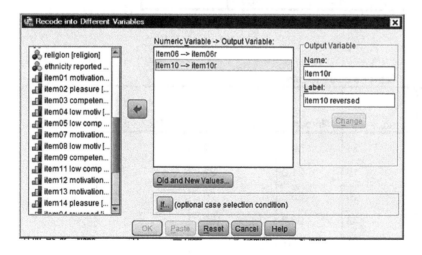

Fig. 5.7. Recode into different variables.

- Click on **Old and New Values** to get Fig. 5.8.
- Now click on the **Value** box (under **Old Value**) and type **4**.
- Click on the **Value** box under **New Value** and type **1**.
- Click on **Add**.

This is the first step in recoding. You have told the computer to change values of 4 to 1. Now do these steps over to recode the values **3** to **2, 2** to **3**, and **1** to **4**. If you did it right, the screen will look like Fig. 5.8 in the **Old --> New** box. Check your box carefully to be sure the recodes are exactly like Fig. 5.8.

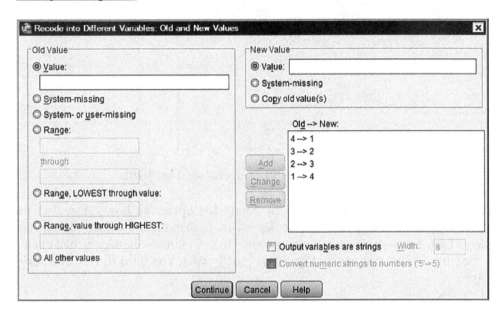

Fig. 5.8. Recode: Old and new values.

- Click on **Continue** and then **OK**.

Now check your **Data** file to see if there is an *item06r* and an *item10r* in the last two columns with numbers ranging from 1 to 4. To double check the recodes, compare the *item06* and *item10* columns in your data file with the *item06r* and *item10r* columns for a few subjects. Also, you should check your syntax file with Output 5.3a.

Output 5.3a: Recoding and Computing Pleasure Scale Score

```
RECODE item06 item10 (4=1) (3=2) (2=3) (1=4) INTO item06r item10r.
VARIABLE LABELS  item06r 'item06 reversed' /item10r 'item10 reversed'.
EXECUTE.
```

Now let's compute the average *pleasure scale*.

- Click on **Transform → Compute Variable**.
- In the **Target Variable** box of Fig. 5.9, type *pleasure*.

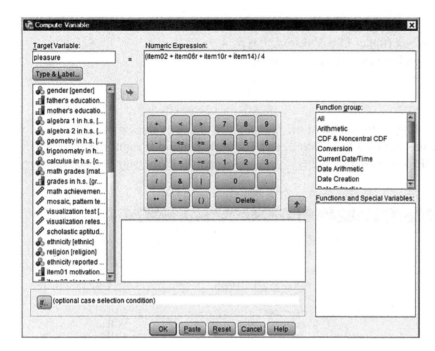

**Fig. 5.9.
Compute
variable.**

- Click on **Type & Label** and give it the name *pleasure scale* (see Fig. 5.10).
- Click on **Continue** to return to Fig. 5.9.
- Click on *item02* and the arrow to move it into the **Numeric Expression box**. Then click on +, click *item06r* (<u>not</u> *item06*) and then the arrow. Click +, then click on item 10r and the arrow. Click +. Last, check on *item14*, the arrow and click +. Finally, in the key pad click / and then 4. Be sure that what shows in Fig. 5.9 is <u>exactly</u> what you have in your **Numeric Expression** box.
- Finally, click on **OK.**

**Fig. 5.10. Compute variable:
Type and label.**

- Now provide **Value Labels** for the *pleasure scale* using commands similar to those you used for *father's educ revised.*
- Type 1, then *very low*, and click **Add.**
- Type 4, then *very high*, and click **Add.** See Fig. 5.6 if you need help.

In the **Compute** method we just used, the computer added items 02, 06r, 10r, and 14 and then divided the sum by four, giving the result a new name, *pleasure.* Be sure your formula is <u>exactly</u> like the one shown. For example, <u>you must have the parentheses, and you must have zero (not the letter O) for *item02* and *item06r*</u>, and you must use the reversed items 06r and 10r.

It is faster to type the formula in the **Numeric Expression** box in Fig. 5.9; but you are more likely to make a mistake.

It is prudent to <u>calculate the pleasure score by hand for a few participants to be sure it was done correctly</u>. The computer will not make calculation mistakes but <u>sometimes you may not tell it exactly what you intended</u>. Check your syntax with the one in Output 5.3b.

Output 5.3b: Computation of Pleasure Scale

```
COMPUTE pleasure=(item02 + item06r + item10r + item14)/4.
VARIABLE LABELS  pleasure 'pleasure scale'.
EXECUTE.
```

Interpretation of Output 5.3

The method we used to compute summated or composite scales will not compute an average score for a particular participant if he or she is missing data for *any* of the questions. The computed score will be missing. This can result in a sizable decrease in subjects who have composite scores if several participants did not answer even one or a few questions. An alternative is to use the **Mean** function, shown in Problem 5.4 and in the callout box beside Fig. 5.11, because it utilizes all of the available data. However, one should not use the **Mean** function if participants have a lot of missing data.

Problem 5.4: Compute Parents' Revised Education with the Mean Function

We have decided to combine *father's* and *mother's education* scores because, as we will find out later, they are highly correlated. Thus, for some purposes, it is better to treat them as one variable. We also want to demonstrate the use of the **Mean** function, which is a type of **Compute** function a little different from what we used to create the *pleasure scale*. Note that, in this problem, we will use the original *father's* and *mother's education* variables (not the revised ones). This provides us with a variable that has more range.

5.4. Compute *parents' education* using the **Mean** function, which is an alternative to using the **compute** function.

- Click on **Transform** → **Compute** to get Fig. 5.11.
- Click on **Reset**.
- In the **Target Variable box**, type *parEduc.*
- Click on **Type & Label** to get Fig. 5.10 again. Label the new variable *parents' education.*
- Click on **Continue**.
- In the **Function Group:** box, scroll down, and highlight **Statistical.**
- In the **Functions and Special Variables** box, highlight **Mean.**
- Click the up arrow to move it into the **Numeric Expression Box.**
- Enter *faed* and *maed* in the brackets. Either type them or click them over. <u>Note the comma between the variables.</u>
- Click on **OK.**

Also, you should label, at least, the highest and lowest **Values**.
- Go to the **Variable View** (in the bottom left-hand corner) of your hsbdata file.
- In the *parents' education* variable row, click on **None** under the **Values** column, and then
- Type 2 and *less than h.s. grad;* click **Add.**

- Type 10 and *Ph.D./M.D.;* click **Add.**
- Click on **OK. (**Note you can get values of 2.5 and 3.5, etc., so leave the decimals at 2.)

Output 5.4: Computation of Parents' Education

> The Mean function computes an average score for each participant who has a score for any of the variables used.

```
COMPUTE ParEduc = MEAN(faed,maed) .
VARIABLE LABELS parEduc "parents' education" .
EXECUTE .
```

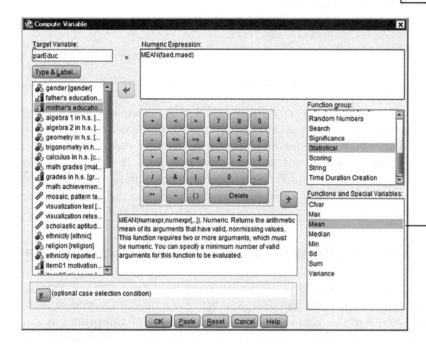

Fig. 5.11. Compute variable.

Interpretation of Output 5.4

Note that you have created another new variable (*parEduc*), which is the seventh and last one you will create for the hsbdata set. It can be found as the 46th variable in the **Variable View** and in the far right column of the **Data View**.

You will see when we print the **Descriptives** in Problem 5.5, that all 75 participants have a *parents' education* value because none of them are missing both *father's* and *mother's education*. It seems reasonable to use only *mother's education* if *father's education* is unknown. It would be even more helpful to compute *parents' education* if there were a lot of students whose *father's education* was unknown, as is sometimes the case. Because almost all students know *mother's education*, by using the **Mean** function, almost all would have a parents' education score. On the other hand, the **Mean** function should be used cautiously because, for example, if a student answered only one of the four *pleasure scale* items, they would get an average *pleasure score* based on that one item. If the item was not representative (i.e., usually rated higher or lower than the others), then the *pleasure* score would be misleading. SPSS allows you to specify the minimum number of variables that must have valid (nonmissing) values by typing .n after **MEAN**. For example, if you decided that at least three of the pleasure scale items must have data, you would type MEAN.3(*item02, item06r, item10r, item14*).

Problem 5.5: Check for Errors and Normality for the New Variables

5.5. Run **Descriptives** in order to understand the new variables, check for errors, and see if they are distributed normally.

Using Chapter 4 (Problem 4.1) as a guide, compute the descriptive statistics (**Minimum, Maximum, Mean, Standard Deviation, Variance,** and **Skewness**) for the new variables *math courses taken, father's educ revised, mother's educ revised, pleasure scale,* and *parents' education.*

Output 5.5: Descriptive Statistics

```
DESCRIPTIVES
  VARIABLES=mathcrs faedRevis maedRevis pleasure parEduc
  /STATISTICS=MEAN STDDEV VARIANCE MIN MAX SKEWNESS.
```

Descriptives

Descriptive Statistics

	N	Minimum	Maximum	Mean	Std.	Variance	Skewness	
	Statistic	Statistic	Statistic	Statistic	Statistic	Statistic	Statistic	Std. Error
math courses taken	75	0	5	2.11	1.673	2.799	.325	.277
father's educ revised	73	1.00	3.00	1.7397	.85028	.723	.533	.281
mother's educ revised	75	1.00	3.00	1.4667	.68445	.468	1.162	.277
pleasure scale	75	1.50	4.00	3.1300	.60454	.365	-.682	.277
parents' education	75	2.00	10.00	4.3933	2.31665	5.367	.923	.277
Valid N (listwise)	73							

Interpretation of Output 5.5

The **Descriptives** table provides, as did Output 4.1, the requested statistics and the Ns for each variable, as well as the listwise N.

Check for Errors. It is especially important to check new computed variables for errors. Note that *father's education revised* has an N of 73 (2 missing). That is what we would expect given that the original *father's education* variable had $N = 73$. However, *parents' education* has no missing data because we used the **Mean** function. Check also the minimum and maximum scores for each variable to see if they lie within the acceptable range of values. For example, because there are five math courses, the number of *math courses taken* has to be between 0 and 5, and it is. Note that, although the codebook and **Variable View** say the *pleasure score* can vary between 1.00 and 4.00, actually the lowest score in this group was 1.50. That is okay, but although not necessarily an error it would be a problem if the lowest score was 3.5 out of 4 or if the highest score was only 1.5. Some variability is necessary for useful statistical analyses.

Check assumptions. Note that *math courses taken* and the *pleasure scale* have **skewness** scores less than 1.0, so we can consider them to be approximately normally distributed. The skewness for *mother's education revised* is 1.16, so it is moderately skewed, as was *mother's education.* However, we will usually use it as an *independent* variable in an ANOVA, so normality is not required. The skewness for *parents' education* is within our acceptable limits at .92, so that is another reason to use it rather than *mother's* or *father's education.*

Describing the Sample Demographics and Key Variables

Using the information that you computed in Chapters 4 and 5, we can now describe this sample of the High School and Beyond (hsb) data. In an article or research report such as a thesis, you will, at a minimum, state the number of participants and provide summary information about the age, gender, and ethnicity characteristics of the sample. We do not have age as a variable in this data set; all the participants were high school seniors and are assumed to be about 18 years old. We do have *gender* and *ethnicity*. For a more complete description of sample demographics, we will add mother's and father's education (revised). This information probably would be described in the Methods section of an article or thesis and could include a table as shown in the box labeled **How to Write about Sample Demographics**. The data for *gender* and *ethnicity* are found in Output 4.5; the revised *mother's education* and *father's education* frequencies are found in Output 5.2. Note that there is always text preceding a table and that the text highlights and often simplifies the material in the table; <u>never repeat everything in the table or include a table without referring to it in the text</u>.

How to Write About Sample Demographics

Method

Participants

Data from 75 high school seniors (34 males and 41 females) were gathered. The majority of the group (54.7%) was of European-American ethnicity. Table 1 shows the frequencies and percentages of students by gender, ethnicity, and parent education. Note that data on education were missing for two fathers. Percentages for Father's Education refer to percentage of those for whom data are available. Most of the mothers (64%) and fathers (52.1%) had a high school education or less. Approximately 26% of the fathers but less than 11% of the mothers had a bachelor's degree or more.

Table 5.1

Demographics of a Sample of 75 High School Seniors

Characteristic	*n*	%
Gender		
Male	34	45.3
Female	41	54.7
Ethnicity		
European-American	41	54.7
African-American	15	20.0
Latino-American	10	13.3
Asian-American	7	9.3
Multi-ethnic	1	1.3
Missing	1	1.3
Mother's education		
H.S. grad or less	48	64.0
Some college	19	25.3
Bachelor's or more	8	10.7
Father's education		
H.S grad or less	38	52.1
Some college	16	21.9
Bachelor's or more	19	26.0

The results section of a research report or thesis will often provide descriptive data and, perhaps, a table about the key variables in the study. This description of the variables may, but likely will not, directly address the research questions for the study. Several key variables, whether or not students had taken each of five types of mathematics courses and how they performed in all their math courses, were dichotomous. Other key variables, such as various test scores and attitudes about mathematics, were essentially continuous and most were approximately normally distributed. In the box labeled **How to Write about Key Variables**, we show one way to describe the variables and summarize them in tables. The data for math courses taken and grades come from Output 4.4. The data on the test scores and math attitudes come from Outputs 4.1b and 5.5.

Note that means, standard deviations, and skewness are all rounded to *two* decimal places and *right* justified. Statistical symbols with English letters (e.g., *N, n, M, SD*) are italicized in the text and tables.

How to Write About Key Variables

Results

Table 5.2 shows the number and percentage of the 75 high school seniors who had taken each of five mathematics courses. More than three-fourths of them (79%) had taken algebra 1. Approximately half had taken algebra 2 (47%) and/or geometry (48%), but only 27% had taken trigonometry and relatively few (11%) had taken calculus. Although not shown in Table 5.2, 41% were judged to have high math grades (As and Bs), and 59% had low math grades.

Table 5.2

Number and Percentage of Students Who Took High School Mathematics Courses

Math course	Taken in h.s.		Not taken	
	n	%	*n*	%
Algebra 1	59	79	16	21
Algebra 2	35	47	40	53
Geometry	36	48	39	52
Trigonometry	20	27	55	73
Calculus	8	11	67	89

Means, standard deviations, and skewness of eight key variables are shown in Table 5.3. The four achievement test scores vary widely in means and SDs given differences in scale, but all are approximately normally distributed. The three mathematics attitude scales have means of approximately 3 on 1 – 5 rating scales; the average motivation scale ratings are somewhat lower than those for the students' perceived competence and pleasure with math. Note that the competence ratings are quite highly skewed. On the average students took 2.11 math courses.

Table 5.3

Means, Standard Deviations, and Skewness for Key Variables

Variable	*M*	*SD*	Skewness
Achievement tests			
Math achievement test	12.56	6.67	0.04
Mosaic pattern test	27.41	9.57	0.53
Visualization test	5.24	3.91	0.13
SAT mathematics	490.53	94.55	
Mathematics attitudes			
Competence scale	3.29	0.66	-1.63
Motivation scale	2.87	0.64	-0.57
Pleasure scale	3.13	0.60	-0.68
Math courses taken	2.11	1.67	0.33

Using Figures to Help Describe the Data

In theses, dissertations and technical reports, it can be helpful to provide graphic representations, such as histograms, frequency polygons, boxplots and piecharts, of your descriptive data. (In journal articles, there is seldom enough space for figures of your <u>descriptive</u> data.) For example, because it has several nominal levels, it might be helpful to provide a **Bar Chart** of the ethnicity data rather than include it as numbers in Table 5.1.

To make a bar chart for ethnicity using SPSS, do the following:
- Click on **Analyze → Descriptive Statistics → Frequencies.**
- Click on *ethnicity* and click on the **arrow** to move it to the **Variable** box.
- Click on **Charts**, then **Bar Charts.**
- Click on **Continue.**
- Click **OK.**

This bar chart is similar to Fig. 3.5 (for religion) and is based on the *ethnicity* data in Table 5.1. You could display this figure (APA calls all charts, graphs, photos, and plots "figures") and write about it in APA format as shown in the box. However, in APA format, the <u>figure caption would be</u> double spaced and at <u>the bottom of the same page as the figure</u>. For journal submissions each figure and caption are on a separate page at the end of the manuscript after references, author notes, and tables. In a thesis or dissertation a figure and its caption would be embedded in the text of the manuscript as soon as possible after it is mentioned in the text. More information about how to make tables and figures in APA format is presented in two paperback books by Nicol and Pexman (2010). See our For Further Reading list after Appendix C. For journal articles, figures will probably have to be redone in Word or some other program because the SPSS figures are not exactly APA format. For Technical reports and student papers, SPSS figures are probably okay.

How to Write about Descriptive Figures

Figure 5.1 shows the relative frequencies of the student ethnicities in this sample. Note that more than half (56.2%) of the students with valid ethnicity codes were European Americans; 20.5% were African Americans; 13.7% were Latino Americans, and 9.6% were Asian Americans. There was also one multi-ethnic student and one had missing data.

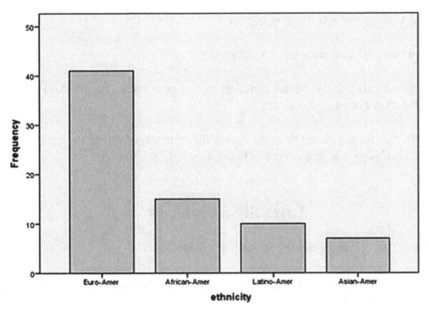

Figure 5.1. Frequencies of the ethnicities of 75 high school students in the High School and Beyond study.

Saving the Updated HSB Data File

You should *always* save your **data file** if you entered new data or made any changes. If you forget to **Save,** you will have to do these **Recodes** and so forth over again! To save, follow these steps:

- Click on the **Data Editor** button at the bottom of your screen.
- Then click **File → Save As.**
- Give your data file a new name; for example, hsbdataB.sav.
- **Select Drive A:** to save on your flash drive (or use C: or a network drive if you have the capability).
- Click **Save**.

Interpretation Questions

5.1.   Using your initial HSB data file (or the file in Chapter 1), compare the original data to your new variables: (a) How many math courses did Participant 1 take? (b) What should *faedr* be for Participants 2, 5, and 8? (c) What should the *pleasure scale* score be for Participant 1? (d) Why is comparing a few initial scores to transformed scores important?

5.2   Why did you recode *father's* and *mother's education*? When would you *not* want to recode a normal/scale level variable into two or three categories?

5.3   Why did you reverse questions 6 and 10?

5.4   Why did you compute *parents' education*?

5.5.   When would you use the **Mean** function to compute an average? And when would the **Mean** function not be appropriate?

5.6.   In Output 5.5, do the *pleasure scale* scores differ markedly from the normal distribution? How do you know? Is *math courses taken* normally distributed?

Extra SPSS Problems

Using the college student data, solve the following problems:

5.1.   Compute a new variable labeled *average overall* evaluation (*aveEval*) by computing the average score (*evalinst + evalprog + evalphys + evalsocl)/4*.

5.2   Compute a similar variable (*meanEval*) using the **Mean** function. Compare the two (5.1 and 5.2) scores. Why do they differ?

5.3   **Count** the number of types of TV shows that each student watches.

5.4   Recode the *student's current gpa* into three categories: 1 = 1.00 – 1.99, 2 = 2.00 – 2.99, 3 = 3.00 – 4.00. Produce a frequency table for the recoded values.

CHAPTER 6

Selecting and Interpreting Inferential Statistics

To understand the information in this chapter, it is necessary to remember or to review the sections in Chapter 1 about **variables** and Chapter 3 about levels of **measurement** (nominal, dichotomous, ordinal, and normal/scale). It is also necessary to remember the distinction we made between difference and associational research questions and between **descriptive and inferential statistics**. This chapter focuses on inferential statistics, which, as the name implies, refers to statistics that make inferences about population values based on the sample data that you have collected and analyzed. What we call **difference inferential statistics** lead to inferences about the differences (usually mean differences) between groups in the populations from which the samples were drawn. **Associational inferential statistics** lead to inferences about the association or relationship between variables in the population. Thus, the purpose of inferential statistics is to enable the researcher to make generalizations beyond the specific sample data. Before we describe how to select statistics, we introduce design classifications.

General Design Classifications for Difference Questions

Many research questions focus on whether there is a significant difference between two or more groups or conditions. When a group comparison or difference question is asked, the independent variable and design can be classified as between groups or within subjects. Understanding this distinction is one essential aspect of determining the proper statistical analysis for this type of question.

Labeling difference question designs. It is helpful to have a brief descriptive label that identifies the design for other researchers and also guides us toward the proper statistics to use. We do not have comparable design classifications for the descriptive or associational research questions, so this section only applies to difference questions. Designs are usually labeled in terms of (a) the overall type of design (between groups or within subjects), (b) the number of independent variables, and (c) the number of levels within each independent variable. The dependent variable is not part of the label of the design.

Between-groups designs. These are designs where each participant in the study is in one and only one condition or group. For example, in a study investigating the "effects" of fathers' education on *math achievement*, there may be three groups (or levels or values) of the independent variable, *father's education*. These levels are: (a) *high school or less*, (b) *some college*, and (c) *BS or more*. In a between-groups design, each participant is in only one of the three conditions or levels. If the investigator wished to have 20 participants in each group, then 60 participants would be needed to carry out the research.

Within-subjects designs. These designs are conceptually the opposite of between-groups designs. In within-subjects designs (also called **repeated measures,** or **related samples** designs), each of the conditions or levels of the independent variable is somehow connected to each of the other conditions or levels of the independent variable. Usually, this is because each participant in the study receives or experiences all of the conditions or is assessed on the dependent variable at each of the times at which these assessments occur; however, these designs also include examples where the participants are matched by the experimenter or are related in some other way (e.g., twins, husband and wife, or mother and child). In that case, each type of person (e.g., husband vs.

wife or child with developmental disability vs. mental-age matched comparison child) is one level of the independent variable in a **related samples** design. When each participant is assessed on the same measure more than once, within-subjects designs are also referred to as **repeated-measures** designs. Repeated measures designs are common in longitudinal research and intervention research. Comparing performance on the same dependent variable assessed before and after intervention (pretest and posttest) is a common example of a repeated-measures design. We might call the independent variable in such a study "time of measurement" or "change over time." In the HSB dataset, one of the variables is repeated (*visualization score* with two levels, *visualization* and *visualization retest*) and one is related samples (*education*, each student has both a *mother's education* and *father's education*). We will use a paired or matched statistic to see if *mother's education* is on the average higher or lower than *father's education*.

Single-factor designs. If the design has only one independent variable (either a between-groups design or a within-subjects design), then it should be described as a basic or single-factor or one-way design. **Factor** and **way** are other names for group difference independent variables. Note that the number of factors or "ways" refers to the number of *independent variables* not the number of *levels* of an independent variable. For example, a between-groups design with one independent variable that has four levels is a single-factor or "one-way" between-groups design with four levels. If the design was a within-subjects design with four levels, then it would be described as a single-factor repeated-measures design with four levels (e.g., the same test being given four times).

Between-groups factorial designs. When there is more than one group difference independent variable, and each level of each factor (independent variable) is possible in combination with each level, the design is called **factorial**. For example, a factorial design could have two independent variables (i.e., factors) *gender* and *ethnicity*, allowing for male and female members of each ethnic group. In these cases, the number of levels of *each* factor (independent variable) becomes important in the description of the design. Each independent variable (IV) is described using one number, which refers to the number of levels for that variable. For example, if *gender* has two levels (male and female) and *ethnicity* has three levels (Euro-American, African American, and Latino-American), then this design is a 2 × 3 between-groups factorial design. In this way of describing the design, the *number* of numbers (in this case two, the 2 and the 3) is the number of factors or ways, and the *numbers themselves* refer to the number of levels of each of those factors. This design could also be called a two-way or two-factor design because there are two independent variables.

Mixed factorial designs. If the design has a between-groups variable and a within-subjects independent variable, it is called a **mixed design.** For example, let's say that the two independent variables are gender (a between-groups variable with 2 levels—male and female) and time of measurement (with pretest and posttest as the two within-subjects levels); this is a 2 × 2 mixed factorial design with repeated measures on the second factor. The mixed design is common in experimental studies with a pretest and posttest, but the analysis can be complex so it is discussed in our intermediate SPSS book (Leech et al., 2011).

So, to summarize, when describing a design, each independent variable (IV) is described using one number, which is the number of levels for that variable. Thus, a design description with two numbers (e.g., 3 × 4) has two independent variables or factors, which have three and four levels. The dependent variable (DV) is not part of the design description, so it was not addressed in these design descriptions.

Selection of Inferential Statistics

How do you decide which of the many possible inferential statistics to use? Although this section may seem overwhelming at first because many statistical tests are introduced, don't be concerned if you don't now know much about the tests mentioned. You should come back to this chapter later, from time to time, when you have to make a decision about which statistic to use, and by then, the tests will be more familiar. We present eight steps, shown in Fig. 6.1, to help guide you in the selection of an appropriate statistical test. The steps and tables are our recommendations; you will see there are often other appropriate choices.

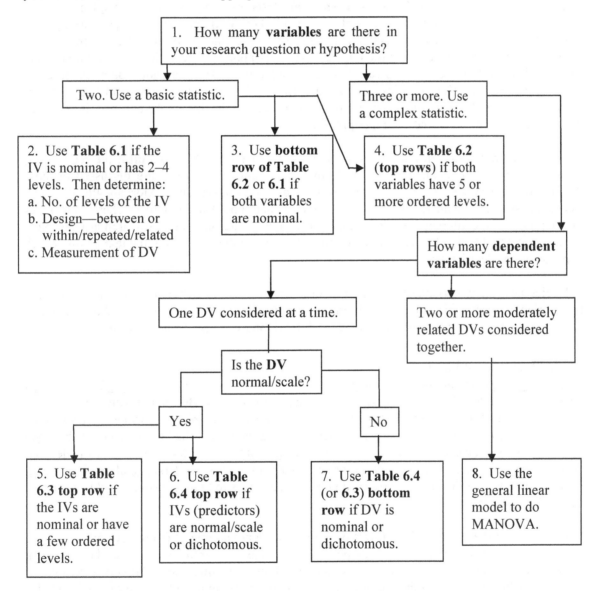

Fig. 6.1. A decision tree to help you select the appropriate inferential statistic from Tables 6.1 to 6.4 (IV = independent variable; DV = dependent variable).

Remember that **difference questions** compare groups and utilize the statistics that we call difference inferential statistics. These statistics (e.g., *t* test and ANOVA) are shown in Tables 6.1 and 6.3, and are discussed in the chapters noted in the tables.

Associational questions utilize what we call associational inferential statistics. The statistics in this group examine the association or relationship between two or more variables and are shown in Tables 6.2 and 6.4.

Using Tables 6.1 to 6.4 to Select Inferential Statistics

As with research questions and hypotheses discussed in Chapter 1, we divide inferential statistics into basic and complex. For **basic (or bivariate) statistics**, there is *one* independent and *one* dependent variable and you will use Table 6.1 or 6.2. For **complex statistics**, there are three or more variables. We decided to call them **complex** rather than **multivariate**, which is more common in the literature, because there is not unanimity about the definition of multivariate, and some statistics with more than two variables (e.g., factorial ANOVA) are not usually classified as multivariate. For complex statistics, you will use Table 6.3 or 6.4. Most of the statistics shown in Tables 6.1 and 6.2 are discussed in the remaining chapters in this book, and text is provided demonstrating how to compute and interpret them.

Two of the complex statistics in Tables 6.3 and 6.4 (**factorial ANOVA** and **multiple regression**) are introduced in this book, but they and other such complex statistics are discussed in more detail in our *IBM SPSS for Intermediate Statistics* book (Leech, Barrett, & Morgan, 4th ed. 2011). These statistics are identified with I.B. (i.e., intermediate book) in the tables. These four tables include most of the inferential statistics that you will encounter in reading research articles. Note the boxes in the decision tree are numbered to correspond to the numbers in the text below, which expands on the decision tree.

1. Decide how many variables there are in your research question or hypothesis. If there are only two variables, use Table 6.1 or 6.2. If there is *more* than one independent and/or dependent variable (i.e., three or more variables) to be used in this analysis, use Table 6.3 or 6.4.

Basic (Two Variable) Statistics

2. If the independent variable is nominal (i.e., has unordered levels) **or** has a few (2 – 4) ordered levels, use Table 6.1. Then your question is a **basic** two variable **difference question** to compare groups. You must then determine: (a) whether there are two *or* more than two levels (also called categories or groups or samples) of your independent variable, (b) whether the design is between groups or within subjects, and (c) whether the measurement level of the dependent variable is (i) normal/scale and parametric assumptions are not markedly violated *or* (ii) ordinal or (iii) nominal *or* dichotomous (see Chapter 3 if you need help). The answers to these questions lead to a specific box and statistic in Table 6.1.

For example, if there are (a) three levels of the independent variable, if (b) the design is between groups (i.e., these are different unrelated participants in the three groups), and if (c) the dependent variable is normally distributed, the appropriate statistic is **one-way ANOVA** (analysis of variance), which is shown in the top row, second box from the right, and discussed in Chapter 11. Another example could be that (a) the independent variable has two levels, (b) the design is within-subjects (repeated measures), and (c) the dependent variable data are ordinal or markedly violate the parent's assumptions. In this case, the appropriate statistic would be the **Wilcoxon** test shown in Table 6.1. An example of the selection of an **independent samples *t* test** is presented at the end of this chapter. Examples of selection, computation, and interpretation of all the statistics noted with "Ch. x" in Tables 6.1–6.4 are discussed in the referenced chapter.

3. If <u>both variables are nominal or dichotomous</u>, you could ask <u>either a difference question</u> (use the bottom row of Table 6.1; e.g., **chi-square**) <u>or an associational question</u> and use the bottom row of Table 6.2 to select **phi** or **Cramer's *V*.** Note, in the second to bottom row of Table 6.2, we have included **eta**, an associational statistic used with one nominal and one normal or scale variable. Later we will see it used as an effect size measure with ANOVAs. There are many other nonparametric associational measures, some of which we will see in Chapter 8.

Table 6.1. *Selection of an Appropriate Inferential Statistic for Basic, Two Variable, Difference Questions or Hypotheses[a]*

Scale of Measurement of **Dependent Variable** ↓	COMPARE ↓	One Factor or Independent Variable With **Two Levels** or **Categories**/Groups/Samples		One Independent Variable **Three or More Levels** or Groups	
		Independent Samples or Groups **(Between)**	Repeated Measures or Related Samples **(Within)**	Independent Samples or Groups **(Between)**	Repeated Measures or Related Samples **(Within)**
Dependent Variable Approximates **Normal/Scale** Data and Assumptions Not Markedly Violated	MEANS	INDEPENDENT SAMPLES *t* TEST Ch. 10 or ONE-WAY ANOVA Ch. 11	PAIRED SAMPLES *t* TEST Ch. 10	ONE-WAY ANOVA Ch. 11	GLM REPEATED MEASURES ANOVA I.B.[b]
Dependent Variables Clearly **Ordinal** or Parametric Assumptions Markedly Violated	MEAN RANKS	MANN–WHITNEY Ch. 10	WILCOXON Ch. 10	KRUSKAL–WALLIS Ch. 11	FRIEDMAN I.B.[b]
Dependent Variable **Nominal** or **Dichotomous**	COUNTS	CHI-SQUARE Ch. 8	MCNEMAR	CHI-SQUARE Ch. 8	COCHRAN Q TEST

[a] It is acceptable to use statistics that are in the box(es) below the appropriate statistic, but there is usually some loss of power. It is <u>not</u> acceptable to use statistics in boxes above the appropriate statistic or ones in another column.
[b] I.B. = Our intermediate book, Leech et al. (2011) *IBM SPSS for Intermediate Statistics: Use and Interpretation (4th ed.).* The other chapters mentioned in the table are the chapters where those statistics are discussed in this *IBM SPSS Introductory Statistics* book.

4. If <u>both variables have many (we suggest five or more) ordered levels,</u> use Table 6.2 (top two rows). Your research question would be a **basic** two variable (bivariate) **associational question**. Which row you use depends on *both* variables. If both are normal/scale, then you would probably select the **Pearson product moment correlation** or **bivariate regression** (top row). Regression should be used if one has a clearly directional hypothesis, with an independent and dependent variable. Correlation is chosen if one is simply interested in how the two variables are related. If one or both variables are ordinal (ranks or grossly skewed) or other assumptions are markedly violated, the second row (**Kendall's tau** or **Spearman rho**) is a better choice.

Table 6.2. *Selection of an Appropriate Inferential Statistic for Basic, Two Variable, Associational Questions or Hypotheses*

Measurement of **Both Variables** ↓	RELATE ↓	Two Variables or Scores for the Same or Related Subjects
Variables Are Both **Normal/Scale** and Assumptions Not Markedly Violated	SCORES	PEARSON (r) or BIVARIATE REGRESSION Ch. 9
Both Variables at Least **Ordinal** Data or Assumptions Markedly Violated	RANKS	KENDALL TAU or SPEARMAN (Rho) Ch. 9
One Variable Is **Normal/Scale** and One Is **Nominal**		ETA Ch. 8
Both Variables Are **Nominal** or **Dichotomous**	COUNTS	PHI or CRAMER'S *V* Ch. 8

Complex (Three or More Variable) Questions and Statistics

It is possible to break down a complex research problem or question into a series of basic (bivariate) questions and analyses. However, <u>there are advantages to combining them into one complex analysis; additional information is provided and a more accurate overall picture of the relationships is obtained.</u>

5. If you have one <u>normally</u> distributed (scale) dependent variable (DV) and two (or perhaps three or four) independent variables (IVs), each of which is <u>nominal</u> or has a few (2 – 4) ordered levels, you will use the top row of Table 6.3 and one of three types of **factorial ANOVA**. These analysis of variance (ANOVA) statistics answer **complex difference questions**.

Note, in Table 6.3, that there are no complex difference statistics available in this program if the dependent variable is ordinal. **Log-linear** analysis is a nonparametric statistic somewhat similar to the between-groups factorial ANOVA for the case where all the variables are nominal or dichotomous (see Table 6.3).

Table 6.3. *Selection of the Appropriate Complex (Two or More Independent Variables) Statistic to Answer Difference Questions or Hypotheses*

Dependent Variable(s) ↓	Two or More Independent Variables		
	All Between Groups	All Within Subjects	Mixed (Between & Within)
One **Normal/Scale** Dependent Variable	GLM, Factorial ANOVA or ANCOVA Ch. 11 and I.B.[a]	GLM (ANOVA) With Repeated Measures on All Factors I.B.	GLM (ANOVA) With Repeated Measures on Some Factors I.B.
Ordinal Dependent Variable	None Common	None Common	None Common
Dichotomous Dependent Variable	LOG-LINEAR	None Common	None Common

[a] I.B. = Leech et al. (2011) *IBM SPSS for Intermediate Statistics: Use and Interpretation* (4th ed.).

6. The statistics in Table 6.4 are used to answer **complex associational questions**. If you have <u>two or more independent or predictor variables and one normal (scale) dependent variable</u>, the top row of Table 6.4 and **multiple regression** are appropriate.

7. If the <u>dependent variable</u> is <u>dichotomous or nominal</u>, consult the bottom row of Table 6.4, and use **discriminant analysis** or **logistic regression**, both discussed in Leech et al. (2005).

Table 6.4. *Selection of the Appropriate Complex Associational Statistic for Predicting a Single Dependent/Outcome Variable from Several Independent Variables*

One Dependent or Outcome Variable ↓	Several Independent or Predictor Variables		
	Normal or Scale	Some Normal Some Dichotomous (Two category)	All Dichotomous
Normal/Scale (Continuous)	MULTIPLE REGRESSION Ch. 9 and I.B. [a]	MULTIPLE REGRESSION Ch. 9 and I.B.	MULTIPLE REGRESSION Ch. 9 and I.B.
Dichotomous	DISCRIMINANT ANALYSIS I.B.	LOGISTIC REGRESSION I.B.	LOGISTIC REGRESSION I.B.

[a] I.B. = Our intermediate book, Leech et al. (2011) *IBM SPSS for Intermediate Statistics: Use and Interpretation (4th ed.).*

8. Multivariate analysis of variance, **MANOVA**, is used if you have two or more normal (scale) dependent variables treated simultaneously. This complex statistic is discussed in our intermediate SPSS book (Leech et al., 2011).

Exceptions

Occasionally you will see a research article in which a dichotomous *dependent variable* was used with a *t* test or ANOVA, or as either variable in a Pearson correlation. Because of the special nature of dichotomous variables, this is not necessarily wrong, as would be the use of a nominal (three or more unordered levels) dependent variable with these parametric statistics. However, we think that it is usually a better practice to use the same statistics with dichotomous variables that you would use with nominal variables. The exception is that it is appropriate to use dichotomous (dummy) independent variables in multiple and logistic regression (see Table 6.4 again).

The General Linear Model

Whether or not there is a relationship between variables can be answered in two ways. For example, if each of two variables provides approximately normally distributed data with five or more levels, based on Fig. 6.1 and Table 6.2, the statistic to use is either the Pearson correlation or bivariate (simple) regression, and that would be our recommendation. Instead, some researchers choose to divide the independent variable into two or more levels or groups, such as low, medium, and high, and then do a one-way ANOVA.

Conversely, in a second example, others who start with an independent variable that has only a few (say two through four *ordered* categories) may choose to do a correlation instead of a one-way ANOVA. Although these choices are not necessarily wrong, we do not think they are usually the best practice. In the first example, information is lost by dividing a continuous independent variable into a few categories. In the second example, there would be a restricted range, which tends to decrease the size of the correlation coefficient.

In the previous examples, we recommended one of the choices, but the fact that there *are* two choices raises a bigger and more complex issue. Statisticians point out, and can prove mathematically, that the distinction between difference and associational statistics is an artificial one. Figure 6.2 (and Fig. 1.1) shows that, although we make a distinction between difference and associational inferential statistics, they both serve the purpose of exploring and describing (top box) relationships and both are subsumed by the general linear model (middle box).

Statisticians state that all common parametric statistics are relational. Thus, the full range of methods used to analyze one continuous dependent variable and one or more independent variables, either continuous or categorical, are mathematically similar. The model on which this is based is called the **general linear model**. The relationship between the independent and dependent variables can be expressed by an equation with weights for each of the independent/predictor variables plus an error term.

The bottom part of Fig. 6.2 indicates that a *t* test or one-way ANOVA with a dichotomous independent variable is analogous to bivariate regression. Finally, as shown in the lowest row of boxes in Fig. 6.2, a one-way or factorial ANOVA can be computed mathematically as a multiple regression with multiple dichotomous predictors (dummy variables). Note in Fig. 6.1 and Tables 6.1 and 6.3 that SPSS uses the GLM program to perform a variety of statistics, including factorial ANOVA and MANOVA.

Although we recognize that our distinction between difference and associational parametric statistics is a simplification, we think it is useful because it corresponds to a distinction made by most researchers when they are conceptualizing their studies. We hope that this glimpse of an advanced topic is clear and helpful.

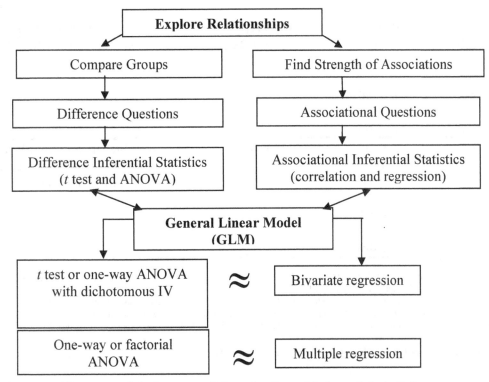

Fig. 6.2. A general linear model diagram of the selection of inferential statistics.

Interpreting the Results of a Statistical Test

In Chapters 8–11, we present information about how to check assumptions, do the commands, interpret the previous statistics, and write about them. For each statistic, the program produces a number or **calculated value** based on the specific data in your study. They are labeled *t, F,* and so on, or sometimes just value by SPSS.

Statistical Significance
The calculated value is compared to a **critical value** (found in a statistics table or stored in the computer's memory) that takes into account the degrees of freedom, which are usually based on the number of participants. Using this comparison, the program provides a probability value (called *sig.* for significance). It is the probability of a Type I error, which is the probability of rejecting the null hypothesis when it is actually true. Figure 6.3 shows how to interpret any inferential test once you know the probability level (*p* or *sig.*) from the computer or statistics table. In general, if the calculated value of the statistic (*t, F,* etc.) is relatively large, the probability or *p* is small (e.g., .05, .01, .001). If the probability is *less than* the preset alpha level (usually .05), we can say that the results are **statistically significant** or that they are significant at the .05 level. We can also say that the null hypothesis of no difference or no relationship can be rejected. Note that, using this program's computer printouts, it is quite easy to determine statistical significance because the actual significance or probability level (*p*) is printed so you do

not have to look up a critical value in a table. Because SPSS labels this *p* value or **Sig.**, all of the common inferential statistics have a common metric, the significance level or **Sig**. Thus, regardless of what specific statistic you use, if the sig. or *p* is small (e.g., less than an alpha set at .05), the finding is statistically significant, and you can reject the null hypothesis of no difference or no relationship.

SPSS Value[1]	Meaning	Null Hypothesis	Interpretation
1.00	$p = 1.00$	Don't Reject	Not Statistically Significant (could be due to chance)
.50	$p = .50$		
.06	$p = .06$		
.049	$p < .05$ or $p = .049$	Reject[2]	Statistically Significant[3] (not likely due to chance but not necessarily important or practical)
.01	$p = .01$		
.000	$p < .001$		

1. SPSS uses **Sig.** to indicate the significance or probability level (*p*) of all inferential statistics. This figure provides just a sample of Sig. values, which could be any value from 0 to 1.
2. .05 is the typical alpha level that researchers use to assess whether the null hypothesis should be rejected or not. However, sometimes researchers use more liberal levels (e.g., .10 in exploratory studies) or more conservative levels (e.g., .01).
3. Statistically significant does *not* mean that the results have practical significance or importance. See next section.

Fig. 6.3. Interpreting inferential statistics using Sig.

Practical Significance versus Statistical Significance

Students, and sometimes researchers, misinterpret statistically significant results as being practically or clinically important. But statistical significance is not the same as practical significance or importance. With large samples, you can find statistical significance even when the differences or associations are very small/weak. Thus, in addition to statistical significance, you should examine effect size. We will see that it is quite possible, with a large sample, to have a statistically significant result that is weak (i.e., has a small **effect size.**) Remember that the null hypothesis states that there is *no* difference or *no* association. A statistically significant result with a small effect size means that we can be very confident that there is at least a little difference or association, but that relationship may not be of any practical importance.

Confidence Intervals

One alternative to null hypothesis significance testing (NHST) is to create confidence intervals. These intervals provide more information than NHST and *may* provide more practical information. For example, suppose one knew that an increase in reading scores of five points, obtained on a particular instrument, would lead to a functional increase in reading performance. Two different methods of instruction were compared. The result showed that students who used the new method scored significantly higher statistically than those who used the other method. According to NHST, we would reject the null hypothesis of no difference between methods and conclude that the new method is better. If we apply **confidence intervals** to this same study, we can determine an interval that contains the *population mean difference* 95% of the time. If the lower bound of that interval is greater than five points, we can conclude that using this method of instruction would lead to a practical or functional increase in reading levels. If, however, the confidence interval ranged from, say, 1 to 11, the result would be statistically significant, but the mean difference in the population could be as little as 1 point, or as big as 11 points. Given these results, we could not be confident that there would be a *practical* increase in reading using the new method.

Effect Size

A statistically significant outcome does not give information about the strength or size of the outcome. Therefore, it is important to know, in addition to information on statistical significance, the size of the effect. **Effect size** is defined as the strength of the relationship between the independent variable and the dependent variable, and/or the magnitude of the difference between levels of the independent variable with respect to the dependent variable. Statisticians have proposed many effect size measures that fall mainly into two types or families, the *r* family and the *d* family.

The *r* family of effect size measures. One method of expressing effect sizes is in terms of strength of association. The most well-known variant of this approach is the **Pearson correlation coefficient, *r*.** Using Pearson *r*, effect sizes always have an absolute value less than 1.0, varying between −1.0 and +1.0 with 0 representing no effect and +1 or −1 the maximum effect. This *family* of effect sizes includes many other associational statistics such as Spearman's rho (r_s), phi (ϕ), eta (η), and the multiple correlation (R).

The *d* family of effect size measures. The *d* family focuses on magnitude of difference rather than on strength of association. If one compares two groups, the effect size (*d*) can be computed by subtracting the mean of the second group (B) from the mean of the first group (A) and dividing by the pooled standard deviation of the two groups. The general formula is below on the left. If the two groups have equal *n*s, the pooled *SD* is the average of the *SD*s for the two groups. When *n*s are unequal, the formula below on the right is the appropriate one. Be sure to follow the rules of algebra, doing multiplications before addition. The answer to the denominator is the SD weighted more for the larger sample; it should be a number between the SDs of the two groups.

$$d = \frac{M_A - M_B}{SD_{pooled}} \qquad\qquad d = \frac{M_A - M_B}{\sqrt{\dfrac{(N_A - 1)SD_A^2 + (N_B - 1)SD_B^2}{N_A + N_B - 2}}}$$

There are many other formulas for d family effect sizes, but they all express effect size in standard deviation units. Thus, a *d* of .5 means that the groups differ by one half of a standard deviation. Using *d*, effect sizes usually vary from 0 to + or −1 but *d* can be more than 1 if the effect is very large.

Issues about effect size measures. Unfortunately, as just indicated, there are many different effect size measures and little agreement about which to use. Although *d* is the most commonly discussed effect size measure for differences between groups, it is not available on SPSS outputs. However, *d* can be calculated by hand from information in the printout, using the previous appropriate formula. The correlation coefficient, *r,* and other measures of the strength of association, such as phi (ϕ), eta^2 (η^2), and R^2, are available in the outputs if requested.

There is disagreement among researchers about whether it is best to express effect size as the unsquared or squared *r* family statistic (e.g., *r* or r^2). The squared versions have been used because they indicate the percentage of variance in the dependent variable that can be predicted from the independent variable(s). However, some statisticians argue that these usually small percentages give you an underestimated impression of the strength or importance of the effect. Thus, we (like Cohen, 1988) decided to use the unsquared statistics (r, ϕ, η, and R) as our r family indexes.

Relatively few researchers reported effect sizes before 1999 when the APA Task Force on Statistical Inference stated that effect sizes should *always* be reported for your primary results (Wilkinson & The Task Force, 1999). The 5th edition (APA, 2001) adopted this recommendation of the Task Force so, now, most journal articles discuss the size of the effect as well as whether or not the result was statistically significant.

Interpreting Effect Sizes

Assuming that you have computed an effect size measure, how should it be interpreted? Based on Cohen (1988) and Vaske, Gliner, and Morgan (2002), Table 6.5 provides guidelines for interpreting the size of the "effect" for five common effect size measures: d, r, ϕ, R and η.

Table 6.5. *Interpretation of the Strength of a Relationship (Effect Sizes)*

General Interpretation of the Strength of a Relationship	*The d Family* [a]	*The r Family* [b]					
	d	r^2	r and ϕ	R^2	R	η^2	η (eta) [d]
Much larger than typical	$\geq \lvert 1.00 \rvert$ [c, e]	.49	$\geq \lvert .70 \rvert$	.49+	$\lvert .70 \rvert$+	.21	$\lvert .45 \rvert$+
Large or larger than typical	$\lvert .80 \rvert$	.25	$\lvert .50 \rvert$	.26	$\lvert .51 \rvert$	.14	$\lvert .37 \rvert$
Medium or typical	$\lvert .50 \rvert$	.09	$\lvert .30 \rvert$	.13	$\lvert .36 \rvert$	.06	$\lvert .24 \rvert$
Small or smaller than typical	$\lvert .20 \rvert$	.01	$\lvert .10 \rvert$	.02	$\lvert .14 \rvert$	.01	$\lvert .10 \rvert$

[a] d values can vary from 0.0 to + or – infinity, but d greater than 1.0 is relatively uncommon.

[b] r family values can vary from 0.0 to + or – 1.0, but except for reliability (i.e., same concept measured twice), r is rarely above .70. In fact, some of these statistics (e.g., phi) have a restricted range in certain cases; that is, the maximum phi is less than 1.0.

[c] We interpret the numbers in this table as a range of values. For example, a d greater than .90 (or less than −.90) would be described as "much larger than typical," a d between, say, .70 and .90 would be called "larger than typical," and d between, say, .60 and .70 would be "typical to larger than typical." We interpret the other three columns similarly.

[d] Partial etas are multivariate tests equivalent to R. Use R column.

[e] Note. | | indicates absolute value of the coefficient. The absolute magnitude of the coefficient, rather than its sign, is the information that is relevant to effect size. R and η usually are calculated by taking the square root of a squared value, so that the sign usually is positive.

Note that these guidelines are based on the effect sizes usually found in studies in the behavioral sciences and education. Thus, they do not have absolute meaning; large, medium, and small are only relative to typical findings in these areas. For that reason, we suggest using "larger than typical" instead of large, "typical" instead of medium, and "smaller than typical" instead of small. The guidelines do not apply to all subfields in the behavioral sciences, and they definitely do not apply to fields, designs, or contexts where the usually expected effects are either larger or smaller. It is advisable to examine the research literature to see if there is information about typical effect sizes on the topic and adjust the values that are considered typical accordingly.

Cohen (1988) provided research examples of what he labeled small, medium, and large effects to support the suggested d and r family values. Most researchers would not consider a correlation (r) of .5 to be very strong because only 25% of the variance in the dependent variable is predicted. However, Cohen argued that a d of .8 (and an r of .5, which he showed are mathematically similar) are "grossly perceptible and therefore large differences, as (for example, is) the mean difference in height between 13- and 18-year-old girls" (p. 27). Cohen stated that a small effect may be difficult to detect, perhaps because it is in a less well-controlled area of research. Cohen's medium size effect is "… visible to the naked eye. That is, in the course of normal experiences, one would become aware of an average difference in IQ between clerical and semi-skilled workers …" (p. 26).

Effect size and practical significance. The effect size indicates the strength of the relationship or magnitude of the difference and thus is relevant to the issue of practical significance. Although some researchers consider effect size measures to be an index of practical significance, we think that even effect size measures are not direct indexes of the importance of a finding. As implied earlier, what constitutes a large or important effect depends on the specific area studied, the context, and the methods used. Furthermore, practical significance always involves a judgment by the researcher and/or the consumers (e.g., clinicians, clients, teachers, school boards) of research that takes into account such factors as cost and political considerations. A common example is that the effect size of taking daily aspirin on heart attacks is quite small but the practical importance is high because preventing heart attacks is a life or death matter, the cost of aspirin is low, and side effects are relatively uncommon. On the other hand, a curriculum change could have a large effect size but be judged impractical because of high costs and/or extensive opposition to its implementation.

Confidence intervals of the effect size. Knowing the confidence interval around an effect size can provide information useful to making a decision about practical significance or importance. If the confidence interval is narrow, one would know that the effect size in the population is close to the computed effect size. On the other hand, if the confidence interval is large (as is usually the case with small samples) the population effect size could fall within a wide range, making it difficult to interpret the computed effect size for purposes of estimating practical significance. Similar to the example described earlier, if the lower bound of the confidence interval was more than a minimum effect size agreed to indicate a practically significant effect, one could then be quite confident that the effect was important or practical. Unfortunately, SPSS does not provide confidence intervals for effect size measures and it is not easy to compute them by hand.

Steps in Interpreting Inferential Statistics

When you interpret inferential statistics, we recommend:

1. Decide whether to reject the null hypothesis. However, that is not enough for a full interpretation. If you find that the outcome is statistically significant, you need to answer at least two *more* questions. Figure 6.4 summarizes the steps described later about how to more fully interpret the results of an inferential statistic.

2. What is the direction of the effect? Difference inferential statistics compare groups so it is necessary to state which group performed better. We discuss how to do this in Chapters 10 and 11. For associational inferential statistics (e.g., correlation), the sign is very important, so you must indicate whether the association or relationship is positive or negative. We discuss how to interpret associational statistics in Chapters 8 and 9.

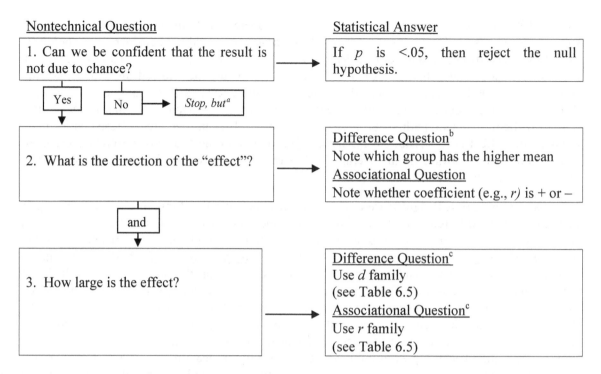

Nontechnical Question   Statistical Answer

1. Can we be confident that the result is   If *p* is <.05, then reject the null
not due to chance?   hypothesis.

Yes   No → *Stop, but*[a]

2. What is the direction of the "effect"?   Difference Question[b]
                                                Note which group has the higher mean
                                                Associational Question
                                                Note whether coefficient (e.g., *r)* is + or −

and

3. How large is the effect?   Difference Question[c]
                                                Use *d* family
                                                (see Table 6.5)
                                                Associational Question[c]
                                                Use *r* family
                                                (see Table 6.5)

[a] If you have a small sample *(N)*, it is possible to have a nonsignificant result (it may be due to chance) and yet a large effect size. If so, an attempt to replicate the study with a larger sample may be justified.

[b] If there are three or more means or a significant interaction, a post hoc test (e.g., Tukey) will be necessary for complete interpretation.

[c] Interpretation of effect size is based on Cohen (1988) and Table 6.5. A "large" effect is one that Cohen stated is "grossly perceptible." It is larger than typically found but does not necessarily explain a large amount of variance. You might use confidence intervals in addition to or instead of effect sizes.

Fig. 6.4. Steps in the interpretation of an inferential statistic.

3. <u>What is the size of the effect?</u> It is desirable to include the effect size and/or the confidence interval in the description of all your results or at least provide the information to compute them. Unfortunately, SPSS does not always provide effect sizes and confidence intervals, so for some statistics we have to compute or estimate the effect size by hand, or use an effect size calculator, several of which are available online.

4. Although not shown in Fig. 6.4, the <u>researcher or the consumer of the research should make a judgment about whether the result has practical or clinical significance or importance.</u> To do so, they need to take into account the effect size, the costs of implementing change, and the probability and severity of any side effects or unintended consequences.

An Example of How to Select and Interpret Inferential Statistics

As a review of what you read in Chapter 1 and this chapter, we now provide an extended example based on the HSB data. We will walk you through the process of identifying the variables, research questions, and approach, and then show how we selected appropriate statistics and interpreted the results.

Research problem. <u>Suppose your research problem was to investigate the relation of *gender* and *math courses* taken to *math achievement.*</u>

Identification of the variables and their measurement. The research problem specifies three variables: *gender*, *math courses taken*, and *math achievement*. The latter appears to be the outcome or dependent variable, and gender and math courses taken are the independent or predictor variables because they occurred before the math achievement exam, which we said was taken near the end of the students' senior year. As such, *gender* and *math courses taken* are *presumed* to have an effect on math achievement scores.

What is the level of measurement for these three variables? *Gender* is clearly dichotomous (*male* or *female*). *Math courses taken* has six ordered values, from zero to five courses. These are scale data because we found in Chapter 5 that the scores were not highly skewed. Likewise, the *math achievement* test has many levels, with more scores somewhere in the middle than at the high and low ends so was approximately normally distributed. We confirmed in Chapters 4 and 5 that math courses taken and math achievement were at least approximately normally distributed by determining the skewness of each.

Research questions. There are a number of possible research questions that could be asked and statistics that could be used with these three variables, including all of the types of questions in Appendix B, the descriptive statistics discussed in Chapter 3, and several of the inferential statistics presented in this chapter. However, we focus on three research questions and three inferential statistics because they answer this research problem and fit our earlier recommendations for good choices. First, we discuss two basic research questions, given the previous specification of the variables and their measurement. Then, we discuss a complex research question that could be asked instead of research questions 1 and 2.

1. Is there a difference between *males* and *females* (the two levels of the variable, *gender)* on their average *math achievement scores*?

Type of research question. Using the text, Fig. 6.1, and Table 6.1, you should see that the first question is phrased as a **basic difference question** because there are only two variables and the focus is a group difference (the difference between the male group and the female group).

Selection of an appropriate statistic. If you examine Table 6.1, you will see that the first question should be answered with an **independent samples *t* test** because (a) the independent variable has only two values (male and female), (b) the design is between groups (males and females form two independent groups), and (c) the dependent variable (*math achievement*) is normal/scale data. We would also check other assumptions of the *t* test, especially homogeneity of variances, to be sure that they are not markedly violated.

Interpretation of the results for question 1. Let's assume that about 50 students participated in the study and that $t = 2.05$. The output will give you the exact **Sig.** In this case, $p < .05$ and thus *t* is statistically significant. However, if you had 25 participants, this *t* would not have been significant (because the *t* value necessary for statistical significance is influenced strongly by sample size. Small samples require a larger *t* to be significant.).

Deciding whether the statistic is significant only means the result is unlikely to be due to chance. You still have to state the direction of the result and the effect size and/or the confidence interval (see Fig. 6.4). To determine the direction, we need to know the mean (average) *math achievement* scores for males and females. In the HSB data, males have the higher mean, as you saw in Chapters 4. Given that the difference is significant, you can be quite confident that males in the population are at least a little better at math achievement, on average, than females. So you should state that males scored higher than females. If the difference was not statistically significant, it is best *not* to make any comment about which mean was higher because the difference could be due to chance. Likewise, if the difference was not significant, we recommend that you report but do not discuss or interpret the effect size.[1] You should also provide the means and standard deviations so that the effect size can be better understood.

Because the *t* was statistically significant, we would calculate *d* and discuss the **effect size,** as shown earlier. In this situation, we would compute the pooled (weighted average) standard deviation for male and female *math achievement* scores. Let's say that the difference between the means was 2.0 and the pooled standard deviation was 6.0; then *d* would be .33, a small to medium size effect. This means that the difference is less than typical of the statistically significant findings in the behavioral sciences. A *d* of .33 may or may not be a large enough difference to use for recommending programmatic changes (i.e., may or may not be practically significant).

Confidence intervals might help you decide if the difference in *math achievement* scores was large enough to have practical significance. For example, say you found (from the lower bound of the confidence interval) that you could only be confident that there was a 1/2 point difference between males and females. Then you could decide whether that was a big enough difference to justify, for example, a programmatic change.

2.   Is there an association between *math courses taken* and *math achievement?*

Type of research question. This second question is phrased as a **basic associational question** because there are only two variables and both have many ordered levels. Thus, use Table 6.2 for the second question.

Selection of an appropriate statistic. As you can see from Table 6.2, the second research question should be answered with a **Pearson correlation** because both *math courses taken* and *math achievement* are normally distributed variables.

Interpretation of the results for research question 2. The interpretation of *r* is based on decisions similar to those made above for *t*. If *r* = .30 (with 50 subjects), it would be statistically significant at the *p* < .05 level. If the *r* is statistically significant, you still need to discuss the direction of the correlation and effect size. Because the correlation is positive, we would say that students with a relatively *high* number of math courses taken tend to perform at the high end on the math achievement test and those with few math courses taken tend to perform poorly on the math achievement test. The **effect size** of *r* = .30 is medium or typical.

Note that if *N* were 25, the *r* of .30 would not be significant, but the effect size (.30) would still be typical. On the other hand, if *N* were 500 and *r* = .30, *p* would be <.0001. With *N* = 500, even *r* = .10 would be statistically significant, indicating that you could be quite sure the association was not zero, but the effect size would be small, or less than typical.

Complex research question and statistics. As you will see in later chapters, there are advantages to considering the two independent variables (*gender* and *math courses taken*) together rather than separately as in questions 1 and 2. There are several statistics that you will compute that could be used to consider *gender* and *math courses taken* together. A research question which subsumes both questions 1 and 2 could be:

---

[1] At times when one has a small sample, one would present the effect size and talk about the need to replicate the study with a larger sample.

3.   Is there a combination of *gender* and *math courses* that predicts *math achievement*?

Selection of an appropriate statistic. Multiple regression could be used to answer this question. As you can see in Table 6.4, multiple regression is appropriate because we are trying to predict a normally distributed/scale variable (*math achievement*) from two independent variables, which are *math courses taken* (normal or scale) and *gender* (a dichotomous variable).

Based on our discussion of the general linear model (GLM), a **two-way factorial ANOVA** would be another statistic that could be used to consider both *gender* and *math courses taken* simultaneously. However, to use ANOVA, the many levels of math courses taken would have to be recoded into a few categories or levels (perhaps high, medium, and low). Because information is lost when you do such a recode, we would not recommend factorial ANOVA for this example. Another possible statistic to use for this example is **analysis of covariance** (ANCOVA) using gender as the independent variable and *math courses taken* as the covariate; ANCOVA is discussed in Leech et al. (2011).

Interpretation of the results for research question 3. We provide an introduction to multiple regression in Chapter 9 and to factorial ANOVA in Chapter 11, but extended treatment is beyond the scope of this book (see Leech et al., 2011). For now, let's just say that we would obtain important new information about the relationships among these three variables by doing these complex statistics rather than by doing only the *t* test and correlation described earlier and in the next section. In the HSB data, we would find that the fact that males take more math courses than do females seems to statistically account for the difference in math achievement of males versus females. Findings like this, which clarify potentially misleading results, are one of the reasons that complex statistics can be useful.

Writing About Your Outputs

One of the goals of this book is to help you write a research report or thesis using the outputs. Thus, we have provided an example later that could be two paragraphs from a research paper based on the expanded HSB data used in the assignments in this book.

Before demonstrating how you might write about the results of research questions 1 and 2, we would like to make several important points. There are several books listed in the bibliography that will help you write a research paper and make appropriate tables. Note especially the APA manual (2010), Nicol and Pexman (2010), and Morgan, Reichert, and Harrison (2002). The example that follows and the samples provided in each output interpretation section give only one way to write about outputs. There are other good ways.

Based on your outputs, you should first write about descriptive statistics about the demographics (e.g., gender, age, ethnicity) of the participants in your sample in your **Method** section. You should add to any literature-based evidence about the reliability and validity of your measures or instruments. You also should include in your report whether statistical assumptions of the inferential statistics were met or how adjustments were made.

The **Results** section includes a description (but not a discussion) of the findings in words, tables, and maybe figures. Your Results section should include the following numbers about each statistically significant finding (in a table or the text):
   1. The value of the statistic (e.g., $t = 2.05$ or $r = .30$) to two decimals.
   2. The degrees of freedom (often in parentheses) and for chi-square the N (e.g., $\chi^2 = 5.26$,

$df = 2, N = 49$).

3. The p or Sig. value (e.g., $p = .048$), preferably the exact p value to 2 or 3 decimal places.
4. If the statistic is significant, the direction of the finding (e.g., by showing which mean is larger or the sign of the correlation.)
5. An index of effect size from either the d family or the r family, and, if the statistic is significant, a statement about the relative size of the "effect." (See Table 6.5 and accompanying text.)

When not shown in a table, the prior information should be provided in the text, as shown later. *In addition* to the numerical information, you must describe your significant results in words, including the variables related, the direction of the finding, and an interpretive statement about the size/strength of the effect based on Table 6.5 or, better still, based on the effect sizes found in the literature on your topic. Realize that our effect size terms are only rough estimates of the magnitude of the "effect" based on what is typical in the behavioral sciences; they are not necessarily applicable to your topic.

If your paper includes a table, it is usually not necessary or advisable to include all the details about the value of the statistic, degrees of freedom, and p in the text because they are in the table. If you have a table, you must refer to it by number (e.g., Table 1) in the text and you must describe the main points, but don't repeat all of it or the table is not necessary. You can mention relationships that are not significant (acknowledging their statistical nonsignificance), but do not discuss the direction of the finding or interpret the meaning of nonsignificant findings because the results could well be due to chance. Do provide effect sizes or at least the information (e.g., ns, means, and standard deviations) necessary for other researchers to compute the effect size, in case your study is included in a future meta-analysis.

The **Discussion** chapter puts the findings in context in regard to the research literature, theory, and the purposes of the study. You should also discuss limitations of the study and attempt to explain why the results turned out the way they did.

An Example of How to Write about Results

Based on what we reported earlier about the results of research questions 1 and 2, we might make the following statements in our Results section:

Results

For research question 1, there was a statistically significant difference between male and female students on math achievement, $t(48) = 2.05$. $p = .04$, $d = .33$. Males ($M = 14.70$) scored higher than females ($M = 12.70$), and the effect size was small to medium according to Cohen's (1988) guidelines. The confidence interval for the difference between the means was .50 to 6.50, indicating that the difference could be as little as half a point, which is probably not a practically important difference, but also could be as large as six and one half points.

For research question 2, there was a statistically significant positive correlation between math courses taken and math achievement, $r(48) = .30$, $p = .03$. The positive correlation means that, in general, students who took more math courses tended to score high on the math achievement test and students who did not take many math courses scored low on math achievement. The effect size of $r = .30$ is considered medium or typical.

We present examples of how to write about the results of each statistic that you compute in the appropriate chapter.

Conclusion

Now you should be ready to study each of the statistics in Tables 6.1 to 6.4 and learn more about their computation and interpretation. It may be tough going at times, but hopefully this overview has given you a good foundation. It would be wise for you to review this chapter, especially the tables and figures, from time to time as you learn about the various statistical methods. If you do, you will have a good grasp of how the various statistics fit together, when to use them, and how to interpret the results. You will need this information to understand the chapters that follow.

Interpretation Questions

6.1.   Compare and contrast a between-groups design and a within-subjects design.

6.2.   What information about variables, levels, and design should you keep in mind in order to choose an appropriate statistic?

6.3.   Provide an example of a study, including the variables, level of measurement, and hypotheses, for which a researcher could <u>appropriately</u> choose two different statistics to examine the relations between the same variables. Explain your answer.

6.4.   When $p < .05$, what does this signify?

6.5.   Interpret the following related to effect size:
(a) $d = .25$ (c) $R = .53$ (e) $d = 1.15$
(b) $r = .35$ (d) $r = .13$ (f) $\eta = .38$

6.6.   What statistic would you use if you wanted to see if there was a difference between three ethnic groups on math achievement? Why?

6.7.   What statistic would you use if you had two independent variables, income group (<$10,000, $10,000–$30,000, >$30,000) and ethnic group (Hispanic, Caucasian, African American), and one normally distributed dependent variable (self-efficacy at work)?

6.8.   What statistic would you use if you had one independent variable, geographic location (North, South, East, West), and one dependent variable (satisfaction with living environment, Yes or No)?

6.9   What statistic would you use if you had three normally distributed (scale) independent variables (weight of participants, age of participants, and height of participants) plus one dichotomous independent variable (gender) and one dependent variable (positive self-image), which is normally distributed?

6.10. A teacher *ranked* the students in her Algebra I class from 1 = highest to 25 = lowest in terms of their grades on several tests. After the next semester, she checked the school records to see what the students received from their Algebra II teacher. The research question is "Is there a relationship between rank in Algebra I and grades in Algebra II?" What statistic should she use?

CHAPTER 7

Methods to Provide Evidence for Reliability and Validity

In this chapter we start with a brief overview of measurement reliability and validity. Then we demonstrate four statistics that provide evidence for some of the several aspects of the reliability and validity of your data. These statistics are often described in the **Method** chapter of a research report because they precede the testing of your research hypothesis. Including information about the reliability and validity of your data will help support the answers to your research questions

Problem 7.1 demonstrates the use of **Cohen's kappa**, which is a good method to assess evidence for interrater *reliability* of a nominal variable. Problem 7.2 uses **correlation** and the **paired samples *t* test** to illustrate one method to assess interrater *reliability* for normally distributed (scale) variables. Problem 7.3 uses **factor analysis** to show how one could reduce several variables to a smaller number of composite variables that represent several theoretically related aspects of a complex concept and provide support for later analyses of the research questions. In Problem 7.4, **Cronbach's alpha** is used to provide evidence for the internal consistency reliability of composites, multi-item subscales, or sets of variables resulting from a factor analysis or from a theoretical combination of variables (e.g. several items on a questionnaire designed to measure the same concept). This chapter illustrates how to compute, interpret and write about these statistics in terms of the evidence they provide to support reliability and validity.

Problems 7.1 and/or 7.2 will be helpful when you are using observations to "code" specific categories of behavior or whenever there is at least some subjectivity to a classification system. In this case the consistency or reliability of the data needs to be checked by having two observers or raters independently record their scores and then check how well they agree with one another (their interrater or interobserver reliability).

It is common for a researcher to develop a smaller number of new summated variables from an initially larger number of items such as the 14 Likert-type ratings we designed to measure attitudes about mathematics motivation, competence, and pleasure. The statistics described in Problems 7.3 and 7.4 are relatively complex but useful both for assessing the reliability and validity of established instruments such as published questionnaires. Even with an established questionnaire, one would check one's own data, at least for the internal consistency reliability (alpha) of the subconcepts such as the math attitudes of competence, motivation, and pleasure described in Chapter 1.

If one were developing a new or modified instrument, one would probably first try to find support for the validity of the theoretical groupings of the items to see how well the factor analysis fits the proposed structure or organization of the subconstructs based on the literature or theory. Then, one would check the reliability of the factors using Cronbach's alpha, as we have in Problems 7.3 and 7.4.

It is important to realize that the statistics performed here are based on, and in some cases, the same as those in Chapters 8–11. The Pearson correlation which was introduced briefly in Chapter 6 (especially in Table 6.2 and research question 2) is used in Problems 7.2–7.4 so it is important to understand a little more about correlation before we introduce the problems in this chapter. (Correlation is discussed more fully in Chapter 9.)

Correlation Coefficients, these statistics can vary from −1.00 (a perfect negative correlation or association) through .00 (no correlation) to +1.00 (a perfect positive correlation). Note that +1 and −1 are equally high or strong, but they lead to different interpretations. A high *positive correlation* between two items on a questionnaire would mean that persons with high ratings on the first item tended to have higher ratings on the second item, those with lower item ratings on item one had lower item two ratings, and those in between had ratings that were neither especially high nor especially low. On the other hand, a high *negative correlation* would mean that students rated high on one item tended to rate low on the other item. With a *zero correlation* there are no consistent associations. A person rated high on one item might be rated low, medium, or high on the other item.

Measurement Reliability

This chapter illustrates several of the methods for computing measurement reliability. It is important to assess the reliability of your data prior to conducting inferential statistics to help answer your research questions. If reliability tests indicate that your data have low reliability, the results from inferential testing would be suspect. To increase the chances that your new data will be reliable, it is best, whenever possible, to use existing measures that have already been tested. Regardless, it is always important to assess the degree of measurement reliability for your data set. We use the term measurement reliability to point out that the data only provide evidence for reliability; it is inappropriate to say that a test or measure is 'reliable" or "unreliable." Research methods books, such as Gliner, Morgan, and Leech (2009) provide extended discussions of reliability and validity and the several methods used to provide evidence to support them.

Interrater Reliability

Reliability for one nominal variable assessed twice. There are several methods of computing interrater or interobserver reliability. In Problem 7.1, **Cohen's kappa** is used to assess interobserver agreement when the data are nominal or unordered categories. In this chapter we check the reliability of the *ethnicity* measure by examining the agreement between codes in the school records and ethnicity self-reported by the students.

Reliability for one ordered variable measured twice. In Problem 7.2, you will compute a **correlation coefficient** (as one part of a paired sample *t*) to check the interrater reliability of *visualization and mosaic scores*.[1] As mentioned earlier, *interrater reliability* is needed because behaviors or classification systems involve some degree of subjective judgment (e.g., when there are open-ended questions that must be classified or ratings or categories observers must determine based on observations). If there were more than two raters the appropriate statistic would be the ICC (intraclass correlation coefficient), which could also be used with two raters. ICC is not demonstrated in this chapter.

Internal Consistency Reliability

In Problem 7.4, we will compute the most commonly used type of reliability, **Cronbach's alpha**. This measure indicates the internal consistency of a multiple-item scale. Alpha is typically used when you have several Likert-type items that are summed to make a composite score or **summated scale**. Alpha is based on the mean or average correlation of each item in the scale with every other item. In the social science literature, alpha is widely used, in part because it provides a measure of reliability that can be obtained during the study from just one testing session or one administration of a questionnaire. In Problem 7.4, you will compute alphas for the three revised math attitude scales (*motivation*, *competence*, and *pleasure*) that items 1 to 14 were intended to assess.

---

[1] Several other types of reliability evidence can be illustrated by this correlation. If *visualization 2* was each participant's score from retaking the test a month or so after they initially took it, then the correlation would be a measure of *test–retest reliability*. On the other hand, if *visualization 2* was a score on an alternative, parallel or equivalent version of the *visualization test*, then this would be a measure of *equivalent forms reliability*.

Assumptions for Measures of Reliability

When two or more items or assessments are viewed as measuring the same underlying variable (construct), reliability can be assessed; for example, if on a questionnaire four items were intended to measure stress, one could assess the reliability of the resulting data. Reliability is used to indicate the extent to which scores are consistent with one another and the extent to which the data are free from measurement error. It is assumed that each item or score is composed of a true score measuring the underlying construct, plus error; there is almost always some error in the measurement. Therefore, one assumption is that the measures or items are related systematically to one another in a linear manner because they are believed to be measures of the same construct.

Measurement Validity

In this chapter we discuss one method to provide evidence supporting measurement validity. Measurement validity is concerned with establishing evidence for the use of a measure or instrument in a particular setting with a specific population for a given purpose. We use the term measurement validity; others might use terms such as *test validity*, *score validity*, or just *validity*. We use the modifier *measurement* to point out that the scores only provide evidence for validity; it is inappropriate to say that a test or measure is "valid" or "invalid." Thus, when we address the issue of measurement validity with respect to a particular test, we are addressing the issue of the evidence for the validity of the scores on that test for a particular purpose, and not the validity of the test or instrument in general.

Reliability or consistency is a necessary prerequisite for measurement validity. However, an instrument may produce consistent data (provide evidence for reliability), but the data may not be valid because they are not an accurate measure of the intended concept. In research articles, there is usually more evidence for the reliability of the instrument than for the validity of the instrument because evidence for validity is more difficult to obtain. To establish validity, one ideally needs a "gold standard" or "criterion" related to the particular purpose of the measure. To obtain such a criterion is often not an easy matter or sometimes even possible, so other types of evidence to support the validity of a measure are necessary. Increasingly, validity has been conceptualized as a unitary concept; however, many types of evidence should be gathered to help assess validity for a given set of data.

Several broad types of evidence to support validity are discussed in research methods textbooks. No one type of evidence alone is insufficient. Validation should integrate all the pertinent evidence from as many of the types of evidence as possible. Preferably, validation should include some evidence in addition to content evidence, which is probably the most common and easiest to obtain. **Content evidence** refers to whether the content that makes up the instrument is a reasonable representation of the concept that one is attempting to measure. Does the instrument accurately represent the major aspects of the concept and not include material that is irrelevant to it? There is no statistic that demonstrates evidence based on the content of the measure. Because this type of evidence depends on the logical, but subjective, agreement of a few experts, we consider it necessary but not sufficient evidence. The experts review the measure for clarity and fit with the construct to be measured. The 14 math attitude questions presented in Chapter 1 and used in Problems 7.3 and 7.4 were developed and refined using experts to provide evidence for content validity.

Evidence Based on Internal Structure

An example of internal structure evidence will be demonstrated in this chapter. This is a type of evidence for validity, not a separate indicator of validity. Evidence from several types of analysis, including factor analysis, can be useful here. Most questionnaires have an overall construct to be measured; in this chapter, the example is student self-perceptions regarding mathematics. Many times, the overall construct will have subconstructs; multiple areas that measure aspects of the overall construct. In this example, the subconstructs were the perceptions of math competence, motivation, and pleasure. **Factor analysis,** demonstrated in Problem 7.3, can provide evidence for validity based on internal structure when a construct is complex and several aspects (or factors) of it are measured. If the clustering of items supports the theory-based grouping of items, factorial evidence of validity is provided. Therefore, from this example, a factor analysis would help us identify the degree to which the data supported the subconstructs by indicating if the respondents answered similarly to the questions for competence and also if the respondents answered similarly to the questions for motivation and similarly for pleasure.

- First log on and get **hsbdataB** (you saved it after computing new vaiables in Chapter 5).
- If you haven't completed Chapter 5, use **Alternative hsbdataB**.

Problem 7.1: Cohen's Kappa to Assess Reliability with Nominal Data

When we have two nominal variables with the *same* possible values (usually two raters' observations or scores using the same codes) you can compute Cohen's kappa to check the interrater reliability or agreement between the codes. Kappa has a few assumptions about the underlying nature of the data: (a) Participants are independent of each other, (b) the raters, reporters, or observers providing the data do so independently of one another, and (c) the rating categories are <u>mutually exclusive</u> and exhaustive. Data typically are nominal, but they can be ordinal; however, kappa treats them as unordered. If the data are normally distributed, other statistics are preferable. Imagine that the ethnicity variable was based on school records. Then, a new variable was obtained by asking students to self-report their ethnicity. Ethnicity does involve some subjectivity, especially if only one ethnicity can be used to represent each person when they may identify with more than one ethnicity. The question is, how reliable is the interobserver classification data for ethnicity?

7.1. What is the interrater reliability coefficient for the *ethnicity* codes (based on school records) and *ethnicity reported by the student*? Is there consistency between the two measures of ethnicity?

To compute kappa:
- Click on **Analyze → Descriptive Statistics → Crosstabs...** to get Fig. 7.1.
- Click on **Reset** to clear any previous entries.
- Move *ethnicity (ethnic)* to the **Rows** box and *ethnicity reported by students (ethnic 2)* to the **Columns** box. (See Fig. 7.1.)

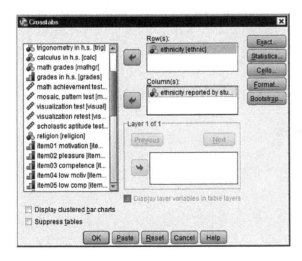

Fig. 7.1 Crosstabs.

- Click on **Statistics** as in the upper right corner of Fig. 7.1 to get Fig. 7.2.
- Click on **Kappa** in the **Statistics** dialog box in Fig. 7.2.

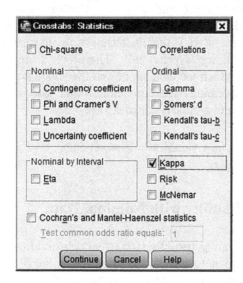

Fig. 7.2. Crosstabs statistics.

- Click on **Continue** to go back to the Crosstabs window. (Fig. 7.1)
- Then click on **Cells** in Fig. 7.1 to get Fig. 7.3 and request the **Observed** under **Counts** and **Total** under **Percentages**. Leave the rest of the window as is.

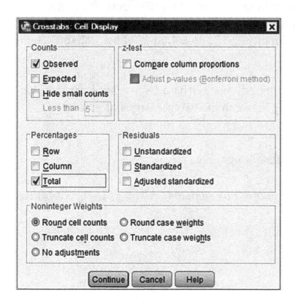

Fig. 7.3. Crosstabs: Cell display.

- Click on **Continue** and then **OK**. Compare your syntax and output to Output 7.1.

Output 7.1: Cohen's Kappa With Nominal Data

```
CROSSTABS
  /TABLES=ethnic  BY ethnic2
  /FORMAT= AVALUE TABLES
  /STATISTICS=KAPPA
  /CELLS= COUNT TOTAL
  /COUNT ROUND CELL.
```

Crosstabs

Case Processing Summary

| | Cases | | | | | |
| | Valid | | Missing | | Total | |
	N	Percent	N	Percent	N	Percent
ethnicity * ethnicity reported by student	71	94.7%	4	5.3%	75	100.0%

ethnicity * ethnicity reported by student Crosstabulation

| | | | ethnicity reported by student | | | | |
			Euro-Amer	Afican-Amer	Latino-Amer	Asian-Amer	Total
ethnicity	Euro-Amer	Count	40	1	0	0	41
		% of Total	56.3%	1.4%	.0%	.0%	57.7%
	African-Amer	Count	2	11	1	0	14
		% of Total	2.8%	15.5%	1.4%	.0%	19.7%
	Latino-Amer	Count	0	1	8	0	9
		% of Total	.0%	1.4%	11.3%	.0%	12.7%
	Asian-Amer	Count	0	1	0	6	7
		% of Total	.0%	1.4%	.0%	8.5%	9.9%
Total		Count	42	14	9	6	71
		% of Total	59.2%	19.7%	12.7%	8.5%	100.0%

One of six disagreements; they are in "squares" off the diagonal.

Agreements between school records and student report.

As a measure of reliability, kappa should be high (usually ≥ .70) not just statistically significant.

Symmetric Measures

		Value	Asymp. Std. Error[a]	Approx. T[b]	Approx. Sig.
Measure of Agreement	Kappa	.858	.054	11.163	.000
N of Valid Cases		71			

a. Not assuming the null hypothesis.

b. Using the asymptotic standard error assuming the null hypothesis.

Interpretation of Output 7.1

The **Case Processing Summary** table shows that 71 students have data on both variables. The **Crosstabulation** table shows that six students' codes disagree with the school records, as indicated by boxes off the diagonal; this table also shows the cases where the school records and the student self-reports are in agreement (they are on the diagonal and circled). There are 65 (40 + 11 + 8 + 6) students with such agreement or consistency.

The **Symmetric Measures** table shows that kappa is .86. This indicates good interobserver reliability because such measures should be high (≥ .70) and positive. Statistical significance is not relevant for reliability measures.

Example of How to Write About Problem 7.1
Method
Kappa was used to investigate the interrater reliability coefficient for the *ethnicity* codes (based on school records) and *ethnicity reported by the student* (kappa = .86). This indicates that there is strong evidence for reliability between the students' reports and the school records.

Problem 7.2: Correlation and Paired *t* to Assess Interrater Reliability

As mentioned earlier, there are several ways to assess interrater reliability when one has normally distributed (scale) data. One way is to use a paired *t* test. We could demonstrate interrater reliability for the *visualization test* scores using correlation. However, the paired computing test in SPSS may be a better way to go because it produces and displays not only the reliability <u>correlation</u> but also the comparison of the <u>means</u> for the two raters. Thus, the correlation will tell us whether the test scores were strongly associated. In addition, the *t* test will tell us whether, on the average, scores of the second rater were the same (versus systematically higher or lower) than the first rater. Thus, two raters may provide reliable data for the same construct (high positive correlation), but one may be an easier rater, such that students seem to perform at a higher level. The paired *t* enables one to determine this, providing more information about the tests. Another advantage of the paired *t* is that several such reliability checks can be made with one SPSS run with a relatively compact and easily interpretable output. Here we only check the reliability of two variables, *visualization* and *mosaic.* Each of these tests had somewhat subjective scoring so were observed by two researchers in order to check interrater reliability.

7.2.   What is the interrater reliability of the *visualization test* and *mosaic pattern test* scores? Do average *visualization* and *mosaic* scores by the second rater differ from average visualization and mosaic scores by the first rater?

To compute reliability and mean differences with the paired *t* test program:
- Select **Analyze → Compare Means → Paired Samples T Test...**
- Click on both *visualization test* and *visualization 2* and move them to the **Paired Variables:** box.
- Next, click on *mosaic* and *mosaic2* and move them to the **Paired Variable** box (see Fig. 7.4).

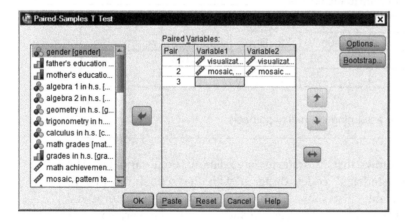

Fig. 7.4. Paired-samples *t* test.

- Click on **OK.**

Compare your output to Output 7.2.

Output 7.2: Test–Retest Reliability for Visualization Scores

```
T-TEST PAIRS=visual mosaic WITH visual2 mosaic2 (PAIRED)
  /CRITERIA=CI(.9500)
  /MISSING=ANALYSIS.
```

Paired Samples Statistics

		Mean	N	Std. Deviation	Std. Error Mean
Pair 1	visualization test	5.2433	75	3.91203	.45172
	visualization 2	5.1067	75	3.77518	.43592
Pair 2	mosaic, pattern test	27.413	75	9.5738	1.1055
	mosaic pattern test 2	27.4800	75	9.34816	1.07943

Notice that the means for *visualization test* and *visualization 2* and also for *mosaic pattern test* and *mosaic pattern test 2* are very similar.

These are interrater reliability coefficients. Focus on the <u>size</u> of the correlations, not the Sig.

Paired Samples Correlations

		N	Correlation	Sig.
Pair 1	visualization test & visualization 2	75	.938	.000
Pair 2	mosaic, pattern test & mosaic pattern test 2	75	.957	.000

Paired Samples Test

		Paired Differences					t	df	Sig. (2-tailed)
		Mean	Std. Deviation	Std. Error Mean	95% Confidence Interval of the Difference				
					Lower	Upper			
Pair 1	visualization test – visualization 2	.13667	1.36331	.15742	-.17700	.45033	.868	74	.388
Pair 2	mosaic, pattern test – mosaic pattern test 2	-.06667	2.77334	.32024	-.70476	.57142	-.208	74	.836

Interpretation of Output 7.2

The first table, **Paired Samples Statistics**, shows the **Means** for the two raters of the students' *visualization test* and of their *mosaic pattern test.* These means will be compared in the third table. In addition, the *N*s, *SD*s, and standard errors are shown.

The second table shows the **Paired Samples Correlations**, which will be used to assess the interrater reliabilities of the *visualization* scores and the *mosaic pattern test* scores. Note that *r*s are .94 and .96, which are very high positive correlations and provide good support for reliability. These correlations indicate that students who were scored high by the first observer on either test were very likely to be scored high by the second observer, and students who were scored low were very likely to be scored low. It indicates that the visualization and mosaic tests are systematically measuring primarily the same thing no matter which observer (rater) is scoring them. However, it cannot indicate *what construct or skill* the raters or observers' scores are measuring. This would be the goal of *validity* measurement.

The **Paired Samples Test** table shows that the means of the two raters of the *visualization test* and the two raters of the *mosaic pattern test* provide very similar average scores; the means are not significantly different (*p* = .39 and .84). It is usually desirable for the means of two assessments of the same variable to be similar, indicating that one rater was not a harder or easier scorer (grader) than the other.

An Example of How to Write about Problem 7.2
Method
The interrater reliability coefficient for both the visualization test data, *r*(73) = .94, and the mosaic pattern test data, *r*(73) = .96, indicated strong evidence for reliability.

Problem 7.3: Exploratory Factor Analysis to Assess Evidence for Validity

In Problem 7.3, we perform a principal axis factor analysis on the math attitude variables. Exploratory factor analysis (EFA) is appropriate when one has the belief that there are latent constructs underlying the variables, usually these constructs are groups of items. In this example, we have beliefs about the constructs underlying the math attitude questions; we believe that there are three constructs: *motivation, competence,* and *pleasure.* Now, we want to see if the items that were written to measure each of these constructs actually do "hang together." That is, we wish to determine empirically whether participants' responses to the motivation questions are more similar to each other than to their responses to the competence items, and so on. Conducting factor analysis can assist us in validating the data. If the data do fit reasonably well into the three constructs that we believe exist, then this gives us internal structure evidence to support the validity of the math attitude measures in this sample. We "allow" the factor analysis to find factors that best fit the data, even if this deviates from our original predictions.

Conditions and Assumptions for Factor Analysis
There are two main conditions necessary for factor analysis. The first is that there need to be relationships among the variables or items. Further, the larger the sample size, especially in relation to the number of variables, the more reliable the resulting factors. Principal axis factor analysis, used in Problem 7.3 should never be used if the number of items (variables) is greater than the number of participants. The methods of extracting factors that are used in this book do not make strong distributional assumptions; normality is important only to the extent that skewness or outliers affect the observed correlations. Because factor analysis is based on correlations, independent sampling is required and the variables should be related to each other (in pairs) in a linear fashion. Each of the variables should be correlated at

a moderate level with <u>some</u> of the other variables. Factor analysis would not be a sensible thing to do if the correlations all hover around zero. Bartlett's test of sphericity addresses this assumption. However, if correlations are all too high, this may cause problems with obtaining a mathematical solution; this is tested with the Determinant. See the Interpretation of Output 7.3 for more testing assumptions.

The question for Problem 7.3 could be stated as

7.3 Can we reduce the 14 math attitude questions to a smaller number of groups of variables or factors? Do the results provide evidence to support the validity of our conceptualization of three factors (*competence*, *motivation*, and *pleasure*) underlying the math attitude questions?

To answer this question, we will conduct a factor analysis using the principal axis factoring method and specify the number of factors to be three (because our conceptualization is that there are three math attitude scales or factors: *motivation*, *competence*, and *pleasure*).

- **Analyze → Dimension Reduction → Factor...** to get Fig. 7.5.
- Next, select the variables *item01* through *item14*. <u>Do not</u> include *item04r* or any of the other reversed items because we are including the unreversed versions of those same items.

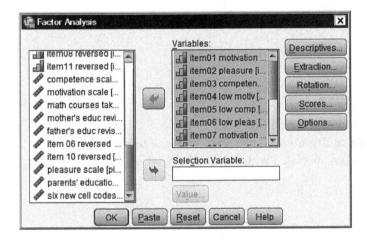

Fig. 7.5. Factor analysis.

- Now click on **Descriptives...** to produce Fig. 7.6.
- Then click on the following: **Coefficients, Determinant,** and **KMO and Bartlett's test of sphericity** (under **Correlation Matrix**).
- Click on **Continue** to return to Fig. 7.5.

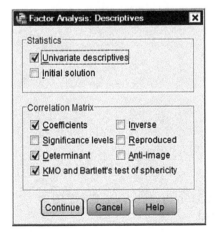

Fig. 7.6. Factor analysis: Descriptives.

- Next, click on **Extraction...** This will give you Fig. 7.7.
- Select **Principal axis factoring** from the **Method** pull-down menu.
- *Unclick* **Unrotated factor solution** (under **Display**).
- Click on **Fixed number of factors** under **Extract,** and type **3** in the box. This setting instructs the computer to extract three factors, which we are hoping will correspond to the three predicted math perception constructs.
- Click on **Continue** to return to Fig. 7.5.

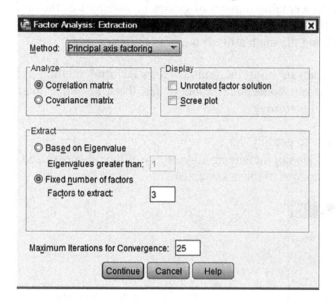

Fig. 7.7. Extraction method to produce principal axis factoring.

- Now click on **Rotation...** in Fig. 7.5, which will give you Fig. 7.8.
- Click on **Varimax**, then make sure **Rotated solution** is also checked. Varimax rotation creates a solution in which the factors are orthogonal (uncorrelated with one another), which can make results easier to interpret
- Click on **Continue** to go back to Fig. 7.5.

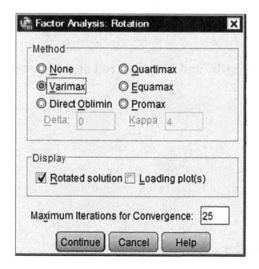

Fig. 7.8. Factor analysis: Rotation.

- Next, click on **Options...**, which will give you Fig. 7.9.
- Click on **Sorted by size**.
- Click on **Suppress absolute values less than** and type **.3** (point 3) in the box (see Fig. 7.9). Suppressing small factor loadings makes the output easier to read.

- Click on **Continue** then **OK**. Compare Output 7.3 with your output and syntax.

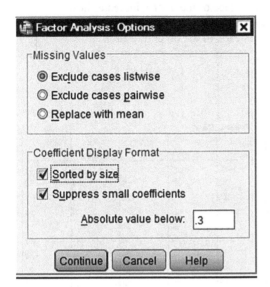

Fig. 7.9. Factor analysis: Options.

Output 7.3: Factor Analysis for Math Attitude Questions

```
FACTOR
  /VARIABLES item01 item02 item03 item04 item05 item06 item07 item08 item09 item10 item11 item12
item13 item14
  /MISSING LISTWISE
  /ANALYSIS item01 item02 item03 item04 item05 item06 item07 item08 item09 item10 item11 item12
item13 item14
  /PRINT UNIVARIATE CORRELATION DET KMO EXTRACTION ROTATION
  /FORMAT SORT BLANK(.3)
  /CRITERIA FACTORS(3) ITERATE(25)
  /EXTRACTION PAF
  /CRITERIA ITERATE(25)
  /ROTATION VARIMAX
  /METHOD=CORRELATION.
```

Factor Analysis

Descriptive Statistics

	Mean	Std. Deviation	Analysis N
item01 motivation	2.99	.918	71
item02 pleasure	3.58	.822	71
item03 competence	2.82	.915	71
item04 low motiv	2.21	.909	71
item05 low comp	1.61	.948	71
item06 low pleas	2.44	.996	71
item07 motivation	2.77	1.072	71
item08 low motiv	1.96	.917	71
item09 competence	3.32	.770	71
item10 low pleas	1.41	.748	71
item11 low comp	1.38	.763	71
item12 motivation	2.99	.837	71
item13 motivation	2.68	.807	71
item14 pleasure	2.86	.723	71

Pairs of items with relatively high (+ or -) correlations (e.g., > .40) will probably have high loadings from the same factor.

This piece of the matrix indicates how each question is associated (correlated) with each of the other questions.

Correlation Matrix[a]

		Item01 motivation	Item02 pleasure	Item03 competence	Item04 low motiv	Item05 low comp	Item06 low pleas	Item07 motivation	Item08 low motiv	Item09 competence	Item10 low pleas
Correlation	Item01 motivation	1.000	.484	.625	-.305	-.745	-.165	.461	-.340	.209	.071
	Item02 pleasure	.484	1.000	.389	-.166	-.547	-.312	.361	-.176	.219	-.389
	Item03 competence	.625	.389	1.000	-.348	-.743	-.209	.423	-.248	.328	.027
	Item04 low motiv	-.305	-.166	-.348	1.000	.363	.323	-.596	.576	-.120	.102
	Item05 low comp	.745	-.547	-.743	.363	1.000	.260	-.538	.276	-.351	.130
	Item06 low pleas	-.165	-.312	-.209	.323	.260	1.000	-.268	.192	-.131	.217
	Item07 motivation	.461	.361	.423	-.596	-.538	-.268	1.000	-.606	.228	-.169
	Item08 low motiv	-.340	-.176	-.248	.576	.276	.192	-.606	1.000	-.243	.067
	Item09 competence	.209	.219	.328	-.120	-.351	-.131	.228	-.243	1.000	-.109
	Item10 low pleas	.071	-.389	.027	.102	.130	.217	-.169	.067	-.109	1.000
	Item11 low comp	.441	-.401	.513	.398	.605	.418	-.331	.370	-.407	.250
	Item12 motivation	.186	.116	.165	-.391	-.187	-.044	.347	-.392	.406	-.059
	Item13 motivation	.187	.028	.170	-.334	-.169	.001	.361	-.308	.286	-.062
	Item14 pleasure	.040	.475	.068	-.063	-.166	-.469	.180	-.117	-.020	-.447

a. Determinant = .001

Should be greater than .0001. If very close to zero, collinearity is too high. If zero, no solution is possible.

Low correlations (e.g., < .20) usually will not have high loadings from the same factor.

KMO and Bartlett's Test ———— Tests of assumptions.

Kaiser-Meyer-Olkin Measure of Sampling Adequacy.		.770
Bartlett's Test of Sphericity	Approx. Chi-Square	433.486
	df	91
	Sig.	.000

Should be greater than .70 indicating sufficient items for each factor.

Should be significant (less than .05), indicating that the correlation matrix is significantly different from an identity matrix, in which correlations between variables are all zero.

Factor Matrix[a]

a. 3 factors extracted. 12 iterations required.

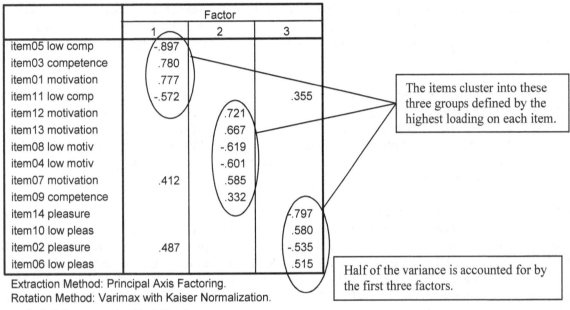

Rotated Factor Matrix[a]

	Factor		
	1	2	3
item05 low comp	-.897		
item03 competence	.780		
item01 motivation	.777		
item11 low comp	-.572		.355
item12 motivation		.721	
item13 motivation		.667	
item08 low motiv		-.619	
item04 low motiv		-.601	
item07 motivation	.412	.585	
item09 competence		.332	
item14 pleasure			-.797
item10 low pleas			.580
item02 pleasure	.487		-.535
item06 low pleas			.515

Extraction Method: Principal Axis Factoring.
Rotation Method: Varimax with Kaiser Normalization.

a. Rotation converged in 5 iterations.

> The items cluster into these three groups defined by the highest loading on each item.

> Half of the variance is accounted for by the first three factors.

Total Variance Explained

Factor	Rotation Sums of Squared Loadings		
	Total	% of Variance	Cumulative %
1	3.017	21.549	21.549
2	2.327	16.621	38.171
3	1.784	12.746	50.917

Extraction Method: Principal Axis Factoring.

> This table shows the percentage of variance explained by each of the three factors and the cumulative percentage, which is 51%.

Factor Transformation Matrix

Factor	1	2	3
1	.747	.552	-.370
2	-.162	.692	.704
3	.645	-.466	.606

Extraction Method: Principal Axis Factoring.
Rotation Method: Varimax with Kaiser Normalization.

> We will ignore this; it was used to convert the initial factor matrix into the rotated factor matrix.

Interpretation of Output 7.3

The SPSS factor analysis program generates a variety of tables depending on which options you have chosen. Our first table includes **Descriptive Statistics** for each variable and the **Analyses N,** which in this case is 71 because several items have one or more participants missing. It is especially important to check the Analysis N when you have a small sample, scattered missing data, or one variable with lots of missing data. In the latter case, it may be wise to run the analysis without that variable. The second table in Output 7.3 is a **correlation matrix** showing how each of the 14 items is associated with each of the other 13. Note that some of the correlations are high (e.g., + or −.60 or greater) and some are low (i.e., near zero). Relatively high correlations indicate that two items are associated and will probably be grouped together by the factor analysis.

Next, several assumptions are tested. The **determinant** (located under the correlation matrix) should be more than .0001 or collinearity is too high. Here, it is .001 so this assumption is met. The **Kaiser-Meyer-Olkin (KMO)** measure should be greater than .70 and is inadequate if less than .50. The KMO test tells us whether or not enough items are predicted by each factor. The **Bartlett** test should be significant (i.e., a significance value of less than .05); this means that the variables are correlated highly enough to provide a reasonable basis for factor analysis.

We rotate the factors so that they are easier to interpret. Rotation makes it so that, as much as possible, different items are explained or predicted by different underlying factors, and each factor explains more than one item. This is a condition called simple structure. Although this is the *goal* of rotation, in reality, this is not always achieved. One thing to look for in the **Rotated Factor Matrix** of factor loadings is the extent to which simple structure is achieved. The Rotated Factor Matrix table, which contains these loadings, is key for understanding the results of the analysis. Note that the analysis has sorted the 14 math attitude questions (*item01* to *item14*) into three somewhat overlapping groups of items, as shown by the circled items. The items are sorted so that the items that have the highest loading (not considering whether the correlation is positive or negative) from factor 1 (four items in this analysis) are listed first, and they are sorted from the one with the highest factor weight or loading (i.e., *item05*, with a loading of −.897) to the one with the lowest loading <u>from that first factor</u> (*item11*). Actually, every item has some loading from every factor, but we requested for loadings less than |.30| (|.30| means the absolute value, or value without considering the sign) to be excluded from the output, so there are blanks where low loadings exist.

Next, the six items that have their highest loading from factor 2 are listed from highest loading (*item12*) to lowest (*item9*). Finally, the four items on which factor 3 loads most highly are listed in order. Loadings resulting from an orthogonal rotation are correlation coefficients between each item and the factor, so they range from −1.0 through 0 to + 1.0. A negative loading just means that the question needs to be interpreted in the opposite direction from the way it is written for that factor (e.g., *item05* "I am a little slow catching on to new topics in math" has a negative loading from the competence factor, which indicates that the people scoring <u>higher</u> on this item are <u>lower</u> in competence). Usually, factor loadings lower than |.30| are considered low, which is why we suppressed loadings less than |.30|. On the other hand, loadings of |.40| or greater are typically considered high. This is just a guideline, however, and one could set the criterion for "high" loadings as low as .30 or as high as .50. Setting the criterion lower than .30 or higher than .50 would be very unusual.

The investigator should examine the content of the items that have high loadings from each factor to see if they fit together conceptually and can be named. Items 5, 3, and 11 were intended to reflect a perception of *competence* at math, so the fact that they all have strong loadings from the same factor provides some support for their being conceptualized as pertaining to the same construct. On the other hand, *item01* was intended to measure *motivation* for doing math, but it is highly related to this same *competence* factor. In retrospect, one can see why this item could also be interpreted as competence. The item reads, "I practice math skills until I can do them well." Unless one felt one <u>could do</u> math problems well, this would not be true. Likewise, *item02*, "I feel happy after solving a hard problem," although intended to measure *pleasure* at doing math (and having its strongest loading there), might also reflect competence at doing math, in that, again, one could not endorse this item unless one had solved hard problems, which one could only do if one were good at math. On the other hand, *item09*, which was originally conceptualized as a competence item, had no really strong loadings so we will not use it as part of the revised motivation scale in Problem 7.4.

Every item has a weight or loading from every factor, but in a "clean" factor analysis almost all of the loadings that are not in the circles that we have drawn on the **Rotated Factor Matrix** will be low (blank or less than |.40|). The fact that both Factors 1 and 3 load highly on *item02,* and the fact that Factors 1 and 2 both load highly on *item07* is <u>common but undesirable,</u> in that one wants only one factor to predict each item. Thus, with modest exceptions, the factor analysis provides internal structure evidence to support the validity of the three math attitude concepts.

The last table we consider is the **Total Variance Explained** table. It shows that the percentage of variance explained by the three factors after rotation is 21.5%, 16.6% and 12.7% with a cumulative total of 50.9% explained by the three factors.

Example of How to Write about Problem 7.3

Method

Principal axis factor analysis with varimax rotation was conducted to assess the underlying structure for the 14 items of the Math Motivation Questionnaire. Three factors were requested, based on the fact that the items were designed to index three constructs: motivation, competence, and pleasure. After rotation, the first factor accounted for 21.5% of the variance, the second factor accounted for 16.6%, and the third factor accounted for 12.7%. Table 7.1 displays the items and factor loadings for the rotated factors, with loadings less than .40 omitted to improve clarity.

The first factor, which seems to index competence, had strong loadings on the first four items. Two of the items indexed low competence and had negative loadings. The second factor, which seemed to index motivation, had high loadings on the next five items in Table 7.1. "I prefer to figure out the problem without help" had its highest loading from the second factor but had a cross-loading over .4 on the competence factor. The third factor, which seemed to index low pleasure from math, loaded highly on the last four items in the table. "I feel happy after solving a hard problem" had its highest loading from the pleasure factor but also had a strong loading from the competence factor. Thus, the result provides some support for validity; namely that there are three concepts (competence, motivation, and pleasure) measured by the 14 items.

Table 7.1
Factor Loadings for the Rotated Factors

Item	Factor Loadings		
	1	2	3
Slow catching on to new topics	−.90		
Solve math problems quickly	.78		
Practice math until do well	.78		
Have difficulties doing math	−.57		
Try to complete math even if takes long		.72	
Explore all possible solutions		.67	
Do not keep at it long if problem challenging		−.62	
Give up easily instead of persisting		−.60	
Prefer to figure out problems without help	.41	.59	
Really enjoy working math problems			−.80
Smile only a little when solving math problem			.58
Feel happy after solving hard problem	.49		−.54
Do not get much pleasure out of math			.52
% of variance	21.55	16.62	12.75

Note. Loadings < .40 are omitted.

Problem 7.4: Cronbach's Alpha to Assess Internal Consistency Reliability

The 14 items used in the factor analysis seem to fit best into three groups that could be labeled, as we hypothesized, competence, motivation, and pleasure. Based on the factor analysis, competence is composed of four items that were rated on Likert scales, from very atypical (1) to very typical (4). Do the scores for these items go together (interrelate) well enough to add them together for future use as a composite or summated variable labeled *revised competence*? Note that this revised scale is somewhat different from the one in Chapter 1 and used later in this book because it does not include item 09 but does include item 01 which was intended to be a motivation item.

7.4a. What is the internal consistency reliability of the math attitude scale data that we have labeled *revised competence*?

Note that you <u>do not use the computed scale score</u>. Instead, use the individual items to create the scale temporarily. Now let's do reliability analysis for the revised competence scale.

- Click on **Analyze → Scale → Reliability Analysis**. You should get a dialog box like Fig. 3.1.
- Now move the variables *item01, item03, item05 reversed, and item11 reversed,* (the competence questions based on the factor analysis) to the **Items** box. Be sure to use items 05 and 11 reversed (<u>not</u> *item05* and *item11*) because a high rating on the original (unreversed) items indicates low motivation. The alpha will be based on the average correlation among each pair of items, so they all need to be scored so that higher scores index the same thing (e.g., higher levels of competence) so you won't be averaging positive and negative correlations.
- Type **Alpha for the Revised Competence Scale** in the **Scale label** box. Be sure the **Model** is **Alpha** (refer to Fig. 7.10).

- Click on **Statistics** in the **Reliability Analysis** dialog box and you will see something similar to Fig. 7.11.

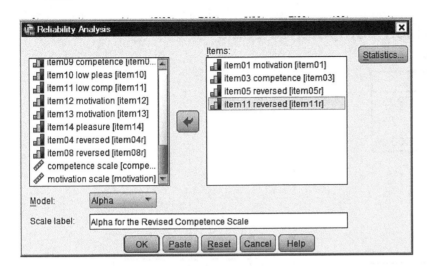

Fig. 7.10. **Reliability analysis.**

- Check the following items: **Item** and **Scale if item deleted** (all under Descriptives for) and **Correlations** (under Inter-Item).

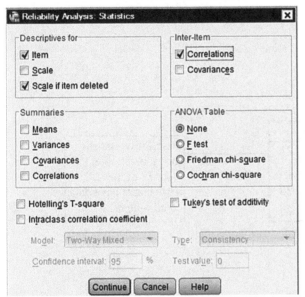

Fig. 7.11. **Reliability analysis: Statistics.**

- Click on **Continue** then **OK**. Compare your syntax and output to Output 7.4a.

Output 7.4a: Cronbach's Alpha for the Revised Competence Scale

```
RELIABILITY
  /VARIABLES=item01 item03 item05r item11r
  /SCALE('Alpha for the Revised Competence Scale') ALL
  /MODEL=ALPHA
  /STATISTICS=DESCRIPTIVE SCALE CORR
  /SUMMARY=TOTAL MEANS CORR.
```

Reliability

Scale: Alpha for the Revised Competence Scale

Case Processing Summary

		N	%
Cases	Valid	73	97.3
	a	2	2.7
	Total	75	100.0

Listwise deletion based on all variables in the procedure.

Reliability Statistics

Cronbach's Alpha	Cronbach's Alpha Based on Standardized Items	N of Items
.856	.853	4

This Cronbach's alpha coefficient is the usual one to report.

Item Statistics

	Mean	Std. Deviation	N
item01 motivation	2.96	.934	73
item03 competence	2.82	.903	73
item05 reversed	3.37	.979	73
item11 reversed	3.63	.755	73

Descriptive statistics for each variable. Note 73 of the participants have data on all 4 items.

Inter-Item Correlation Matrix

	item01 motivation	item03 competence	item05 reversed	item11 reversed
item01 motivation	1.000	.600	.761	.411
item03 competence	.600	1.000	.704	.513
item05 reversed	.761	.704	1.000	.564
item11 reversed	.411	.513	.564	1.000

Note that each of the four items in this revised competence scale correlated positively and relatively highly with the other three items. Duplicate correlations are crossed out.

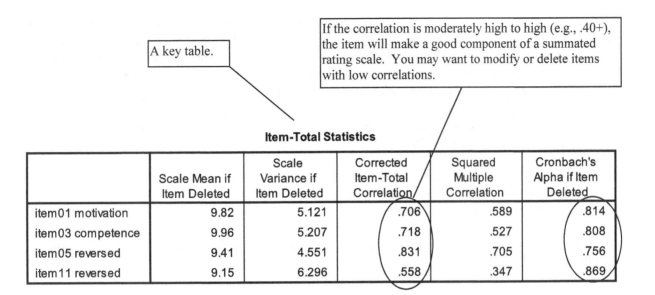

A key table.

If the correlation is moderately high to high (e.g., .40+), the item will make a good component of a summated rating scale. You may want to modify or delete items with low correlations.

Item-Total Statistics

	Scale Mean if Item Deleted	Scale Variance if Item Deleted	Corrected Item-Total Correlation	Squared Multiple Correlation	Cronbach's Alpha if Item Deleted
item01 motivation	9.82	5.121	.706	.589	.814
item03 competence	9.96	5.207	.718	.527	.808
item05 reversed	9.41	4.551	.831	.705	.756
item11 reversed	9.15	6.296	.558	.347	.869

Interpretation of Output 7.4a

The first table shows the number of **Valid** cases, that is, those with no missing data on the selected variables. The second table lists the **Cronbach's Alpha** and an **Alpha Based on Standardized Items**. In general, you will use the unstandardized alpha unless the items in the scale have quite different means and standard deviations. For example, if one were to compute an alpha for *math achievement* ($M = 12.6$, $SD = 6.7$), *grades* ($M = 5.7$, $SD = 1.6$), and *visualization* ($M = 5.2$, $SD = 3.9$), we would use the standardized alpha.

As with other reliability coefficients, alpha should be above .70; however, it is common to see journal articles where one or more scales have somewhat lower alphas (e.g., in the .60–.69 range), especially if there is only a handful of items in the scale. A very high alpha (e.g., greater than .90) probably means that the items are repetitious or that you have more items in the scale than are really necessary for an internally reliable measure of the concept. In this example, the alpha for the *revised competence* scale is .86, which provides strong evidence for internal consistency reliability. How to write about this output is found after Problems 7.4b and 7.4c.

Third is the **Item Statistics** table of descriptive statistics, produced by checking **Item** in Fig. 7.11. The fourth table is a matrix showing the **inter-item correlations** of every item in the scale with every other item. It shows whether all the items are at least moderately correlated.

The **Item Total Statistics** table, which we think is the most important table, is produced if you check **Scale if Item Deleted** under **Descriptives for** in the dialog box displayed in Fig. 7.11. This table provides five pieces of information for each item in the scale. The two we find most useful are the **Corrected Item-Total Correlation** and the **Alpha if Item Deleted**. The former is the correlation of each specific item with the sum/total of the <u>other</u> items in the scale. If this correlation is moderately high or high, say, .40 or above, the item is probably at least moderately correlated with most of the other items and will make a good component of this summated rating scale. Items with lower item-total correlations do not fit into this scale as well, psychometrically. If the item-total correlation is negative or too low (less than .30), it is wise to examine the item for wording problems and conceptual fit. You may want to modify or delete such items. You can tell from the last column what the alpha would be if you deleted that item. Compare this with the alpha for the scale with all items included, which was given earlier in the **Reliability Statistics** table. Deleting a poor item will usually make the alpha go up, but it will usually make only a small difference in the alpha unless the scale has only a few items (e.g., fewer than five) because alpha is based on the number of items as well as their average intercorrelations. Note that we have used item 05 *reversed* and item 11 *reversed* so that all items would be scored with high competence as a high number. If we had instead used item 05 or item 11, the item-total correlation for them probably would have been negative, indicating a problem. Some of the correlations in the **Inter-item Correlation Martix** would also be negative, which would create problems when the alpha was calculated.

Again, we ask if it reasonable to add the item scores based on the factor analysis to form summated measures of the concepts of *motivation* and *pleasure*.

7.4b. What is the internal consistency reliability of the *revised motivation*?

7.4c. What is the internal consistency reliability of the *revised pleasure scale*?

Let's repeat the same steps as before to check the reliability of the following scales and then compare your output to 7.4b and 7.4c.

- For the *revised motivation scale,* use *item04 revised, item07, item08 revised, item12,* and *item13*.
- Remember to change the **Scale Label** to "Alpha for Revised Motivation Scale."
- For the *pleasure scale,* use *item02, item06 reversed, item10 reversed,* and *item14*.
- Change the **Scale Label** to "Alpha for the Revised Pleasure Scale."

Output 7.4b: Cronbach's Alpha for the Math Attitude Revised Motivation Scale

```
RELIABILITY
  /VARIABLES=item04r item07 item08r item12 item13
  /SCALE('Alpha for Revised Motivation Scale') ALL
  /MODEL=ALPHA
  /STATISTICS=DESCRIPTIVE CORR
  /SUMMARY=TOTAL.
```

Reliability

Scale: Alpha for the Revised Motivation Scale

Case Processing Summary

			N	%
Cases	Valid		74	98.7
		a	1	1.3
	Total		75	100.0

Listwise deletion based on all variables in the procedure.

Reliability Statistics

Cronbach's Alpha	Cronbach's Alpha Based on Standardized Items	N of Items
.798	.799	5

Item Statistics

	Mean	Std. Deviation	N
item04 reversed	2.84	.922	74
item07 motivation	2.76	1.057	74
item08 reversed	3.07	.912	74
item12 motivation	2.99	.819	74
item13 motivation	2.68	.796	74

Inter-Item Correlation Matrix

	item04 reversed	item07 motivation	item08 reversed	item12 motivation	item13 motivation
item04 reversed	1.000	.549	.584	.378	.319
item07 motivation	.549	1.000	.586	.344	.361
item08 reversed	.584	.586	1.000	.386	.314
item12 motivation	.378	.344	.386	1.000	.603
item13 motivation	.319	.361	.314	.603	1.000

Item-Total Statistics

	Scale Mean if Item Deleted	Scale Variance if Item Deleted	Corrected Item-Total Correlation	Squared Multiple Correlation	Cronbach's Alpha if Item Deleted
item04 reversed	11.49	7.404	.616	.423	.747
item07 motivation	11.57	6.824	.616	.429	.750
item08 reversed	11.26	7.372	.635	.457	.741
item12 motivation	11.34	8.145	.541	.416	.771
item13 motivation	11.65	8.395	.502	.390	.782

Output 7.4c: Cronbach's Alpha for the Revised Pleasure Scale

```
RELIABILITY
 /VARIABLES=item02 item06r item10r item14
 /SCALE('Alpha for Revised Pleasure Scale')  ALL
 /MODEL=ALPHA
 /STATISTICS=DESCRIPTIVE SCALE CORR
 /SUMMARY=TOTAL MEANS CORR .
```

Reliability

Scale: Alpha for Revised Pleasure Scale

Case Processing Summary

		N	%
Cases	Valid	75	100.0
	Excluded^a	0	.0
	Total	75	100.0

a. Listwise deletion based on all variables in the procedure.

Reliability Statistics

Cronbach's Alpha	Cronbach's Alpha Based on Standardized Items	N of Items
.688	.704	4

Item Statistics

	Mean	Std. Deviation	N
item02 pleasure	3.5200	.90584	75
item06 reversed	2.5733	.97500	75
item10 reversed	3.5867	.73693	75
item14 pleasure	2.8400	.71735	75

Inter-Item Correlation Matrix

	item02 pleasure	item06 reversed	item10 reversed	item14 pleasure
item02 pleasure	1.000	.285	.347	.504
item06 reversed	.285	1.000	.203	.461
item10 reversed	.347	.203	1.000	.436
item14 pleasure	.504	.461	.436	1.000

Item-Total Statistics

	Scale Mean if Item Deleted	Scale Variance if Item Deleted	Corrected Item-Total Correlation	Squared Multiple Correlation	Cronbach's Alpha if Item Deleted
item02 pleasure	9.0000	3.405	.485	.278	.615
item06 reversed	9.9467	3.457	.397	.217	.685
item10 reversed	8.9333	4.090	.407	.211	.662
item14 pleasure	9.6800	3.572	.649	.422	.528

Example of How to Write About Problems 7.4a, 7.4b, and 7.4c

Method

Based on a factor analysis of the 14 mathematics attitude items, three factors were derived. To assess whether the data from the variables in each factor form three reliable scales, Cronbach's alphas were computed. The alpha for the four item competence scale was .86, which indicates that the items would form a scale that has good internal consistency reliability. Similarly, the alpha for the motivation scale (.79) indicated good internal consistency, but the .69 alpha for the pleasure scale indicated minimally adequate reliability.

The Use of Factor Analysis and Alpha to Make Summated Scales

In Problems 7.3 and 7.4, we demonstrated how a researcher might use the results of a factor analysis to indicate how to aggregate (sum or average) the items that have high loadings for each factor and use these composite variables in further research. The implication is that each composite variable is an index of a separate underlying construct such as motivation, competence, or pleasure when studying mathematics.

It is common for a researcher to develop a smaller number of new variables from an initially larger number of items such as the 14 Likert-type ratings we designed to measure attitudes about mathematics motivation, competence, and pleasure. Figure 7.12 shows a flow chart of a method that researchers can use to help decide which items to combine or summate and how to check the internal consistency reliability of the resulting summated scales.

If the competence, motivation and pleasure scales described in Chapter 1 had been used in other studies, we probably would have started by computing three Cronbach's alphas to check the reliability of each of the three initially planned scales: competence, motivation, and pleasure. In fact, we have done that (not shown here), and we found the Item-Total correlation for item 1 of the motivation scale was somewhat low, so we decided to use exploratory factor analyses (EFA) as shown in Problems 7.3 to determine whether the 14 items should be grouped in the way initially predicted. Based on the factor analysis we deleted item 9, and item 1 was moved from the motivation to the competence scale. Because of the changes, the alphas were recomputed for the revised grouping of items in Problem 7.4, as indicated in Fig. 7.12.

Finally, the items in each group or scale should be summed or averaged to form three new composite variables. In our example, each participant's score on the four competence items would be summed to form a new composite competence variable for each person. Likewise, scores on the five motivation items would be summed, and the four low pleasure items would be summed. Now, each participant would have three new variables or measures that could be used in later inferential data analyses *instead of* their scores for the 14 original items.

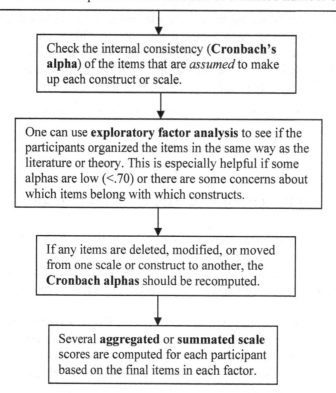

Fig. 7.12. Flow chart diagram of a strategy for making multiple-item summated or composite scales when there are a number of Likert-type items that the researcher thinks can be reduced to a smaller number of conceptually meaningful scales (variables).

Interpretation Questions

7.1.   Write an additional sentence or two describing the disagreements in Output 7.1 that you might include in a detailed research report.

7.2.   Interpret the interrater reliability and paired *t* test results for the *visualization test* and *visualization* scores using Output 7.2. What might be another reason for the pattern of findings obtained, besides those already discussed in this chapter?

7.3.   In Output 7.3 which factor explained the most variance? Why is this important?

7.4.   If one were to delete one of the 14 items based on the factor analysis in Output 7.3, which one would it be? Why?

7.5   If you had to delete one question from the analysis in Output 7.4a, which one would you delete?

7.6.   Interpret the Cronbach alphas in Output 7.4 a, b, and c. What is the internal consistency reliability?

Extra SPSS Problems

Using the College Student data.sav file, do the following problems. Print your outputs after typing your interpretations on them. Please circle the key parts of the output that you discuss.

7.1.   Write a research question that can be answered from the data using a paired sample *t* test. Run the *t* test and provide a full interpretation.

7.2.   Identify four variables that could be combined to make a summated scale. Check the Cronbach's alpha for that scale. Write an interpretation of the resulting output.

Using the Chapter Seven data.sav file, do the following problems. Print your outputs after typing your interpretation on them. Please circle the key parts of the output that you discuss. Use the information in the appropriate "Output Interpretation" and "How to Write" sections.

7.3   Compute Cohen's Kappa to assess reliability using *Rater 1* and *Rater 2*. Interpret your output as in Output 7.1 by writing an explanatory paragraph as you would in the method section of an article or paper.

7.4   Compute interrater reliability by running a paired *t* test for the *essay score 1* with the *essay score 2*. Interpret your output following the guide in the Interpretation of Output 7.2. Write up your results for this analysis as you would in the method section of an article or paper.

7.5   Run an Exploratory Factor Analysis using the extraction method of principal axis factoring as demonstrated in problem 7.3. Run the factor analysis on the 13 items related to stress. In the extraction window (see Fig. 7.7), request "fixed number of factors to extract" as 2. Study your output using the Interpretation of Output 7.3, make a table and write up your results as you would for an article or paper.

7.6   Run Cronbach's alpha for the five happiness scale items from the Chapter Seven data file. Follow the procedures outlined in Problem 7.4. Write up an explanation of your resulting Cronbach's alpha finding as you would in an article or paper.

CHAPTER 8

Cross-Tabulation, Chi-Square, and Nonparametric Measures of Association

In this chapter, you will learn how to make cross-tabulation tables from two variables, both of which have a few levels or values of categorical data. You will learn how to decide if there is a statistically significant relationship between two nominal variables using **chi-square** and you will learn how to assess the strength of this relationship (i.e., the effect size) using **phi** (or **Cramer's V**) and **odds ratios**. You will also compute and interpret **Kendall's tau-b** for ordinal variables and **eta** for one nominal and one normal/scale variable. We will see eta again in Chapter 11 as an effect size measure for ANOVAs. The statistics demonstrated in this chapter are called nonparametric statistics because they are designed to be used with data that are not normally distributed.

- First log on and get **hsbdataB** (you saved it after computing new variables in Chapter 5).
- If you haven't done Chapter 5, use **Alternative hsbdataB**.

Problem 8.1: Chi-Square and Phi (or Cramer's *V*)

The statistics discussed in this first problem are designed to analyze two nominal or dichotomous variables. Remember, nominal variables are variables that have discrete *unordered* levels or categories; each subject is in only one level (you can only be male *or* female). Chi-square (χ^2) or phi/Cramer's *V* are good choices for statistics when analyzing two nominal variables. They are less appropriate if either variable has three or more *ordered* levels because these statistics do not take into account the order and thus sacrifice statistical power if used with ordinal or scale variables.

Chi-square requires a relatively large sample size and/or a relatively even split of the subjects among the levels because the expected counts in 80% of the cells should be greater than five. **Fisher's exact test** should be reported instead of chi-square for small samples if each of the two variables being related has only two levels (2 × 2 cross-tabulation). Chi-square and the Fisher's exact test provide similar information about relationships among variables; however, they only tell us whether the relationship is statistically significant (i.e., not likely to be due to chance). They do not tell the effect size (i.e., the strength of the relationship). Another way to interpret chi-square is as a test of whether there are differences between the groups formed from one variable (gender in this problem) on the incidence or counts of each category of the other variable (see Table 6.1). Chi-square is more difficult to interpret if there are more than two categories or levels in the "columns" variable so chi-square is best for 2 × 2 or 2 × 3 comparisons.

Phi and **Cramer's *V*** provide a test of statistical significance and also provide information about the *strength* of the association between two categorical variables. They can be used as measures of the effect size. If one has a 2 × 2 cross-tabulation, phi is the appropriate statistic. For larger cross-tabs, Cramer's *V* is used. If one variable has only two categories but the other has more than two categories, then Cramer's *V* is equal to phi. The numbers in the cross-tabs description refer to the number of levels in each of the variables. Thus, for *gender* and *religion* in the HSB data set, the cross-tab would be 2 × 3 because *gender* has two levels and *religion* has three levels.

For phi and Cramer's *V*, the strength of association measures belong to the *r* family of effect sizes and are similar to the correlations you will compute in the next chapter (see Table 6.5). Like correlation, a strong phi or Cramer's *V* could be close to 1.00 or –1.00, whereas one close to zero would indicate no relationship. A problem with phi and Cramer's *V* is that, under some conditions, the maximum possible value of these statistics is considerably less than 1.00. This makes them hard to interpret.

Assumptions and Conditions for the Use of Chi-square, Phi, Cramer's *V*, and Odds Ratios

- The data for the variables must be independent. Each subject is assessed only once.
- Data are treated as nominal, even if ordered.
- For chi-square, if the expected frequencies are less than 5, the test of significance is too liberal. At least 80% of the expected frequencies should be 5 or larger. All should be at least 5 if you have a 2 × 2 chi-square; if they are not, use Fisher's exact test.
- Odds ratios and risk ratios are problematic to interpret when the probability of an event is near zero (i.e., < .1) or near 1.

8.1. Do males and females differ on whether they have high or low math grades? If so, how strong is the relationship between gender and high/low math grades?

Let's see if males and females differ in terms of their *math grades*. Remember, both the *gender* and *math grades* variables are dichotomous; they each have two values.

- Click on **Analyze → Descriptive Statistics → Crosstabs...**
- Move *math grades* to the **Rows** box using the arrow key and put *gender* in the **Columns** box. (Where to move these variables is a decision for the researcher. When one of the variables has more levels, it can make interpretation easier if this variable is in the Row(s) box.)

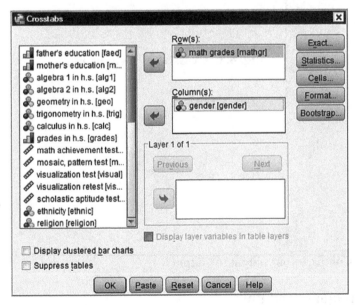

Fig. 8.1. Crosstabs.

- Next, click on **Statistics** in Fig. 8.1.
- Check **Chi-square** and **Phi and Cramer's V**. The window should look like Figure 8.2.

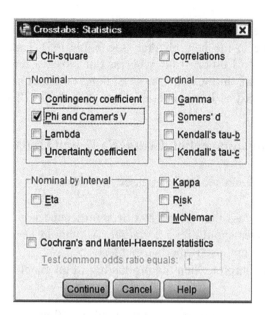

Fig. 8.2. Crosstabs statistics.

- Click on **Continue**.
- Once you return to the **Crosstabs** menu (Fig. 8.1), click on **Cells**.
- Now, ensure that **Observed** is checked; also in Fig. 8.3, check **Expected** under **Counts**, and **Column** under **Percentages**. It helps the interpretation if the total of the percentages of students for each level of the presumed independent variable (gender, in this case) adds up to 100%. Because gender is the column variable, we checked **Column**.

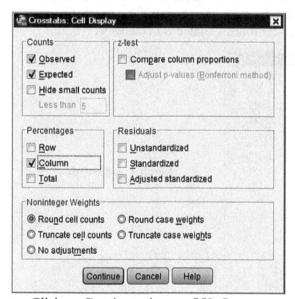

Fig. 8.3. Crosstabs: Cell display.

- Click on **Continue**, then on **OK**. Compare your output to Output 8.1.

Output 8.1: Crosstabs With Chi-Square and Phi

```
CROSSTABS
  /TABLES=mathgr BY gender
  /FORMAT= AVALUE TABLES
  /STATISTICS=CHISQ PHI
  /CELLS= COUNT EXPECTED COLUMN
  /COUNT ROUND CELL .
```

Crosstabs

Case Processing Summary

	Cases					
	Valid		Missing		Total	
	N	Percent	N	Percent	N	Percent
math grades * gender	75	100.0%	0	.0%	75	100.0%

math grades * gender Crosstabulation

			gender		Total
			male	female	
math grades	less A-B	Count	24	20	44
		Expected Count	19.9	24.1	44.0
		% within gender	70.6%	48.8%	58.7%
	most A-B	Count	10	21	31
		Expected Count	14.1	16.9	31.0
		% within gender	29.4%	51.2%	41.3%
Total		Count	34	41	75
		Expected Count	34.0	41.0	75.0
		% within gender	100.0%	100.0%	100.0%

Compare the expected and observed counts.

Chi-Square Tests

	Value	df	Asymp. Sig. (2-sided)	Exact Sig. (2-sided)	Exact Sig. (1-sided)
Pearson Chi-Square	3.645[a]	1	.056		
Continuity Correction[b]	2.801	1	.094		
Likelihood Ratio	3.699	1	.054		
Fisher's Exact Test				.064	.046
Linear-by-Linear Association	3.597	1	.058		
N of Valid Cases	75				

a. 0 cells (.0%) have expected count less than 5. The minimum expected count is 14.05.

b. Computed only for a 2x2 table

This indicates the data met the condition of having an expected count of at least 5 in each cell.

Symmetric Measures

		Value	Approx. Sig.
Nominal by Nominal	Phi	.220	.056
	Cramer's V	.220	.056
N of Valid Cases		75	

Best for 2 × 2 tables

Interpretation of Output 8.1

The case processing summary table indicates that there are no participants with missing data. The **Crosstabulation** table includes the **Counts** and **Expected Counts,** and each cell also has a **% within gender.** For example, there are 24 *males* who had low *math grades* (less than A – B); this is 71% of the 34 male students. On the other hand, 20 of 41 females had low math grades; that is only 49% of the females. It looks like a higher percentage of males had low math grades. The **Chi-Square Tests** tables tell us whether we can be confident that this apparent difference is not due to chance.

Note, in the **Cross-tabulation** table, that the **Expected Count** of the number of *male* students who *had low math grades* is 19.9 and the observed or actual **Count** is 24. Thus, there are 4.1 more *males* who *had low math grades* than would be expected by chance, given the **Total**s shown in the table. There are also the same discrepancies between observed and expected counts in the other three cells of the table. A question answered by the chi-square test is whether these discrepancies between observed and expected counts are bigger than one might expect by chance.

The **Chi-Square Tests** table is used to determine if there is a statistically significant relationship between two dichotomous or nominal variables. It tells you whether the relationship is statistically significant but <u>does not indicate the strength of the relationship,</u> like phi or a correlation does. In Output 8.1, we use the **Pearson Chi-Square** <u>or</u> (for small samples) the **Fisher's Exact Test** to interpret the results of the test. The two-sided (tailed) chi-square test is *not* statistically significant (p = .056), which indicates that we cannot be certain that *males* and *females* are different on whether they have low *math grades*. Note that in this case the **Fisher's Exact Test** leads to different interpretations depending on whether one uses the one-sided column (p = .046, statistically significant) or the two-sided column (p = .064, not significant). You would only use the one-sided (one-tailed) column if you had predicted *before the study* that females would have higher math grades; i.e., your alternative hypothesis was directional. Also note that footnote b states that no cells have expected counts less than 5. That is good because otherwise a condition for using chi-square would be violated. (If so, we could then use the Fisher exact test.) A good guideline is that no more than 20% of the cells should have expected frequencies less than 5. For chi-square with 1 *df* (i.e., a 2 × 2 cross-tabulation as in this case), *none* of the cells should have expected frequencies less than 5. Some statisticians say none less than 10.

The **Symmetric Measures** table provides measures of the strength of the relationships or effect size. If the association between variables is weak, the **Value** of the statistic will be relatively close to zero. If the relationship or effect size is large, the value should be +/– .50 or more. However, remember that the maximum value for phi and Cramer's *V* may be less than 1.00, the theoretical maximum for most measures of association. If both variables have two levels (i.e., 2 × 2 cross-tabs), phi is the appropriate statistic. In Output 8.1, **phi** is .22, and, like the chi-square, it is not statistically significant. Phi, in this case, is a smaller sized effect than is typical in the behavioral sciences (see Table 6.5) according to Cohen (1988).

Example of How to Write about the Results of Problem 8.1

Results

To investigate whether males and females differ on whether they have high or low math grades, a chi-square statistic was conducted. Assumptions were checked and were met. Table 8.1 shows the Pearson chi-square results and indicates that males and females are not significantly different on whether or not they have high math grades (χ^2 = 3.65, *df* = 1, *N* = 75, *p* =.056). Males are not more likely than expected under the null hypothesis to have low or high math grades than are females.

Table 8.1

Chi-square Analysis of Prevalence of High or Low Math Grades among Males and Females

Variable	*n*	Gender		χ^2	*p*
		Males	Females		
Math grades				3.65	.056
Less than A or B	44	24	20		
Most A or B	31	10	21		
Totals	75	34	41		

Problem 8.2: Risk Ratios and Odds Ratios

When you have two dichotomous variables and thus a 2 × 2 contingency table or cross-tabulation, you can compute risk ratios and odds ratios instead of chi-square and phi. These ratios are commonly used to report results in medical, applied health, and prevention science fields. The assumptions for odds ratios are listed under Problem 8.1.

8.2 What is the relative risk of having low *math grades* for students who didn't or did take *algebra 2*? And, what is the odds ratio?

To compute these measures, you again use Fig. 8.1, 8.2, and 8.3, but this time click on **Risk** in the **Statistics** window in Fig. 8.2.

- Click on **Analyze →Descriptive Statistics → Crosstabs...**
- Click on **Reset**.
- Move *algebra 2* to the **Rows** box and *math grades* (not *grades in h.s.*) to the **Columns** box. (See Fig. 8.1.)
- Click on **Statistics** to get Fig. 8.2.
- Check **Risk** in the lower right part of the window. Click <u>off</u> **Chi-Square** and **Phi and Cramer's V** if they are checked.
- Click on **Continue** to get Fig. 8.1 again.

- Click on **Cells** to get Fig. 8.3. (See Problem 8.1)
- Check **Observed** and **Row**. Make sure **Expected** is <u>not</u> checked.
- Click on **Continue**, then **OK**.
- Compare your output and syntax to Output 8.2.

Output 8.2: Crosstabs with Risk Ratios and Odds Ratios

```
CROSSTABS
  /TABLES=alg2  BY mathgr
  /FORMAT= AVALUE TABLES
  /STATISTICS=RISK
  /CELLS= COUNT ROW
  /COUNT ROUND CELL.
```

Crosstabs

Case Processing Summary

	Cases					
	Valid		Missing		Total	
	N	Percent	N	Percent	N	Percent
algebra 2 in h.s. * math grades	75	100.0%	0	.0%	75	100.0%

algebra 2 in h.s. * math grades Crosstabulation

			math grades		
			less A-B	most A-B	Total
algebra 2 in h.s.	not taken	Count	28	12	40
		% within algebra 2 in h.s.	70.0%	30.0%	100.0%
	taken	Count	16	19	35
		% within algebra 2 in h.s.	45.7%	54.3%	100.0%
Total		Count	44	31	75
		% within algebra 2 in h.s.	58.7%	41.3%	100.0%

Risk Estimate

	Value	95% Confidence Interval	
		Lower	Upper
Odds Ratio for algebra 2 in h.s. (not taken / taken)	2.771	1.073	7.154
For cohort math grades = less A-B	1.531	1.012	2.317
For cohort math grades = most A-B	.553	.315	.970
N of Valid Cases	75		

The risk ratio for low math grades (less A – B in the cross-tabulation above) is $70\% / 45.7\% = 1.531$. See interpretation.

The risk ratio for high math grades (most A – B).

Interpretation of Output 8.2

The first two tables are similar to those in Output 8.1, except that the variables are different and there are no **Expected Counts** in the **Crosstabulation** table. Note that all 75 participants had both variables. Forty-four students had low *math grades* (few As and Bs). Of those 44, 28 had not taken *algebra 2* and 16 had taken it. The **Risk Estimate** table shows the odds ratio, the two risk ratios, and confidence intervals for each. The first risk ratio is 1.53, which is computed by dividing 70% by 45.7%. This risk ratio can be interpreted to mean that students who didn't take *algebra 2* are 1.53 times as likely to have low *math grades* as students who did take *algebra 2*. Conversely, of the 31 students with high math grades (mostly As and Bs), 12 didn't take *algebra 2* and 19 did. The second risk ratio is .553, which is 30% divided by 54.3%. This risk ratio is interpreted as students who didn't take *algebra 2* are only about half as likely to have high *math grades* as those who took *algebra 2*. Notice that the **95% Confidence Interval** for each ratio does not include 1.0. That is, the **Lower** and **Upper** bounds are either greater than 1.0 (i.e., 1.012 and 2.317) or less than 1.0 (.315 and .970). This indicates that the risk ratios are statistically significant. If the risk ratio was exactly 1.0, it would indicate that, for example, those who didn't take *algebra 2* are equally likely to have low *math grades* as students who did take *algebra 2*.

The **Odds Ratio** (OR) of 2.77 is a ratio of ratios. In this case, 1.53/.55 = 2.77. This OR means that the odds of getting low *math grades* for those who didn't take *algebra 2* are 2.77 times as high as the odds of getting high *math grades* if one didn't take *algebra 2*.

Odds ratios and risk ratios are common examples of a third group or family of effect size measures, called **risk potency** measures. Remember that we discussed in Chapter 6 the *r* family of effect sizes, including phi, Cramer's *V*, and eta used in this chapter, and the *d* family, which is used to indicate effect size in Chapters 10 and 11. Although odds ratios and risk ratios are common effect size measures when both variables are dichotomous (also called binary), especially in the health-related literature, they are somewhat difficult to interpret clearly. Furthermore, there are no agreed-upon standards for what represents a large ratio because the ratio may approach infinity if the outcome is very rare or very common, even when the association is near random.

How to Write about Output 8.2
Results
Because whether or not students took algebra 2 and whether their math grades were high or low were both binary variables and neither alternative was rare, an odds ratio was computed. The OR was 2.77, indicating that the odds of students getting low math grades if they didn't take algebra 2 were 2.77 times as high as the odds for those who did take algebra 2. The 95% confidence interval was 1.07 to 7.15.

Problem 8.3: Other Nonparametric Associational Statistics

In addition to phi and Cramer's V, there are several other nonparametric measures of association that we could have chosen in Fig. 8.2. They attempt, in different ways, to measure the strength of the association between two variables. If both variables are nominal and you have a 2 × 2 cross-tabulation, like the one in Output 8.1, phi is the appropriate statistic to use from the symmetric measures table. For larger cross-tabulations (like a 3 × 3) with nominal data, Cramer's V is the appropriate statistic. Note that with a 2 × 3 or a 3 × 2 cross-tabulation, phi and Cramer's V are the same. If the variables are ordered (i.e., ordinal), you have several other choices. We will use Kendall's tau-b in this problem. The primary assumption of Kendall's tau-b is that data are at least ordinal.

8.3. What is the relationship or association between *father's education* and *mother's education*?

- **Analyze → Descriptive Statistics → Crosstabs...**
- Click on **Reset** to clear the previous entries.
- Put *mother's education revised* in the **Rows** box and *father's education revised* in the **Columns** box.
- Click on **Cells** and ask that the **Observed** and **Expected** cell counts and **Total** percentages be printed in the table. Click on **Continue** and then **Statistics.**
- Request the following **Statistics: Kendall's tau-b** coefficient under **Ordinal**, and **Phi and Cramer's *V*** under **Nominal** (for comparison purposes). Do not check **Chi-square.**
- Click on **Continue** then **OK.** Compare your syntax and output to Output 8.3.

Output 8.3: Crosstabs and Nonparametric Associational Statistics

```
CROSSTABS
  /TABLES=maedRevis  BY faedRevis
  /FORMAT= AVALUE TABLES
  /STATISTICS=PHI BTAU
  /CELLS= COUNT EXPECTED TOTAL
  /COUNT ROUND CELL.
```

Crosstabs

Case Processing Summary

	Cases					
	Valid		Missing		Total	
	N	Percent	N	Percent	N	Percent
mother's educ revised * father's educ revised	73	97.3%	2	2.7%	75	100.0%

mother's educ revised * father's educ revised Crosstabulation

			father's educ revised			
			HS grad or less	Some college	BS or more	Total
mother's educ revised	HS grad or less	Count	33	9	4	46
		Expected Count	23.9	10.1	12.0	46.0
		% of Total	45.2%	12.3%	5.5%	63.0%
	Some college	Count	5	7	7	19
		Expected Count	9.9	4.2	4.9	19.0
		% of Total	6.8%	9.6%	9.6%	26.0%
	BS or more	Count	0	0	8	8
		Expected Count	4.2	1.8	2.1	8.0
		% of Total	.0%	.0%	11.0%	11.0%
Total		Count	38	16	19	73
		Expected Count	38.0	16.0	19.0	73.0
		% of Total	52.1%	21.9%	26.0%	100.0%

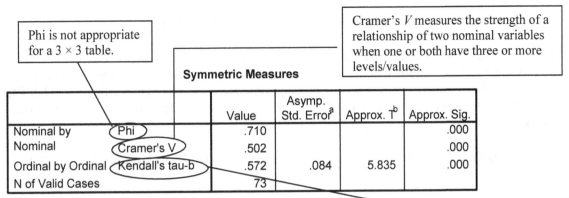

Phi is not appropriate for a 3 × 3 table.

Cramer's *V* measures the strength of a relationship of two nominal variables when one or both have three or more levels/values.

Symmetric Measures

		Value	Asymp. Std. Error[a]	Approx. T[b]	Approx. Sig.
Nominal by Nominal	Phi	.710			.000
	Cramer's V	.502			.000
Ordinal by Ordinal	Kendall's tau-b	.572	.084	5.835	.000
N of Valid Cases		73			

a. Not assuming the null hypothesis.

b. Using the asymptotic standard error assuming the null hypothesis.

Kendall's tau-b measures the strength of the association if both variables are ordinal.

Interpretation of Output 8.3

There are several nonparametric measures of association that we could have chosen from Fig. 8.2. All of them except chi-square attempt, in different ways, to measure the *strength* of the association between two variables roughly on the −1 to +1 scale used by the Pearson correlation (see Chapter 9). However, several of them, including phi and Cramer's *V*, have maximum values considerably less than 1 under some conditions.

For tables <u>with nominal data</u> (like a 3 × 3 cross-tabulation of *religion* and *ethnicity*), **Cramer's *V*** would be the appropriate statistic. In Problem 8.3, we requested **Kendall's tau-b** because both *mother's education* and *father's education* are ordered variables and ordinal data. Cramer's *V* (and phi) treat the cross-tabulated variables as if they were nominal even if they are ordered, so they would not be good choices for this problem. We requested them so you could compare them to Kendall's tau-b.

If the association between variables is weak, the value of the statistic will be close to zero and the significance level (**Sig.**) will be greater than .05, the usual cutoff to say that an association is statistically significant. However, if the association is statistically significant, the *p* will be small (< .05). In this case, *p* is < .001 for Kendall's tau-b, which is clearly significant, and the effect size (tau-b = .572) is large; the interpretation of tau-b is similar to that of *r* (see Table 6.5).

Example of How to Write about Problem 8.3
Results

To investigate the relationship between father's education and mother's education, Kendall's tau-b was conducted. The analysis indicated a statistically significant positive association between father's education and mother's education, tau (71) = .572, *p* < .001. This means that more highly educated fathers were married to more highly educated mothers and less educated fathers were married to less educated mothers. This tau is considered to be a large effect size (Cohen, 1988).

Problem 8.4: Cross-Tabulation and Eta

There is an important associational statistic, eta, that is used when one variable is nominal and the other is approximately normal or scale. We will use this statistic to describe the association between *gender* and *math courses taken* (an approximately normal variable with six levels). **Eta squared** will be an important statistic in later chapters when we interpret the *effect size* of various ANOVAs.

8.4. What is the association between *gender* and number of *math courses taken*? How strong is it?

Follow these steps:
- Click on **Analyze → Descriptive Statistics → Crosstabs...**
- Click on **Reset** to clear the previous entries.
- Put *math courses taken* in the **Rows** box using the arrow key and put *gender* in the **Columns** box (similar to Fig. 8.1).
- Next, click on **Statistics** and select **Eta**.
- Click on **Continue**.
- Now, click on **Cells** and select **Expected** and **Observed**.
- Click on **Continue**.
- Click on **OK**. Compare your syntax and output to Output 8.4.

Output for Problem 8.4: Eta for Gender and Math Courses Taken

```
CROSSTABS
  /TABLES=mathcrs  BY gender
  /FORMAT= AVALUE TABLES
  /STATISTICS=ETA
  /CELLS= COUNT EXPECTED
  /COUNT ROUND CELL.
```

Crosstabs

Case Processing Summary

	Cases					
	Valid		Missing		Total	
	N	Percent	N	Percent	N	Percent
math courses taken * gender	75	100.0%	0	.0%	75	100.0%

math courses taken * gender Crosstabulation

			gender		Total
			male	female	
math courses taken	0	Count	4	12	16
		Expected Count	7.3	8.7	16.0
	1	Count	3	13	16
		Expected Count	7.3	8.7	16.0
	2	Count	9	6	15
		Expected Count	6.8	8.2	15.0
	3	Count	6	2	8
		Expected Count	3.6	4.4	8.0
	4	Count	7	5	12
		Expected Count	5.4	6.6	12.0
	5	Count	5	3	8
		Expected Count	3.6	4.4	8.0
Total		Count	34	41	75
		Expected Count	34.0	41.0	75.0

Directional Measures

			Value
Nominal by Interval	Eta	Math courses taken Dependent	.328
		gender Dependent	.419

This is the appropriate eta for this problem. It is always a positive number in the SPSS program.

Interpretation of Output 8.4

The second table shows the actual **Counts** and the **Expected Counts** of the number of persons in each cell. If there are positive discrepancies between the actual and expected counts in the upper left (male) columns and negative discrepancies in the lower left columns or vice versa, that would indicate that there is an association between the two variables. Because of the way the SPSS program computes eta, it ranges from zero to about +1.0. High values of eta indicate a strong association. In this case, the appropriate eta is .328 because *math courses taken* is the dependent variable. It is a medium to large effect size (see Table 6.5). With 75 subjects, an eta of .33 probably would be statistically significant, but this program does not test it. Eta squared would be .11, indicating that the two variables share 11% common variance. We will see eta squared when interpreting the size of the "effect" in analysis of variance.

Example of How to Write about Problem 8.4

Results

Eta was used to investigate the strength of the association between gender and number of math courses taken (eta = .33). This is a medium to large effect size (Cohen, 1988). Males were more likely to take several or all the math courses than females.

Interpretation Questions

8.1.   In Output 8.1: (a) What do the terms "count" and "expected count" mean? (b) What does the difference between them tell you?

8.2.   In Output 8.1: (a) Is the (Pearson) chi-square statistically significant? Explain what it means. (b) Are the expected values in at least 80% of the cells $\geq$ 5? How do you know? Why is this important?

8.3   In Output 8.2: (a) How is the risk ratio calculated? What does it tell you? (b) How is the odds ratio calculated and what does it tell you? (c) How could information about the odds ratio be useful to people wanting to know the practical importance of research results? (d) What are some limitations of the odds ratio as an effect size measure?

8.4.   Because *father's* and *mother's education revised* are at least ordinal data, which of the statistics used in Problem 8.3 is the most appropriate to measure the strength of the relationship: phi, Cramer's *V*, or Kendall's tau-b? Interpret the results. Why are tau-b and Cramer's *V* different?

8.5.   In Output 8.4: (a) How do you know which is the appropriate value of eta? (b) Do you think it is high or low? Why? (c) How would you describe the results?

Extra SPSS Problems

Using the College Student data file, do the following problems. Print your outputs after typing your interpretations on them. Please circle the key parts of the output that you discuss.

8.1.   Run crosstabs and interpret the results of chi-square and phi (or Cramer's *V*), as discussed in Chapter 6 and in the interpretation of Output 8.1, for: (a) gender and marital status and (b) age group and marital status.

8.2.   Select two other appropriate variables; run and interpret the output as we did in Output 8.1.

8.3.   Is there an association between having children or not and watching TV sitcoms?

8.4.   Is there a difference between students who have children and those who do not in regard to their age group?

8.5   Compute an appropriate statistic and effect size measure for the relationship between gender and evaluation of social life.

CHAPTER 9

Correlation and Regression

In this chapter, you will learn how to compute several associational statistics, after you learn how to make **scatterplots** and how to interpret them. An assumption of the **Pearson product moment correlation** is that the variables are related in a linear (straight line) way so we will examine scatterplots to see if that assumption is reasonable. Second, the **Pearson correlation** and the **Spearman rho** will be computed. The Pearson correlation is used when you have two variables that are normal/scale, and the Spearman is used when one or both of the variables are ordinal. Third, you will compute a **correlation matrix** indicating the associations among all the pairs of three or more variables. Fourth, you will compute simple or **bivariate regression**, which is used when one wants to predict scores on a normal/scale dependent (outcome) variable from one normal or scale independent (predictor) variable. Last, we will provide an introduction to a complex associational statistic, **multiple regression**, which is used to predict a scale/normal dependent variable from two or more independent variables.

As stated in Chapter 7, correlations can vary from −1.00 (a perfect negative correlation or association) through .00 (no correlation) to +1.0 (a perfect positive correlation). Note that +1 and −1 are equally high or strong, but they lead to different interpretations. A high **positive correlation** between aptitude and grades would mean that students with higher aptitude tended to have higher grades, those with lower anxiety had lower grades, and those in between had grades that were neither especially high nor especially low. A high **negative correlation** would mean that students with high aptitude tended to have low grades; also, high grades would be associated with low aptitude. With a **zero correlation** there are no consistent associations. A student with high aptitude might have low, medium, or high grades.

Assumptions and Conditions for the Pearson Correlation (*r*) and Bivariate Regression
1. The two variables have a linear relationship. We will show how to check this assumption with a scatterplot in Problem 9.1. (Pearson *r* will not detect a curvilinear relationship unless you transform the variables, which is beyond the scope of this book.)
2. Scores on one variable are normally distributed for each value of the other variable and vice versa. If degrees of freedom are greater than 25, failure to meet this assumption has little consequence. Statistics designed for normally distributed data are called **parametric statistics.** Remember that we checked variables for skewness and normality in Chapter 4.
3. Outliers (i.e., extreme scores) can have a big effect on the correlation.

Assumptions and Conditions for Spearman Rho (*r*$_s$)
1. Data on both variables are at least ordinal. Statistics designed for ordinal data and which do not assume normal distribution of data are called **nonparametric statistics.**
2. Scores on one variable are monotonically related to the other variable. This means that as the values of one variable increase, the other should also increase but not necessarily in a linear (straight line) fashion. The curve can flatten but cannot go both up and down as in a **U** or **J**.

Rho is computed by ranking the data for each variable and then computing a Pearson product moment correlation. The SPSS program will do this for you automatically when you request a Spearman correlation.

- Retrieve **hsbdataB.sav.**

Problem 9.1: Scatterplots to Check the Assumption of Linearity

A **scatterplot** is a plot or graph of two variables that shows how the score for an individual on one variable associates with his or her score on the other variable. If the correlation is *high positive,* the plotted points will be close to a straight line (the **linear regression line**) from the lower left corner of the plot to the upper right. The linear regression line will slope downward from the upper left to the lower right if the correlation is *high negative.* For correlations *near zero*, the regression line will be flat with many points far from the line, and the points form a pattern more like a circle or random blob than a line or oval.

Doing a scatterplot with this program is somewhat cumbersome, as you will see, but it provides a visual picture of the correlation. Each dot or circle on the plot represents a particular individual's score on the two variables, with one variable being represented on the X axis and the other on the Y axis. The plot also allows you to see if there are bivariate outliers (circles/dots that are far from the regression line, indicating that the way that person's score on one variable relates to his/her score on the other is different from the way the two variables are related for most of the other participants), and it may show that a better fitting line would be a curve rather than a straight line. In this case the assumption of a linear relationship is violated and a Pearson correlation would not be the best choice. The Spearman or Kendall's tau correlations would be better.

9.1.   What are the scatterplots and linear regression line for (a) *math achievement* and *grades in h.s.* and for (b) *math achievement* and *mosaic pattern score*?

To develop a scatterplot of *math achievement* and *grades*, follow these commands:

- **Graphs → Legacy Dialogs → Scatter/Dot**. This will give you Fig. 9.1.
- Click on **Simple Scatter.**

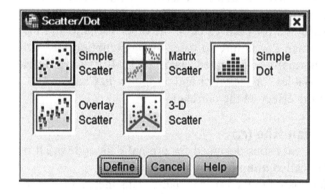

Fig. 9.1. Scatterplot.

- Click on **Define**, which will bring you to Fig. 9.2.
- Now, move *math achievement* to the **Y Axis** and *grades in h.s.* to the **X Axis**. <u>Note: the presumed outcome or dependent variable goes on the Y axis</u>. However, for the correlation itself there is no distinction between the independent and dependent variable.

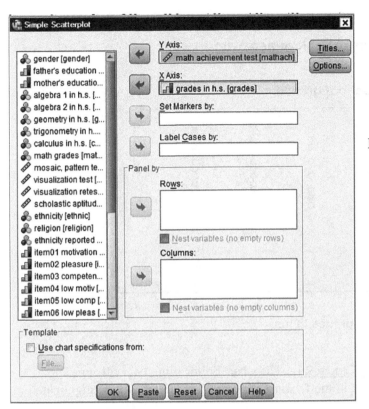

Fig. 9.2. Simple scatterplot.

- Next, click on **Titles** (in Fig. 9.2). Type **Correlation of math achievement with high school grades** (see Fig. 9.3). Note we put the title on two lines.
- Click on **Continue**, then on **OK.** You will get Output 9.1a, the scatterplot. You will not print this now because we want to add the regression line first in order to get a better sense of the relationship and how much scatter or deviation there is.

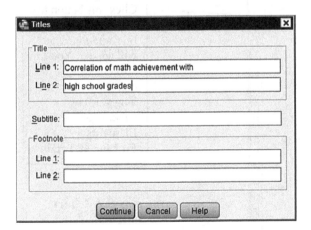

Fig. 9.3. Titles.

Output 9.1a: Scatterplot Without Regression Line

```
GRAPH
  /SCATTERPLOT(BIVAR)=grades WITH mathach
  /MISSING=LISTWISE
  /TITLE= 'Correlation of math achievement with' 'high school grades'.
```

Graph

Correlation of math achievement with

high school grades

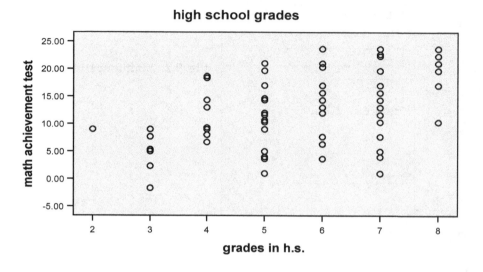

- <u>Double click on the scatterplot in Output 9.1a</u>. The Chart Editor (Fig. 9.4) will appear.
- Click on a circle in the scatterplot in the **Chart Editor;** <u>all the circles will be highlighted in yellow.</u>
- Click on the button circled in Fig. 9.4 to create a **Fit Line**. The **Properties** window (see Fig. 9.5) will appear as well as a blue fit line in the Chart Editor.

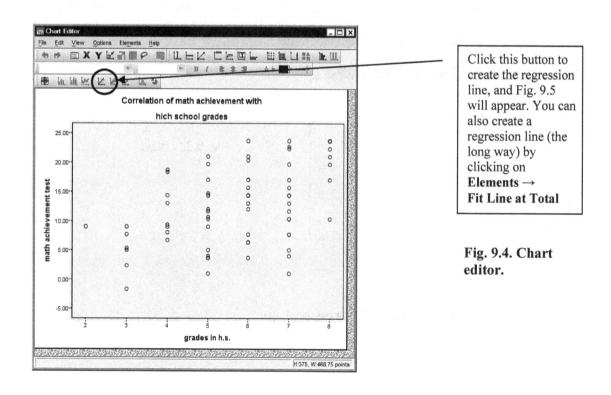

Click this button to create the regression line, and Fig. 9.5 will appear. You can also create a regression line (the long way) by clicking on **Elements → Fit Line at Total**

Fig. 9.4. Chart editor.

- Be sure that **Linear** is checked (see Fig. 9.5).
- Click on **Close** in the **Properties** window and click **File → Close** to close the **Chart Editor** in order to return to the Output window (Output 9.1b).

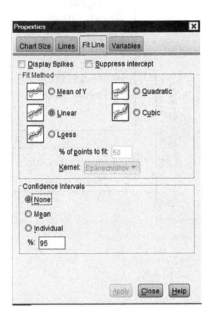

Fig. 9.5. Properties.

- Now <u>add a new scatterplot</u> to Output 9.1b by doing the same steps that you used for Problem 9.1a <u>for a new pair of variables</u>: *math achievement* (**Y-Axis**) with *mosaic* (**X-Axis**).
- Don't forget to click on **Titles** and change the second line before you run the scatterplot so that the title reads: Correlation of math achievement with (1st line) mosaic pattern score (2nd line).
- Then add the linear regression line as you did earlier using Figs. 9.4 and 9.5.
- Now, <u>double click once more on the chart you just created</u>. We want to add a <u>quadratic regression line</u>. The Chart Editor (similar to Fig. 9.4) should appear.
- Again, click on <u>the button circled in Fig. 9.4</u> to bring up the **Properties** window.
- In the **Properties** window (Fig. 9.5), <u>click on **Quadratic**</u> instead of **Linear.**
- Click **Apply** and then **Close**. You will see that a curved line was <u>added</u> to the second scatterplot in Output 9.1b below.

Do your syntax and scatterplots look like the ones in Output 9.1b?

Output 9.1b: Scatterplots With Regression Lines

```
GRAPH
  /SCATTERPLOT(BIVAR)=grades WITH mathach
  /MISSING=LISTWISE
  /TITLE= 'Correlation of math achievement with' 'high school grades'.
```

Graph

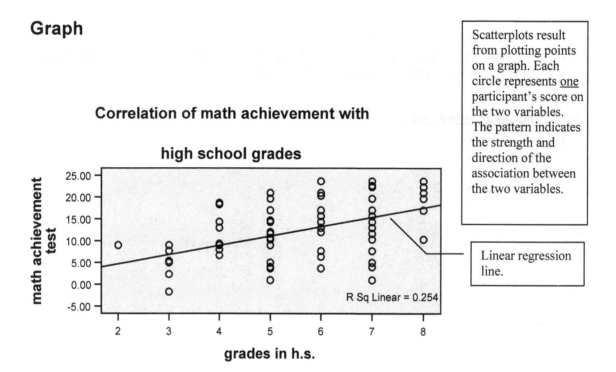

Scatterplots result from plotting points on a graph. Each circle represents <u>one</u> participant's score on the two variables. The pattern indicates the strength and direction of the association between the two variables.

Linear regression line.

```
GRAPH
  /SCATTERPLOT(BIVAR)=mosaic WITH mathach
  /MISSING=LISTWISE
  /TITLE= 'Correlation of math achievement with' 'mosaic pattern score'.
```

Graph

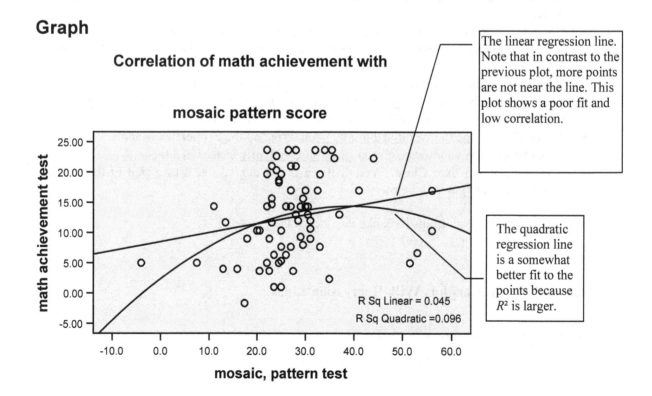

The linear regression line. Note that in contrast to the previous plot, more points are not near the line. This plot shows a poor fit and low correlation.

The quadratic regression line is a somewhat better fit to the points because R^2 is larger.

Interpretation of Output 9.1b

Both scatterplots shown in Output 9.1b show the best fit of a straight or linear regression line (i.e., it minimizes the squared differences between the points and the line). Note that for the first scatterplot (grades in h.s.), the points fit the line pretty well; $r^2 = .25$ and thus r is .50. The second scatterplot shows that mosaic and math achievement are only weakly correlated; the points do not fit the line very well, $r^2 = .05$, and r is .21. Note that in the second scatterplot we asked the program to fit a quadratic (one bend) curve as well as a linear line. It seems to fit the points better; $r^2 = .10$. If so, the linear assumption would be violated and a Pearson correlation may not be the most appropriate statistic.

Problem 9.2: Bivariate Pearson and Spearman Correlations

The **Pearson product moment correlation** is a bivariate parametric statistic used when both variables are approximately normally distributed (i.e., scale data). When you have ordinal data or when assumptions are markedly violated, one should use a nonparametric equivalent of the Pearson correlation coefficient. One such nonparametric, ordinal statistic is the **Spearman rho** (another is Kendall's tau, which we computed in the last chapter). Here you will compute both parametric and nonparametric correlations and then compare them. The variables of interest for Problem 9.2 are *mother's education* and *math achievement*. We found in Chapter 4 that *mother's education* was somewhat skewed, but that *math achievement* was normally distributed.

9.2.   What is the association between *mother's education* and *math achievement*?

To compute Pearson and Spearman correlations follow these commands:

- **Analyze → Correlate → Bivariate...**
- Move *math achievement* and *mother's education* to the **Variables** box.
- Next, under **Correlation Coefficients**, ensure that the **Spearman** and **Pearson** boxes are checked.
- Make sure that the **Two-tailed** (under **Test of Significance**) and **Flag significant correlations** are checked (see Fig. 9.6). Unless one has a clear directional hypothesis, two-tailed tests are used. Flagging the significant correlations (with an asterisk) is optional but helps you quickly identify the statistically significant correlations.

Fig. 9.6. Bivariate correlations.

- Now click on **Options** to get Fig. 9.7.
- Click on **Means and standard deviations** and click on **Exclude cases listwise.** When requesting only one correlation, listwise and pairwise exclusion (of participants with missing data on one or both of these variables) are the same, but, as described later, which one you select may make a difference in a correlation matrix of more than one pair of variables.

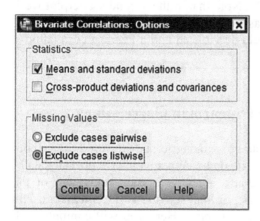

Fig. 9.7. Bivariate correlations: Options.

- Click on **Continue** then on **OK**. Compare Output 9.2 to your output and syntax.

Output 9.2: Pearson and Spearman Correlations

```
CORRELATIONS
  /VARIABLES=mathach maed
  /PRINT=TWOTAIL NOSIG
  /STATISTICS DESCRIPTIVES
  /MISSING=LISTWISE.
```

Correlations

Descriptive Statistics

	Mean	Std. Deviation	N
math achievement test	12.5645	6.67031	75
mother's education	4.11	2.240	75

> There are 75 persons with data on both of these variables.

Correlations[a]

		math achievement test	mother's education
math achievement test	Pearson Correlation	1	.338**
	Sig. (2-tailed)		.003
mother's education	Pearson Correlation	.338**	1
	Sig. (2-tailed)	.003	

> The Pearson correlation: $r = .34$; $p = .003$.

**. Correlation is significant at the 0.01 level (2-tailed).

a. Listwise N=75

> These correlation tables have all the values twice. Ignore the numbers below (or above) the diagonal line; they are duplicates.

Nonparametric Correlations

```
NONPAR CORR
  /VARIABLES=mathach maed
  /PRINT=SPEARMAN TWOTAIL NOSIG
  /MISSING=LISTWISE.
```

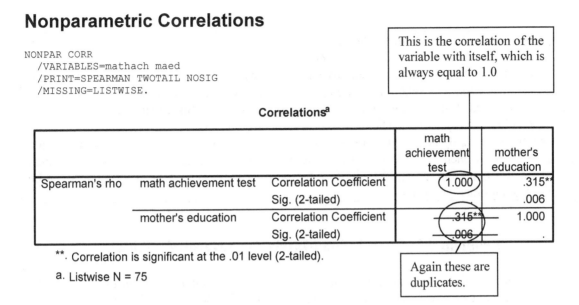

Correlations[a]

			math achievement test	mother's education
Spearman's rho	math achievement test	Correlation Coefficient	1.000	.315**
		Sig. (2-tailed)	.	.006
	mother's education	Correlation Coefficient	.315**	1.000
		Sig. (2-tailed)	.006	.

This is the correlation of the variable with itself, which is always equal to 1.0

Again these are duplicates.

**. Correlation is significant at the .01 level (2-tailed).

a. Listwise N = 75

Interpretation of Output 9.2

The first table provides **descriptive statistics** (mean, standard deviation, and *N*) for the variables to be correlated, in this case *math achievement* and *mother's education*. The two tables labeled **Correlations** are our primary focus. The information is displayed in matrix form, which unfortunately means that every number is presented twice. We have provided a call out box to help you.

The **Pearson Correlation** coefficient is .34; the significance level **(Sig.)** or *p* is .003 and the number of participants with both variables (*math achievement* and *mother's education*) is 75. In a report, this would usually be written as r (73) = .34, p = .003. Note that the degrees of freedom (*N* - 2 for correlations) is put in parentheses after the statistic (*r* for **Pearson** correlation), which is usually rounded to two decimal places and is italicized, as are all statistical symbols using English letters. The statistical significance, or *p* value, follows and is stated as p = .003.

The correlation value for **Spearman's rho** (.32) is slightly different from *r*, but usually, as in this case, it has a similar significance level (p = .006). The nonparametric Spearman correlation is based on ranking the scores (1st, 2nd, etc.) rather than using the actual raw scores. It should be used when the scores are ordinal data or when assumptions of the Pearson correlation (such as normality of the scores) are markedly violated. Note, you should *not* report both the Pearson and Spearman correlations; they provide similar information. Pick the one whose assumptions best fit the data. In this case, because *mother's education* was markedly skewed, Spearman would be the more appropriate choice. Problem 9.1 showed you a way to check the Pearson assumption that there is a linear relationship between the variables (i.e., that it is reasonable to use a straight line to describe the relationship).

It is usually best to choose two-tailed tests, as we did in Fig. 9.6. We also chose to flag (put asterisks beside) the correlation coefficients that were statistically significant so that they could be identified quickly. The output also prints the exact significance level (*p*), which is more specific than just knowing it is statistically significant by seeing the asterisk. It is best in a thesis or paper table to report the exact *p*, but if space is tight you can use asterisks with a footnote, as did Output 9.2.

Example of How to Write about Problem 9.2
Results
    To investigate if there was a statistically significant association between mother's education and math achievement, a correlation was computed. Mother's education was skewed (skewness = 1.13), which violated the assumption of normality. Thus, the Spearman rho statistic was calculated, $r(73) = .32$, $p = .006$. The direction of the correlation was positive, which means that students who have highly educated mothers tend to have higher math achievement test scores and vice versa. Using Cohen's (1988) guidelines, the effect size is medium for studies in this area. The r^2 indicates that approximately 10% of the variance in math achievement test scores can be predicted from mother's education.

Problem 9.3: Correlation Matrix for Several Variables

If you have more than two ordinal or normally distributed variables that you want to correlate, the program will produce a matrix showing the correlation of each selected variable with each of the others. You could print a matrix scatterplot to check the linear relationship for each pair of variables (see Fig. 9.1). We did such a scatterplot (not shown) and found that the assumption of linearity was not markedly violated for this problem.

9.3.   What are the associations among the four variables *visualization, scholastic aptitude test—math, grades in h.s.,* and *math achievement?*

Now, compute **Pearson** correlations among all pairs of the following scale/normal variables: *visualization, scholastic aptitude test—math, grades in h.s.,* and *math achievement.* Move all four into the **Variables** box (see Fig. 9.6). Follow the procedures for Problem 9.2 outlined previously, except:

- Do not check Spearman (under **Correlation Coefficients**) but do check **Pearson**.
- For **Options,** click **Means and standard deviations,** and **Exclude cases listwise.** The latter will only use participants who have no missing data on any of these four variables.

This will produce Output 9.3. To see if you are doing the work right, compare your syntax and output to Output 9.3.

Output 9.3: Pearson Correlation Matrix

```
CORRELATIONS
  /VARIABLES=visual satm grades mathach
  /PRINT=TWOTAIL NOSIG
  /STATISTICS DESCRIPTIVES
  /MISSING=LISTWISE .
```

Correlations

Descriptive Statistics

	Mean	Std. Deviation	N
visualization test	5.2433	3.91203	75
scholastic aptitude test - math	490.53	94.553	75
grades in h.s.	5.68	1.570	75
math achievement test	12.5645	6.67031	75

Correlations^a

		visualization test	scholastic aptitude test - math	grades in h.s.	math achievement test
visualization test	Pearson Correlation	1	.356**	.127	.423**
	Sig. (2-tailed)		.002	.279	.000
scholastic aptitude test - math	Pearson Correlation	.356**	1	.371**	.788**
	Sig. (2-tailed)	.002		.001	.000
grades in h.s.	Pearson Correlation	.127	.371**	1	.504**
	Sig. (2-tailed)	.279	.001		.000
math achievement test	Pearson Correlation	.423**	.788**	.504**	1
	Sig. (2-tailed)	.000	.000	.000	

**. Correlation is significant at the 0.01 level (2-tailed).

a. Listwise N=75

Correlations of the other variables with math achievement.

Interpretation of Output 9.3

Notice that after the **Descriptive Statistics** table, there is a larger **Correlations** table that shows the **Pearson Correlation** coefficients and two-tailed significance (**Sig.**) levels. These numbers are, as in Output 9.2, each given twice so you have to be careful in reading the matrix. It is a good idea to look only at the numbers above (or below) the diagonal (the 1s). You can also benefit from drawing a similar line on your output, so that you will be sure to read only the upper or lower portion of the matrix. There are six different correlations in the table. In the last column, we have circled the correlation of each of the other three variables with *math achievement*. In the second to last column, each of the other three variables is correlated with *grades in h.s.*, but note that the .504 below the diagonal for *grades in h.s.* and *math achievement* is the same as the correlation of *math achievement* and *grades in h.s.* in the last column, so ignore it the second time.

The Pearson correlations on this table are interpreted similarly to the one in Output 9.2. However, because there are six correlations, the odds are increased that one could be statistically significant by chance. Thus, it would be prudent to require a smaller value of p. The Bonferroni correction is a conservative approach designed to keep the significance level at .05 for the whole study. Using Bonferroni, you would divide the usual significance level (.05) by the number of tests. In this case a $p < .008$ (.05/6) would be required for statistical significance. Another approach is simply to set alpha (the p value required for statistical significance) at a more conservative level, perhaps .01 instead of .05. Note that if we had checked **Exclude cases pairwise** in Fig. 9.6, the correlations would be the same, in this instance, because there were no missing data ($N = 75$) on any of the four variables. However, if some variables had missing data, the correlations would be at least somewhat different. Each correlation would be based on the cases that have no missing data <u>on those two variables</u>. One might use pairwise exclusion to include as many cases as possible in each correlation; however, the problem with this approach is that the correlations will include data from somewhat different individuals, making comparisons among correlations difficult. Multivariate statistics, such as multiple regression, use listwise exclusion, including only the subjects with no missing data.

If you checked **One-Tailed Test of Significance** in Fig. 9.6, the **Pearson Correlation** values would be the same as in Output 9.3, but the **Sig**. values would be half what they are here. For example, the Sig. for the correlation between *visualization test* and *grades in h.s.* would be .139 instead of .279. One-tailed tests are only used if you have a clear directional hypothesis (e.g., there will be a *positive* correlation between the variables). If one takes this approach, then all correlations in the direction opposite from that predicted must be ignored, even if they seem to be significant.

Example of How to Write About Problem 9.3

Results

Because each of the four achievement variables was normally distributed and the assumption of linearity was not markedly violated, Pearson correlations were computed to examine the intercorrelations of the variables. Table 9.1 shows that five of the six pairs of variables were significantly correlated. The strongest positive correlation, which would be considered a very large effect size according to Cohen (1988), was between the scholastic aptitude math test and math achievement test, $r(73) = .79$, $p < .001$. This means that students who had relatively high SAT math scores were very likely to have high math achievement test scores. Math achievement was also positively correlated with visualization test scores ($r = .42$) and grades in high school ($r = .50$); these are medium to large size effects or correlations according to Cohen (1988).

Table 9.1

Intercorrelations, Means, and Standard Deviations for Four Achievement Variables ($N = 75$)

Variable	1	2	3	4	*M*	*SD*
1. Visualization	--	.36**	.13	.42**	5.24	3.91
2. SAT math	--	--	.37**	.79**	490.53	94.55
3. Grades	--	--	--	.50**	5.68	1.57
4. Math ach.	--	--	--	--	12.56	6.67

*$p < .05$ **$p < .01$

Problem 9.4: Bivariate or Simple Linear Regression

As stated earlier, the Pearson correlation is the best choice for a statistic when you are interested in the association of two variables that have normal or scale level measurement for the two variables. Correlations do not indicate prediction of one variable from another; however, there are times when researchers wish to make such predictions. To do this, one needs to use bivariate regression (which is also called simple regression or simple linear regression). Assumptions and conditions for simple regression are similar to those for Pearson correlations; the variables should be approximately normally distributed and should have a linear relationship.

9.4.　Can we predict *math achievement* from *grades in high school*?

To answer this question, a bivariate (two variables) regression is the best choice. Follow these commands:

- **Analyze → Regression → Linear...**
- Highlight *math achievement*. Click the arrow to move it into the **Dependent** box.
- Highlight *grades in high school* and click on the arrow to move it into the **Independent(s)** box. The window should look like Figure 9.8.
- Click on **OK.**

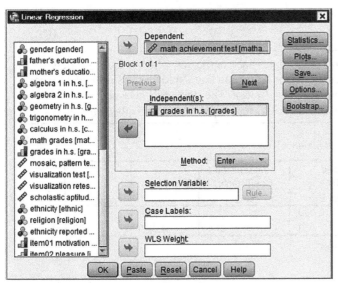

Fig. 9.8. Linear regression.

- Compare your output with Output 9.4

Output 9.4: Bivariate regression

```
REGRESSION
  /MISSING LISTWISE
  /STATISTICS COEFF OUTS R ANOVA
  /CRITERIA=PIN(.05) POUT(.10)
  /NOORIGIN
  /DEPENDENT mathach
  /METHOD=ENTER grades.
```

Regression

> Note that the *R* in this table is a bivariate *r* between the *grades* and *math achievement*. This *R* is the same as the *r* in Output 9.3.

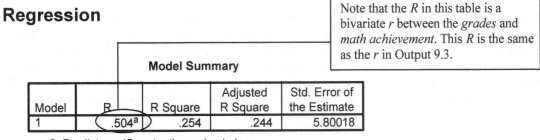

Model Summary

Model	R	R Square	Adjusted R Square	Std. Error of the Estimate
1	.504[a]	.254	.244	5.80018

a. Predictors: (Constant), grades in h.s.

Variables Entered/Removed [b]

Model	Variables Entered	Variables Removed	Method
1	grades in h.s. [a]	.	Enter

a. All requested variables entered.

b. Dependent Variable: math achievement test

ANOVA [b]

Model		Sum of Squares	df	Mean Square	F	Sig.
1	Regression	836.606	1	836.606	24.868	.000[a]
	Residual	2455.875	73	33.642		
	Total	3292.481	74			

a. Predictors: (Constant), grades in h.s.

b. Dependent Variable: math achievement test

> This is the regression coefficient, which is the slope of the best fit line or regression line. Note that it is not equal to the correlation coefficient. The standardized regression coefficient (.504) for simple regression is the correlation.

Coefficients [a]

Model		Unstandardized Coefficients		Standardized Coefficients	t	Sig.
		B	Std. Error	Beta		
1	(Constant)	.397	2.530		.157	.876
	grades in h.s.	2.142	.430	.504	4.987	.000

a. Dependent Variable: math achievement test

Interpretation of Output 9.4

The **Model Summary** table provides R, the standardized regression coefficient, which in bivariate regression is the same as r. The table also includes R^2 and an adjusted R^2 (.24), which indicates the proportion of the variance in math achievement (24%) that can be predicted from *grades in high school*. The **Variables Entered/Removed** table indicates that we have entered one independent or predictor variable, *grades in h.s.* The **ANOVA** table provides the test of the statistical significance of the regression; it indicates that grades is a statistically significant predictor ($p < .001$) of *math achievement*.

In the fourth table, labeled **Coefficients**, the Unstandardized regression Coefficient in bivariate regression is simply the slope of the "best fit" regression line for the scatterplot showing the association between two variables. The Standardized regression Coefficient is equal to the correlation between those same two variables. (In Problem 9.5, multiple regression, we will see that when there is more than one predictor, the relation between correlation and regression becomes more complex, and there is more than one standardized regression coefficient.) The primary distinction between bivariate regression and bivariate correlation (e.g., Pearson) is that, in regression, one wants to predict one variable from another variable, whereas in correlation you simply want to know how those variables are related.

The **Unstandardized Coefficients** give you a formula that you can use to predict the y scores (dependent variable) from the x scores (independent variable). Thus, if one did not have access to the real y score, this formula would tell one the best way of estimating an individual's y score based on that individual's x score. For example, if we want to predict *math achievement* for a similar group knowing only *grades in h.s.*, we could use the regression equation to estimate an individual's achievement score; predicted *math achievement* = .40 + 2.14 × (the person's *grades* score). Thus, if a student has mostly Bs (i.e., a code of 6) for their grades, their predicted *math achievement* score would be 13.24; *math achievement* = .40 + 2.14 × 6.

One should be cautious in doing this because we know (from the **Model Summary** table) that *grades in h.s.* only explains 24% of the variance in *math achievement*, so this would not yield a very accurate prediction. Another use of simple regression is to test a directional hypothesis: high *grades in h.s.* predict high *math achievement*. If one really thinks that this is the direction of the relationship (and not the reverse; i.e. *math achievement* leads to *grades in h.s.*), then regression is more appropriate than correlation.

An Example of How to Write about Output 9.4

Results

Simple regression was conducted to investigate how well grades in high school predict math achievement scores. The results were statistically significant, $F(1, 73) = 24.87$, $p < .001$. The identified equation to understand this relationship was math achievement = .40 + 2.14 × (grades in high school). The adjusted R^2 value was .244. This indicates that 24% of the variance in math achievement was explained by grades in high school. According to Cohen's (1988) guidelines, this is a large effect.

Problem 9.5: Multiple Regression

The purpose of multiple regression is similar to bivariate regression, but with more predictor variables. Multiple regression attempts to predict a normal (i.e., scale) dependent variable from a combination of several normally distributed and/or dichotomous independent/predictor variables. In this problem, we will see if *math achievement* can be predicted well from a combination of several of our other variables, *gender, grades in high school*, and *mother's* and *father's education*. There are many different methods provided to analyze data with multiple regression. We will use one where we assume that all four of the predictor variables are important and that we want to see what is the highest possible multiple correlation of these variables with the dependent variable. For this purpose, we will use the method the SPSS program calls **Enter** (usually called **simultaneous regression***),* which tells the computer to consider all the variables at the same time. Our *IBM SPSS for Intermediate Statistics* book (Leech, Barrett, & Morgan, 4th ed., 2011) provides more examples and discussion of multiple regression assumptions, methods, and interpretation.

Assumptions and Conditions of Multiple Regression

There are many assumptions to consider, but we will only focus on the major ones that are easily tested. These include the following: the relationship between each of the predictor variables and the dependent variable is linear, the errors are normally distributed, and the variance of the residuals (difference between actual and predicted scores) is constant. A condition that can be problematic is **multicollinearity**; it occurs when there are high intercorrelations among some set of the predictor variables. In other words, multicollinearity happens when two or more predictors are measuring overlapping or similar information.

9.5. How well can you predict *math achievement* from a combination of four variables: *grades in high school, father's and mother's education*, and *gender*?

In this problem, the computer will enter or consider all the variables at the same time. We will ask which of these four predictors contribute significantly to the multiple correlation/regression when all are used together to predict *math achievement*.

Let's compute the regression for these variables. To do this, follow these steps:

- Click on the following: **Analyze → Regression → Linear...** The Linear Regression window (Fig. 9.9) should appear.
- Select *math achievement* and click it over to the **Dependent** box (dependent variable).
- Next select the variables *grades in h.s., father's education, mother's education,* and *gender* and click them over to the **Independent(s)** box (independent variables).
- Under **Method**, be sure that **Enter** is selected.
- Click on **Statistics** at the top right corner of Fig. 9.9 to get Fig. 9.10.
- Click on **Estimates** (under **Regression coefficients**), click on **Model fit,** and **Descriptives**. (See Fig. 9.10.)

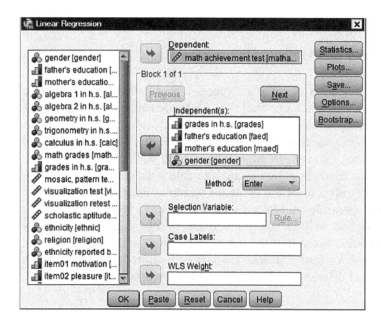

Fig. 9.9. Linear regression.

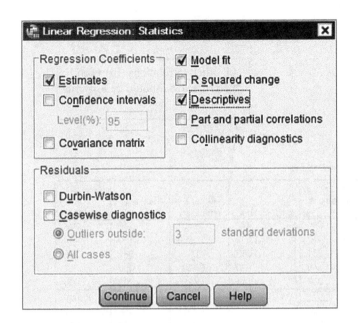

Fig. 9.10. Linear regression: Statistics.

- Click on **Continue**.
- Click on **OK**.

Compare your output and syntax to Output 9.5.

Output 9.5: Multiple Regression

```
REGRESSION
  /DESCRIPTIVES MEAN STDDEV CORR SIG N
  /MISSING LISTWISE
  /STATISTICS COEFF OUTS R ANOVA
  /CRITERIA=PIN(.05) POUT(.10)
  /NOORIGIN
  /DEPENDENT mathach
  /METHOD=ENTER grades faed maed gender.
```

Regression

Descriptive Statistics

	Mean	Std. Deviation	N
math achievement test	12.6621	6.49659	73
grades in h.s.	5.70	1.552	73
father's education	4.73	2.830	73
mother's education	4.14	2.263	73
gender	.55	.501	73

N is 73 because 2 participants have some missing data.

These are the correlations with *math achievement,* the dependent variable. We like them to be medium to high.

All other correlations (between the predictors) should be low, but this one isn't.

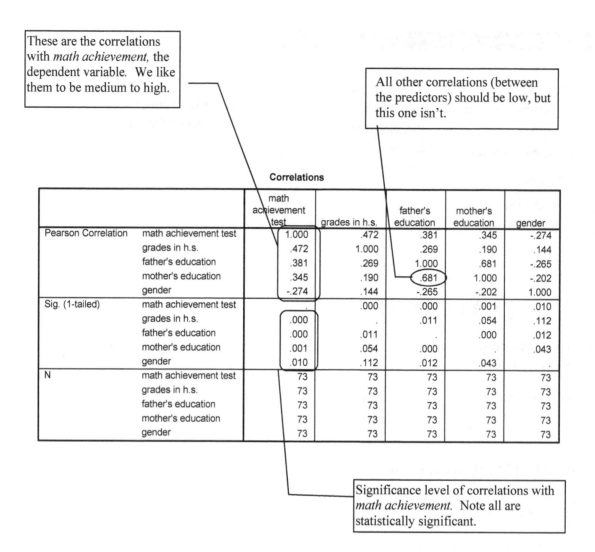

Correlations

		math achievement test	grades in h.s.	father's education	mother's education	gender
Pearson Correlation	math achievement test	1.000	.472	.381	.345	-.274
	grades in h.s.	.472	1.000	.269	.190	.144
	father's education	.381	.269	1.000	.681	-.265
	mother's education	.345	.190	.681	1.000	-.202
	gender	-.274	.144	-.265	-.202	1.000
Sig. (1-tailed)	math achievement test	.	.000	.000	.001	.010
	grades in h.s.	.000	.	.011	.054	.112
	father's education	.000	.011	.	.000	.012
	mother's education	.001	.054	.000	.	.043
	gender	.010	.112	.012	.043	.
N	math achievement test	73	73	73	73	73
	grades in h.s.	73	73	73	73	73
	father's education	73	73	73	73	73
	mother's education	73	73	73	73	73
	gender	73	73	73	73	73

Significance level of correlations with *math achievement.* Note all are statistically significant.

Variables Entered/Removed^b

Model	Variables Entered	Variables Removed	Method
1	gender, grades in h.s., mother's education, father's education^a	.	Enter

This indicates that we used the Enter method in the calculation. If we chose a different method, this box and the outputs would be different.

a. All requested variables entered.

b. Dependent Variable: math achievement test

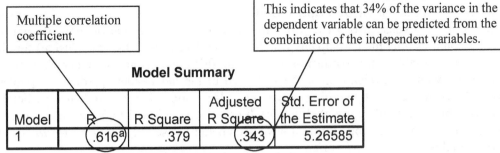

Multiple correlation coefficient.

This indicates that 34% of the variance in the dependent variable can be predicted from the combination of the independent variables.

Model Summary

Model	R	R Square	Adjusted R Square	Std. Error of the Estimate
1	.616[a]	.379	.343	5.26585

a. Predictors: (Constant), gender, grades in h.s., mother's education, father's education

This indicates that the combination of these variables significantly predicts the dependent variable.

ANOVA[b]

Model		Sum of Squares	df	Mean Square	F	Sig.
1	Regression	1153.222	4	288.305	10.397	.000[a]
	Residual	1885.583	68	27.729		
	Total	3038.804	72			

a. Predictors: (Constant), gender, grades in h.s., mother's education, father's education

b. Dependent Variable: math achievement test

Only grades and gender are significantly contributing to the equation. However, all of the variables need to be included to obtain this result.

Coefficients[a]

Model		Unstandardized Coefficients		Standardized Coefficients		
		B	Std. Error	Beta	t	Sig.
1	(Constant)	1.047	2.526		.415	.680
	grades in h.s.	1.946	.427	.465	4.560	.000
	father's education	.191	.313	.083	.610	.544
	mother's education	.406	.375	.141	1.084	.282
	gender	-3.759	1.321	-.290	-2.846	.006

a. Dependent Variable: math achievement test

Interpretation of Output 9.5

This output begins with the usual **Descriptive Statistics** for all five variables in the first table. Note that the N is 73 because two participants are missing a score on one or more variables. Multiple regression uses only the participants who have complete data (listwise exclusion) for all the variables. The next table is a **Correlation** matrix. The first column shows the correlations of the other variables with *math achievement*. Note that all of the independent/predictor variables are significantly correlated with *math achievement*. Also notice that two of the predictor/ independent variables are highly correlated with each other; *mother's* and *father's education* are correlated .68, which is not desirable. It might have been better to use only *mother's* (or *father's*) *education* or a combined *parents' education*.

The **Model Summary** table shows that the multiple correlation coefficient (**R**), using all the predictors simultaneously, is .62 and the **Adjusted R^2** is .34, meaning that 34% of the variance in math achievement can be predicted from the combination of *father's education, mother's education, grades in h.s.,* and *gender*. Note that the adjusted R^2 is lower than the unadjusted R^2 (.38). This is, in part, related to the number of variables in the equation. Because several independent variables were used, a reduction of the number of variables might help us find an equation that explains more of the variance in the dependent variable, once the R^2 is adjusted. It is helpful to use the concept of parsimony with multiple regression and use the smallest number of predictors needed. The **ANOVA** table shows that $F = 10.40$ and is statistically significant, $p < .001$. This indicates that the underlinepredictors significantly combine together to predict *math achievement*.

One of the most important tables is the **Coefficients** table. It shows the **standardized beta coefficients**, which are interpreted much like correlation coefficients. The **t** value and the **Sig.** opposite each independent variable indicates whether that variable is significantly contributing to the equation for predicting *math achievement*. Thus, *grades* and *gender*, in this example, are the only variables that are significantly adding to the prediction when the other three variables are already considered, but the parent education variables add a little. It is important to note that all the variables are being considered together when these values are computed. Therefore, if you delete one of the predictors, even if it is not statistically significant, it can affect the levels of significance for other predictors. For example, if we deleted *father's education*, it is quite possible that *mother's education* would be a statistically significant predictor. The fact that both *father's education* and *mother's education* are correlated with *math achievement* and with each other makes this possibility more likely.

How to Write About Output 9.5

Results

Simultaneous multiple regression was conducted to investigate the best prediction of math achievement test scores. The means, standard deviations, and intercorrelations can be found in Table 9.2a. The combination of variables to predict math achievement from grades in high school, father's education, mother's education, and gender was statistically significant, $F(4, 68) = 10.40$, $p < .001$. The beta coefficients are presented in Table 9.2b. Note that high grades and male gender significantly predict math achievement when all four variables are included. The adjusted R^2 value was .343. This indicates that 34% of the variance in math achievement was explained by the model. According to Cohen (1988), this is a large effect.

Table 9.2a

Means, Standard Deviations, and Intercorrelations for Math Achievement and Predictor Variables (N = 73)

Variable	M	SD	Grades in h.s.	Father's education	Mother's education	Gender
Math Achievement	12.66	6.50	.47**	.38**	.35**	−.27*
Predictor variables						
Grades in h.s.	5.70	1.55	- -	.27*	.19	.14
Father's education	4.73	2.83		- -	.68**	−.27*
Mother's education	4.14	2.26			- -	−.20*
Gender	.55	.50				- -

*p < .05; **p < .01.

Table 9.2b

Simultaneous Multiple Regression Analysis Summary for Grades in High School, Father's and Mother's Education, and Gender Predicting Math Achievement (N = 73)

Variable	B	SE B	β	t	p
Grades in h.s.	1.95	.43	.47	4.56	<.001
Father's education	.19	.31	.08	.61	.544
Mother's education	.41	.38	.14	1.08	.282
Gender	3.86	1.32	−.29	−2.85	.006
Constant	1.05	2.53			

Note. $R^2 = .38$; $F(4, 68) = 10.40$, $p < .001$.

Interpretation Questions

9.1.   Why would we graph scatterplots and regression lines?

9.2.   In Output 9.2, (a) What do the correlation coefficients tell us? (b) What is r^2 for the Pearson correlation? What does it mean? (c) Compare the Pearson and Spearman correlations on both correlation size and significance level; (d) When should you use which type in this case?

9.3.   In Output 9.3, how many of the Pearson correlation coefficients are significant? Write an interpretation of (a) one of the significant and (b) one of the nonsignificant correlations in Output 9.3. Include whether or not the correlation is significant, your decision about the null hypothesis, *and* a sentence or two describing the correlations in nontechnical terms. Include comments related to the sign and to the effect size.

9.4.   Using Output 9.4, find the regression (B) coefficient or weight and the standardized regression (Beta) coefficient. (a) How do these compare to the correlation between the same variables in Output 9.3? (b) What does the regression (B) weight tell you? (c) Give an example of a research problem in which the Pearson correlation would be more appropriate than bivariate regression, and one in which bivariate regression would be more appropriate than Pearson correlation.

9.5.   In Output 9.5, what do the Beta weights (standardized regression weights or coefficients) tell you about the ability of the predictors to predict the dependent variable?

Extra SPSS Problems

Using the College Student data set, do the following problems. Print your outputs after typing your interpretations on them. Please circle the key parts of the output that you discuss.

9.1.   What is the correlation between student's height and parent's height? Also produce a scatterplot. Interpret the results, including statistical significance, direction, and effect size.

9.2.   Write a question that can be answered via correlational analysis with two approximately normal or scale variables. Run the appropriate statistics to answer the question. Interpret the results.

9.3.   Make a correlation matrix using at least four appropriate variables. Identify, using the variable names, the two strongest and two weakest correlations. What were the r and p values for each correlation?

9.4.   Is there a combination of gender and same-sex parent's height that significantly predicts student's height?

9.5.   Is there a combination of hours of TV watching, hours of studying, and hours of work that predicts current GPA?

CHAPTER 10

Comparing Two Groups with *t* Tests and Similar Nonparametric Tests

In this chapter, we will use a number of statistics to compare two groups or samples. In Problem 10.1, we will use a **one-sample *t* test** to compare one group or sample to a hypothesized population mean. Then, in Problems 10.2–10.5, we will examine two parametric and two nonparametric/ordinal statistics that compare two groups of participants. Problem 10.2 compares two independent groups (between-groups design), males and females, using the **independent samples *t* test**. Problem 10.3 uses the **Mann–Whitney** nonparametric test, which is similar to the independent *t* test. Problem 10.4 is a within-subjects design that uses a **paired samples *t*** to compare the average levels of education of students' mothers and fathers. Problem 10.5 shows how to use the nonparametric **Wilcoxon** test for a within-subjects design.

The top right side of Table 10.1 distinguishes between **between-groups** and **within-subjects designs.** This helps determine the specific statistic to use. The other determinant of which statistic to use has do with statistical assumptions. If the assumptions are not markedly violated, you can use a parametric test. If the assumptions are markedly violated, one can use a nonparametric test, which does not have the same assumptions, as indicated by the left side of Table 10.1. Another alternative is to transform the variable so that it meets the assumptions. That is beyond the scope of this book, but is covered in Leech et al. (2011). Note that chi-square was demonstrated in Chapter 8 so we will not use it here. The McNemar test, which is rarely used, will not be demonstrated, but is available in SPSS (see Fig. 10.6).

Table 10.1. *Selection of an Appropriate Inferential Statistic for Basic, Two Variable Difference Questions or Hypotheses*

	Level of Measurement of Dependent Variable	*Compare*	*One Factor or Independent Variable with Two Categories or Levels/Groups/Samples*	
			Independent Samples or Groups (Between)	*Repeated Measures or Related Samples (Within)*
Parametric Statistics	Dependent Variable Approximates **Normal (Scale) Data** and Assumptions Not Markedly Violated	Means	INDEPENDENT SAMPLES *t* TEST (or ONE-WAY ANOVA)	PAIRED SAMPLES *t* TEST
Nonparametric Statistics	Dependent Variable Clearly **Ordinal Data** or Parametric Assumptions Are Markedly Violated	Mean Ranks	MANN–WHITNEY	WILCOXON
	Dependent Variable Is **Nominal** or (dichotomous) Data	Counts	CHI-SQUARE	MCNEMAR

In the next chapter, you will learn about ANOVA (*F*), which can be used to look at differences between the means of <u>two or more groups</u>. You might ask, why would you compute a *t* test when one-way ANOVA can be used to compare *two* groups as well as three or more groups? Because $F = t^2$, both statistics provide the same information. Thus, the choice is mostly a matter of personal preference. However, *t* tests can be either one tailed or two-tailed, while one cannot have one-tailed ANOVAs. Thus, if you have a clear directional hypothesis that predicts which group will have the higher mean, you may want to use a *t* test rather than one-way ANOVA when comparing two groups. In addition, the *t* test output provides an adjustment to deal with the problem of unequal variances, whereas the remedy for such problems in ANOVA may be less satisfactory. Finally, it is more customary to use a *t* test if one is comparing only two groups. You *must* use ANOVA if you want to compare three or more groups.

- Retrieve **hsbdataB** from your data file.

Problem 10.1: One-Sample *t* Test

Sometimes you want to compare the mean of a sample with a hypothesized population mean to see if your sample is significantly different. For example, the scholastic aptitude test was originally standardized so that the mean was 500 and the standard deviation was 100. In our modified HSB data set, we made up mock *scholastic aptitude test – math* (*SAT Math*) scores for each student. You may remember from Chapter 3 that the mean *SAT Math* score for our sample was 490.53. Is this significantly different from 500?

10.1.   Is the mean *SAT Math* score in the modified HSB data set statistically significantly different from the presumed population mean of 500?

Assumptions of the One-Sample t Test
1. The dependent variable is normally distributed within the population.
2. The data are independent (scores of one participant are not dependent on scores of the others; participants are independent of one another).

To compute the one-sample *t* test, use the following commands:
- **Analyze → Compare Means → One-Sample T Test…**
- Move *scholastic aptitude test – math* to the **Test Variable(s)** box.
- Type 500 in the **Test Value** box (the test value is the score that you want to compare to your sample mean).
- Your window should look like Fig. 10.1.
- Click **OK.**

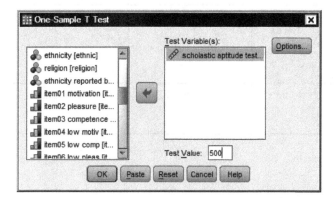

Fig. 10.1. One-sample *t* test.

Compare your output to Output 10.1.

Output 10.1: One-Sample *t* Test

```
T-TEST
  /TESTVAL = 500
  /MISSING = ANALYSIS
  /VARIABLES = satm
  /CRITERIA = CI(.95) .
```

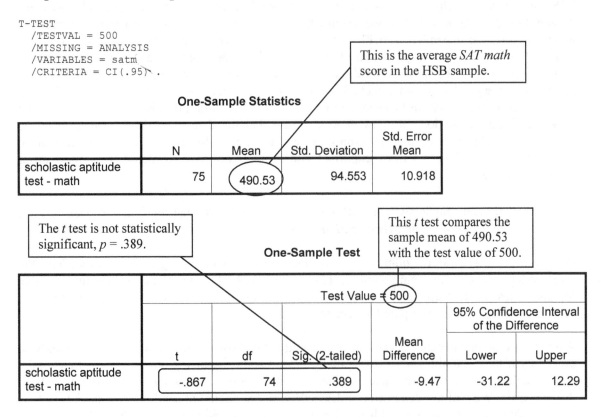

This is the average *SAT math* score in the HSB sample.

One-Sample Statistics

	N	Mean	Std. Deviation	Std. Error Mean
scholastic aptitude test - math	75	490.53	94.553	10.918

The *t* test is not statistically significant, *p* = .389.

This *t* test compares the sample mean of 490.53 with the test value of 500.

One-Sample Test

	Test Value = 500					
					95% Confidence Interval of the Difference	
	t	df	Sig. (2-tailed)	Mean Difference	Lower	Upper
scholastic aptitude test - math	-.867	74	.389	-9.47	-31.22	12.29

Interpretation of Output 10.1

The **One-Sample Statistics** table provides basic descriptive statistics for the variable under consideration. The **Mean** *SAT Math* for the students in the sample was compared to the hypothesized population mean, displayed as the **Test Value** in the **One-Sample Test** table. On the bottom line of this table are the *t* value, *df*, and the two-tailed sig. (*p*) value, which are encircled. Note that *p* = .389, so we can say that the sample (*M* = 491) is not significantly different from the population mean of 500. The table also provides the difference (*M* = −9.47) between the sample and population means and the 95% **Confidence Interval**. The difference between the sample and the population mean is likely to be between +12.29 and −31.22 points. Notice that this range includes the value of zero, so it is possible that there is no difference. Thus, the difference is not statistically significant.

Problem 10.2: Independent Samples *t* Test

When investigating the difference between two unrelated or independent groups (in this case males and females) on an approximately normal dependent variable, it is appropriate to choose an independent samples *t* test if the following assumptions are not markedly violated.

Assumptions of the Independent Samples *t* Test
1. The variances of the dependent variable in the two populations are equal.

2. The dependent variable is normally distributed within each population.
3. The data are independent (scores of one participant are not related systematically to scores of the others).

SPSS will automatically test Assumption 1 with the **Levene's test** for equality of variances. Assumption 2 could be tested, as we did in Chapter 4, Problem 4.3, with the **Explore** command, to see whether the dependent variables are at least approximately normally distributed for each gender. Because the *t* test is quite robust to violations of this assumption, especially if the data for both groups are skewed in the same direction, we won't test it here. Assumption 3 probably is met because the genders are not matched or related pairs and there is no reason to believe that one person's score might have influenced another person's. This assumption is best addressed during design and data collection. In addition to ensuring that the data meet these assumptions, the researcher should try to ensure that groups or samples are of similar size, as the assumption of homogeneity of variance is most important and more likely to be violated if samples differ markedly in size.

10.2. Do male and female students differ in regard to their average *math achievement* scores, *grades in high school,* and *visualization test* scores?

One feature of this SPSS program is that it can do several *t* tests in a single output if they have the same independent or grouping variable (e.g., gender). In this problem, we computed three separate *t* tests, one each for *math achievement, grades in high school,* and *visualization test* scores; in each males are compared to females.

With more than one dependent variable, one could have chosen to use MANOVA (see Fig. 6.1), especially if these variables were conceptually related and correlated with each other. MANOVA would enable us to see how a linear *combination* of these three variables was different for boys than for girls. We will not demonstrate MANOVA in this book, but see Leech et al. (2011) *IBM SPSS for Intermediate Statistics* (4th ed.) for how to compute and interpret MANOVA.

For the *t* tests, follow these commands:

- Click on **Analyze → Compare means → Independent Samples T Test...**
- Move *math achievement, grades in h.s.,* and *visualization test* to the **Test** (dependent) **Variable(s)** box and move *gender* to the **Grouping** (independent) **Variable:** box (see Fig. 10.2).

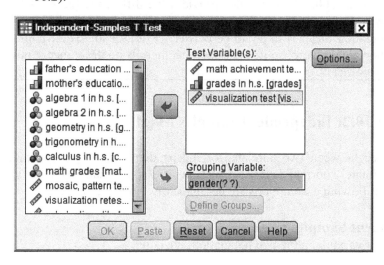

Fig. 10.2. Independent-samples *t* test.

- Next click on **Define Groups** in Fig. 10.2 to get Fig. 10.3.
- Type **0** (for males) in the **Group 1** box and **1** (for females) in the **Group 2** box (see Fig. 10.3). This will enable us to compare males and females on each of the three dependent variables.

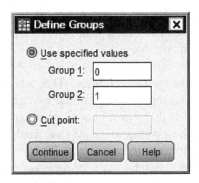

Fig. 10.3. Define groups.

- Click on **Continue** then on **OK**. Compare your output to Output 10.2.

Output 10.2: Independent Samples *t* Test

```
T-TEST GROUPS=gender(0 1)
  /MISSING=ANALYSIS
  /VARIABLES=mathach grades visual
  /CRITERIA=CIN(.95) .
```

Each circle contains a pair of means to be compared.

T-Test

Group Statistics

	gender	N	Mean	Std. Deviation	Std. Error Mean
math achievement test	male	34	14.7550	6.03154	1.03440
	female	41	10.7479	6.69612	1.04576
grades in h.s.	male	34	5.50	1.638	.281
	female	41	5.83	1.515	.237
visualization test	male	34	6.4265	4.47067	.76671
	female	41	4.2622	3.10592	.48506

This is *not* the *t* test. It is a test of the assumption of equal variances.

Circled numbers are discussed in the Interpretation box.

Independent Samples Test

		Levene's Test for Equality of Variances		t-test for Equality of Means					95% Confidence Interval of the Difference	
		F	Sig.	t	df	Sig. (2-tailed)	Mean Difference	Std. Error Difference	Lower	Upper
math achievement test	Equal variances assumed	.537	.466	2.697	73	.009	4.0070	1.48548	1.04648	6.96760
	Equal variances not assumed			2.724	72.472	.008	4.0070	1.47092	1.07515	6.93894
grades in h.s.	Equal variances assumed	.574	.451	-.903	73	.369	-.33	.365	-1.056	.397
	Equal variances not assumed			-.897	68.145	.373	-.33	.367	-1.062	.403
visualization test	Equal variances assumed	6.510	.013	2.466	73	.016	2.1643	.87778	.41486	3.91369
	Equal variances not assumed			2.385	57.150	.020	2.1643	.90727	.34761	3.98094

Interpretation of Output 10.2

The first table, **Group Statistics**, shows descriptive statistics for the two groups (males and females) separately. Note that the means within each of the three pairs look somewhat different. This might be due to chance, so we will check the *t* tests in the next table.

The second table, **Independent Samples Test**, provides two statistical tests. The left two columns of numbers are the **Levene's test** for the assumption that the variances of the two groups are equal. This is *not* the *t* test; it only assesses an assumption! If this *F* test is *not* significant (as in the case of *math achievement* and *grades in high school*), the assumption is not violated, and one uses the **Equal variances assumed** line for the *t* test and related statistics. However, if Levene's *F* is statistically significant (Sig. < .05), as is true for *visualization test*, then variances are significantly different statistically and the assumption of equal variances is violated. In that case, the **Equal variances *not* assumed** line is used, and the *t*, *df*, and **Sig.** are adjusted by the program. The appropriate lines to use are circled in the output.

Thus, in the section titled **t-test for equality of means**, the appropriate values are: *t* = 2.39, degrees of freedom (*df*) = 57.15, and *p* = .020 for *visualization test*. This *t* is statistically significant so, based on examining the means, we can say that boys have higher *visualization* scores than girls. Likewise, the *t* for *math achievement* is statistically significant because *p* = .009. Thus, males have higher means. However, for *grades in high school* the *t* is not statistically significant, so we conclude that there is not enough evidence to say that there is a systematic difference between boys and girls on grades.

The **95% Confidence Interval of the Difference** is shown in the two right-hand columns of the **Independent Samples** table. The confidence interval tells us that if we repeated the study 100 times, 95 of the times the true (population) difference would fall within the confidence interval, which for *math achievement* is between 1.05 points and 6.97 points. Note that if the **Upper** and **Lower** bounds have the same sign (either + and + or – and –), we know that the difference is statistically significant because this means that the null finding of zero difference lies *outside* of the confidence interval. On the other hand, if zero lies between the upper and lower limits, there could be no difference, as is the case for *grades in h.s.* The lower limit of the confidence interval on *math achievement* tells us that the difference between males and females could be as small as 1.05 points out of 25, which is the maximum possible score.

Effect size measures for *t* tests are not provided in the printout but can be estimated relatively easily. See Chapter 6 for the formula and interpretation of *d*. For math achievement, the difference between the means (4.01) would be divided by about 6.4, an estimate of the pooled (weighted average) standard deviation. Thus, *d* would be approximately .60, which is, according to Cohen (1988), a medium to large sized "effect." Because you need means and standard deviations to compute the effect size, you should include a table with means and standard deviations in your results section for a full interpretation of *t* tests.

How to Write about Output 10.2

Results

Table 10.2 shows that males were different from females on *math achievement* ($p = .009$), which was statistically significant. Inspection of the two group means indicates that the average math achievement score for female students ($M = 10.75$) is significantly lower than the score ($M = 14.76$) for males. The difference between the means is 4.01 points on a 25-point test. The effect size d is approximately .6, which is a typical size for effects in the behavioral sciences. Males did not differ from females on grades in high school ($p = .369$), but males did score higher on the visualization test ($p = .020$), which was statistically significant. The effect size, d, is again approximately .6.

Table 10.2

Comparison of Male and Female High School Students on a Math Achievement Test, Grades, and a Visualization Test ($n = 34$ males and 41 females)

Variable	M	SD	t	df	p	d
Math achievement			2.70	73	.009	.6
Males	14.76	6.03				
Females	10.75	6.70				
Grades			−.90	73	.369	.2
Males	5.50	1.64				
Females	5.83	1.52				
Visualization			2.39[a]	57.2[a]	.020	.6
Males	6.43	4.47				
Females	4.26	3.11				

[a]The t and df were adjusted because variances were not equal.

Problem 10.3: The Nonparametric Mann–Whitney U Test

What should you do if the t test assumptions are markedly violated (e.g., what if the dependent variable data are grossly skewed, otherwise non-normally distributed, or are ordinal)? One answer is to run the appropriate nonparametric statistic, which in this case is called the Mann–Whitney (M–W) U test. The M–W is used with a between-groups design with two levels of the independent variable.

10.3 Do boys and girls differ on *visualization, math achievement*, and *grades*?

For this problem, we will assume that the scores for the three dependent variables were ordinal level data or that other assumptions of the t test were violated but that the assumptions of the Mann–Whitney test were met.

Assumptions of the Mann–Whitney Test

1. It is assumed there is an underlying continuity from low to high in the dependent variable, before ranking, even if the actual data are discrete numbers such as 1, 2, 3, 4, 5, on a Likert rating.
2. The data are independent (scores of one participant are not dependent on scores of the others).

- Click on **Analyze → Nonparametric Tests → Legacy Dialogs → 2 Independent Samples…**
- Move *visualization test, math achievement,* and *grades in h.s.* (the dependent variables) to the **Test Variable List:**
- Next, click on *gender* (the independent variable) and move it over to the **Grouping Variable:** box.
- Click on **Define Groups** and enter 0 and 1 for groups because males are 0 and females are 1.
- Ensure that **Mann–Whitney U** is checked. Your window should look like Fig. 10.4.

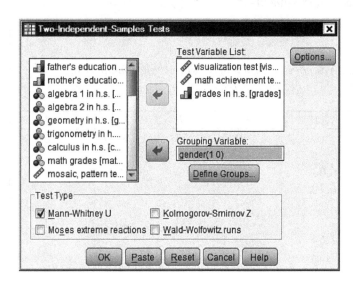

Fig. 10.4. Nonparametric tests for two independent samples.

- Click on **OK.**

Compare your syntax and output to Output 10.3 to check your work.

Output 10.3: Nonparametric Test: Mann–Whitney *U*

```
NPAR TESTS
  /M-W= visual mathach grades BY gender(0 1)
  /MISSING ANALYSIS.
```

NPar Tests

Mann-Whitney Test

> Mean ranks to be compared. The group with the higher rank had the higher grades or test scores.

Ranks

	gender	N	Mean Rank	Sum of Ranks
visualization test	male	34	43.65	1484.00
	female	41	33.32	1366.00
	Total	75		
math achievement test	male	34	45.10	1533.50
	female	41	32.11	1316.50
	Total	75		
grades in h.s.	male	34	35.78	1216.50
	female	41	39.84	1633.50
	Total	75		

Test Statistics[a]

	visualization test	math achievement test	grades in h.s.
Mann-Whitney U	505.000	455.500	621.500
Wilcoxon W	1366.000	1316.500	1216.500
Z	-2.052	-2.575	-.818
Asymp. Sig. (2-tailed)	.040	.010	.413

Note z and Sig. for each dependent variable.

a. Grouping Variable: gender

Interpretation of Output 10.3

The **Ranks** table shows the mean or average ranks for males and females on each of the three dependent variables. The 75 students are ranked from 75 (highest) to 1 (lowest) so that, in contrast to the typical ranking procedure, a high mean rank indicates the group scored higher.

The second table provides the **Mann–Whitney** U, **z score**, and the **Sig.** (significance) level or p value. Asymptotic ("Asymp.") significance refers to the fact that the significance levels are not exact. Note that the mean ranks of the genders differ significantly on *visualization test* and *math achievement* but not on *grades in high school*, as was the case for the similar t tests in Problem 10.2. The Mann–Whitney test is only slightly less powerful than the t test, so it is a good alternative if the assumptions of the t test are violated, as was actually the case with *visualization test*. Note that you would not report both t tests and Mann–Whitney tests for the same variables because they provide very similar information.

Although an effect size measure is not provided in the output, it is easy to compute an r from the z provided in the **Test Statistics** table, using the conversion formula, $r = z/\sqrt{N}$. For these three comparisons, the r effect sizes are −.24 (i.e., 2.05/8.66), −.30, and −.09 for *visualization test*, *math achievement*, and *grades in h.s.*, respectively. You can see from Table 6.5 that these are small to medium/typical, medium, and small/minimal, respectively. These r effect sizes are somewhat smaller than for the corresponding t tests in Output 10.2.

How to Write About Output 10.3

Results

Because the dependent variables were ordinal and the variances were unequal, Mann–Whitney U tests were performed to compare the genders. The 34 male students have higher mean ranks (43.65) than the 41 females (33.32) on the visualization test, $U = 505$, $p = .04$, $r = −.24$, which was a statistically significant difference and, according to Cohen (1988), is a small to medium effect size. Likewise, there was a significant difference, which was statistically significant, in the mean ranks of males (45.10) and females (32.11) on math achievement, $U = 455.5$, $p = .01$, $r = −.30$, which is considered a medium effect size. However, male and female students did not show a statistically significant difference on grades in high school. Mean ranks were 35.78 and 39.84, respectively, $U = 621.5$, $p = .41$, $r = .09$.

Problem 10.4: Paired Samples *t* Test

In this problem, you will compare the average scores of each HSB student's father's and mother's scores on the same measure, namely, their educational level. Because *father's* and *mother's education* are not independent of each other, the paired *t* test is the appropriate test to perform. The paired samples *t* test is also used when the two scores are used for interrater reliability, such as Problem 7.2 in Chapter 7. Other examples would be in a longitudinal study or in a single group quasi-experimental study in which the same assessment is used as the pretest, before the intervention, and as the posttest, after the intervention.

Assumptions and Conditions for Use of the Paired Samples *t* test

1. The independent variable is dichotomous and its levels (or groups) are paired, or matched, in some way (e.g., husband–wife, pre–post, etc.).
2. The dependent variable is normally distributed in the two conditions.

The first assumption depends on the design; the second can be assessed by examining the skewness of the two variables.

10.4. Do students' fathers or mothers have more education?   Are their education levels correlated?

We will determine if the fathers of these students have more education than their mothers. Remember that the fathers and mothers are paired; that is, each child has a pair of parents whose educations are given in the data set. (Note that you can do more than one paired *t* test at a time, so we could have compared the *visualization test* and *visualization 2* scores in the same run as we compared *father's* and *mother's education*.)

- Select **Analyze → Compare Means → Paired Samples T Test**
- Move <u>both</u> of the variables, *father's education* and *mother's education*, to the **Paired Variables:** box (see Fig. 10.5).
- Click on **OK**.

Compare your syntax and output to Output 10.4.

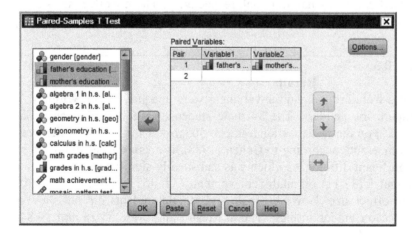

Fig. 10.5. Paired-samples *t* test.

Output 10.4: Paired Samples *t* Tests

```
T-TEST PAIRS= faed WITH maed (PAIRED)
  /CRITERIA=CI(.9500)
  /MISSING=ANALYSIS.
```

T-Test

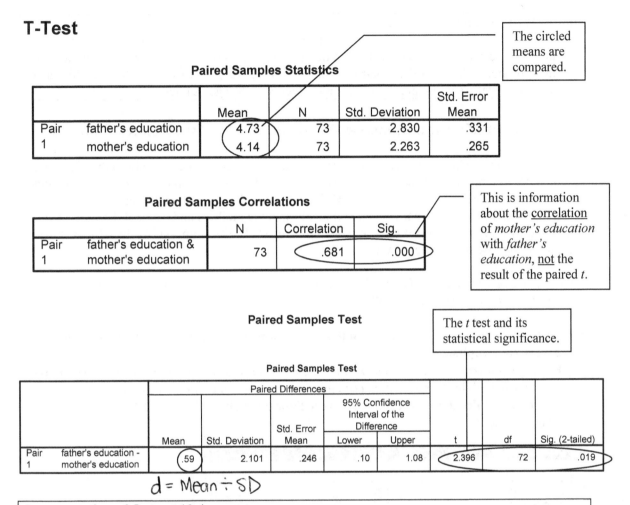

Paired Samples Statistics

The circled means are compared.

		Mean	N	Std. Deviation	Std. Error Mean
Pair 1	father's education	4.73	73	2.830	.331
	mother's education	4.14	73	2.263	.265

Paired Samples Correlations

This is information about the <u>correlation</u> of *mother's education* with *father's education*, <u>not</u> the result of the paired *t*.

		N	Correlation	Sig.
Pair 1	father's education & mother's education	73	.681	.000

Paired Samples Test

The *t* test and its statistical significance.

Paired Samples Test

		Paired Differences					t	df	Sig. (2-tailed)
		Mean	Std. Deviation	Std. Error Mean	95% Confidence Interval of the Difference Lower	Upper			
Pair 1	father's education - mother's education	.59	2.101	.246	.10	1.08	2.396	72	.019

$d = $ Mean $\div$ SD

Interpretation of Output 10.4

The first table shows the descriptive statistics used to compare *mother's* and *father's education* levels. The second table, **Paired Samples Correlations,** provides correlations between the two paired scores. The correlation ($r = .68$) between *mother's* and *father's education* indicates that highly educated men tend to marry highly educated women and vice versa. It doesn't tell you whether men or women have more education. That is what *t* in the third table tells you.

The last table shows the **Paired Samples *t* Test**. The **Sig.** for the comparison of the average education level of the students' mothers and fathers was $p = .019$. Thus, the difference in educational level is statistically significant, and we can tell from the means in the first table that fathers have more education; however, the effect size is small ($d = .28$) and is computed by dividing the mean of the paired differences (.59) by the standard deviation (2.1) of the paired differences. Also, we can tell from the confidence interval that the difference in the means could be as small as .10 or as large as 1.08 points on the 2 to 10 scale.

It is important that you understand that the correlation in the second table provides you with different information than the paired *t*. If not, read this interpretation again.

> **How to Write about Output 10.4**
> **Results**
> A paired or correlated samples t test indicated that the students' fathers had on average significantly more education than their mothers, $t(72) = 2.40$, $p = .019$, $d = .28$. The difference, although statistically significant, is small using Cohen's (1988) guidelines.

Problem 10.5: Nonparametric Wilcoxon Test for Two Related Samples

Let's assume that education levels and visualization test scores are not normally distributed and/or other assumptions of the paired t test are violated. In fact, *mother's education* was quite skewed (see Chapter 4). Let's run the **Wilcoxon signed-ranks** nonparametric test to see if fathers have significantly higher educational levels than the mothers and to see if the *visualization test* is significantly different from the *visualization retest*. The assumptions of the Wilcoxon tests are similar to those for the Mann–Whitney test.

10.5. (a) Are *mother's* and *father's education* levels different? (b) Are the *visualization test* and *visualization 2* scores different?

- To answer these questions, select **Analyze → Nonparametric Tests → Legacy Dialogs → 2 Related Samples...**
- Highlight *father's education* and *mother's education* and move them into the **Test Pairs:** box. Then, highlight *visualization test* and *visualization 2* and move them into the box.
- Ensure that **Wilcoxon** is checked in the **Test Type** dialog box. (See Fig. 10.6.)
- Click on **OK**.

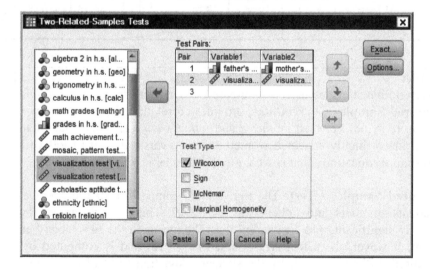

Fig. 10.6. Two related-samples tests

Compare your syntax and output to Output 10.5.

Output 10.5: Wilcoxon Nonparametric Test

```
NPAR TEST
  /WILCOXON=faed visual  WITH maed visual2 (PAIRED)
  /MISSING ANALYSIS.
```

NPar Tests

Wilcoxon Signed Ranks Test

Ranks

		N	Mean Rank	Sum of Ranks
mother's education - father's education	Negative Ranks	27[a]	29.20	788.50
	Positive Ranks	21[b]	18.45	387.50
	Ties	25[c]		
	Total	73		
visualization 2 - visualization test	Negative Ranks	24[d]	37.25	894.00
	Positive Ranks	37[e]	26.95	997.00
	Ties	14[f]		
	Total	75		

a. mother's education < father's education

b. mother's education > father's education

c. mother's education = father's education

d. visualization 2 < visualization test

e. visualization 2 > visualization test

f. visualization 2 = visualization test

This box shows how many individual students had higher, lower, and the same *visualization test* scores compared to their *visualization 2* scores.

Test Statistics[a]

	mother's education - father's education	visualization 2 - visualization test
Z	-2.085[b]	-.373[c]
Asymp. Sig. (2-tailed)	.037	.709

a. Wilcoxon Signed Ranks Test

b. Based on positive ranks.

c. Based on negative ranks.

Note that there was a statistically significant difference ($p = .04$) between the mean rank of *mothers* and *father's education,* but not between *visualization 2* and *visualization test* ($p = .71$).

Interpretation of Output 10.5

Output 10.5 shows the nonparametric (Wilcoxon) analyses, which are similar to the paired *t* tests. Note that the first table shows not only the mean ranks, but also the number of students whose mothers, for example, had less education than their fathers (27). Note that there were lots of ties (25) and almost as many women (21) that have more education than their husbands. However, overall the fathers had more education, as indicated by their lower mean rank (18.45) and the statistically significant *z* ($p = .037$). The second table shows the statistical significance level for the two tests. Note that the *p* or sig. value is quite similar to those for the paired *t* test comparing father's and mother's education. Effect size measures are not provided on the output, but again we can compute an *r* from the *z* scores and *N*s (Total) that are shown in Output 10.5 using the same formula as for Problem 10.3 ($r = z/\sqrt{N}$). For Output 10.5, $r = -.24$ (i.e., $-2.085/8.54$) for the comparison of *mothers'* and *fathers' education,* which is a small to medium effect size. For the comparison of the *visualization* and *visualization 2,* $r = .04$, a small effect size.

How to Write about Output 10.6
Results
Wilcoxon signed ranks tests were used to compare the education of each student's mother and father. Of 73 students, 27 fathers had more education, 21 mothers had more education, and there were 25 ties. This difference indicating more education for fathers is statistically significant, $z = 2.09$, $p = .037$, $r = -.24$, a small to medium effect size according to Cohen (1988). However, there was not a statistically significant difference between the visualization test scores and the visualization 2 scores, $N = 75$, $z = -.373$, $p = .709$, $r = .04$.

Interpretation Questions

10.1.   (a) Under what conditions would you use a one-sample t test? (b) Provide another possible example of its use from the HSB data.

10.2.   In Output 10.2: (a) Are the *variances* equal or significantly different for the three dependent variables? (b) List the appropriate t, df, and p (significance level) for each t test as you would in an article. (c) Which t tests are statistically significant? (d) Write sentences interpreting the gender difference between the means of *grades in high school* and also *visualization*. (e) Interpret the 95% confidence interval for these two variables. (f) Comment on the effect sizes.

10.3.   (a) Compare the results of Output 10.2 and 10.3. (b) When would you use the Mann–Whitney U test?

10.4.   In Output 10.4: (a) What does the paired samples <u>correlation</u> for mother's and father's education mean? (b) Interpret/explain the results for the t test. (c) Explain how the correlation and the t test differ in what information they provide. (d) Describe the results if the r was .90 and the t was zero. (e) What if r was zero and t was 5.0?

10.5.   (a) Compare the results of Outputs 10.4 with Output 10.5. (b) When would you use the Wilcoxon test?

Extra SPSS Problems

Using the College Student data file, do the following problems. Print your outputs after typing your interpretations on them. Please circle the key parts of the output that you use for your interpretation.

10.1.   Is there a significant difference between the genders on average student height? Explain. Provide a full interpretation of the results.

10.2.   Is there a difference between the number of hours students study and the hours they work? Also, is there an association between the two?

10.3.   Write another question that can be answered from the data using a paired sample t test. Run the t test and provide a full interpretation.

10.4.   Are there differences between males and females in regard to the average number of hours they (a) study, (b) work, and (c) watch TV? Hours of study is quite skewed so compute an appropriate nonparametric statistic.

CHAPTER 11

Analysis of Variance (ANOVA)

In this chapter, you will learn how to compute two types of analysis of variance (ANOVA) and a similar nonparametric statistic. In Problem 11.1, we will use the **one-way** or **single factor ANOVA** to compare three levels of *father's education* on several dependent variables (e.g., *math achievement*). If the ANOVA is statistically significant, you will know that there is a difference somewhere, but you will not know which pairs of means were significantly different. In Problem 11.2, we show you when and how to do appropriate **post hoc** tests to see which pairs of means were different. In Problem 11.3, you will compute the **Kruskal–Wallis (K-W)** test, a nonparametric test similar to one-way ANOVA. In Problem 11.4, we will introduce you to two-way or **factorial ANOVA**. This complex statistic is discussed in more detail in our companion book, Leech et al. (2011), *IBM SPSS for Intermediate Statistics* (4th ed.).

- Retrieve your **hsbdataB.sav** file.

Problem 11.1: One-Way (or Single Factor) ANOVA

In this problem, you will examine a statistical technique for comparing two or *more* independent groups on the dependent variable. The appropriate statistic, called **One-Way ANOVA**, compares the *means* of the samples or groups in order to make inferences about the population means. One-way ANOVA also is called single factor analysis of variance because there is only one independent variable or factor. The independent variable has nominal levels or a few ordered levels. The overall ANOVA test does not take into account the order of the levels, but additional tests (contrasts) can be done that do consider the order of the levels. More information regarding contrasts can be found in Leech et al. (2011).

Remember that, in Chapter 10, we used the independent samples *t* test to compare two groups (males and females). The one-way ANOVA *may* be used to compare two groups, but ANOVA is necessary if you want to compare three or more groups (e.g., three levels of *father's education*) in a single analysis. Review Fig. 6.1 and Table 6.1 to see how these statistics fit into the overall selection of an appropriate statistic.

Assumptions of ANOVA

1. Observations are independent. The value of one observation is not related to any other observation. In other words, one person's score should not provide any clue as to how any of the other people would score. Each person is in only one group and has only one score on each measure; there are no repeated or within-subjects measures.
2. Variances on the dependent variable are equal across groups.
3. The dependent variable is normally distributed for each group.

Because ANOVA is robust, it can be used when variances are only approximately equal if the number of subjects in each group is approximately equal. ANOVA also is robust if the dependent variable data are approximately normally distributed. Thus, if assumption #2, or, even more so, #3 is not fully met, you may still be able to use ANOVA. There are also several choices of post hoc tests to use depending on whether the assumption of equal variances has been violated. **Dunnett's C** and **Games–Howell** are appropriate post hoc tests if the assumption of equal variances is violated.

11.1 Are there statistically significant differences among the three *father's education revised* groups on *grades in h.s.*, *visualization test* scores, and *math achievement*?

We will use the **One-Way ANOVA** procedure because we have one independent variable with three levels. We can do several one-way ANOVAs at a time so we will do three ANOVAs in this problem, one for each of the three dependent variables. Note that you could do MANOVA (see Fig. 6.1) instead of three ANOVAs, especially if the dependent variables are correlated and conceptually related, but that is beyond the scope of this book. See our companion book (Leech et al., 2011).

To do the three one-way ANOVAs, use the following commands:

- **Analyze → Compare Means → One-Way ANOVA...**
- Move *grades in h.s., visualization test,* and *math achievement* into the **Dependent List:** box in Fig. 11.1.
- Click on *father's educ revised* and move it to the **Factor** (independent variable) box.
- Click on **Options** to get Fig. 11.2.
- Under **Statistics,** choose **Descriptive** and **Homogeneity of variance test**.
- Under **Missing Values**, choose **Exclude cases analysis by analysis**.

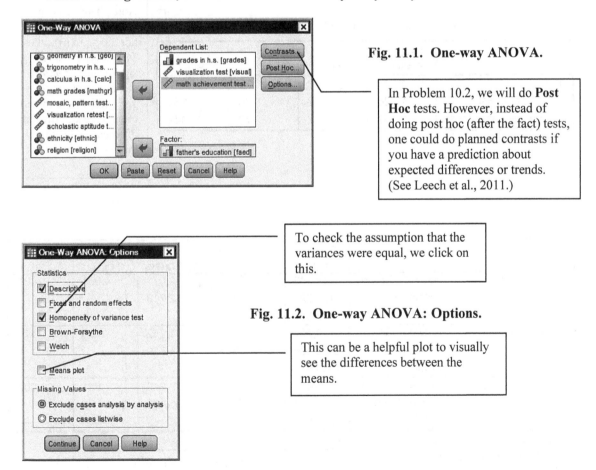

Fig. 11.1. One-way ANOVA.

In Problem 10.2, we will do **Post Hoc** tests. However, instead of doing post hoc (after the fact) tests, one could do planned contrasts if you have a prediction about expected differences or trends. (See Leech et al., 2011.)

To check the assumption that the variances were equal, we click on this.

Fig. 11.2. One-way ANOVA: Options.

This can be a helpful plot to visually see the differences between the means.

- Click on **Continue** then **OK**. Compare your output to Output 11.1.

Output 11.1: One-Way ANOVA

```
ONEWAY grades visual mathach BY faedRevis
  /STATISTICS DESCRIPTIVES HOMOGENEITY
  /MISSING ANALYSIS.
```

Oneway

Descriptives

Means to be compared.

		N	Mean	Std. Deviation	Std. Error	95% Confidence Interval for Mean		Minimum	Maximum
						Lower Bound	Upper Bound		
grades in h.s.	HS grad or less	38	5.34	1.475	.239	4.86	5.83	3	8
	Some College	16	5.56	1.788	.447	4.61	6.52	2	8
	BS or More	19	6.53	1.219	.280	5.94	7.11	4	8
	Total	73	5.70	1.552	.182	5.34	6.06	2	8
visualization test	HS grad or less	38	4.6711	3.96058	.64249	3.3692	5.9729	-.25	14.8
	Some College	16	6.0156	4.56022	1.14005	3.5857	8.4456	-.25	14.8
	BS or More	19	5.4605	2.79044	.64017	4.1156	6.8055	-.25	9.75
	Total	73	5.1712	3.82787	.44802	4.2781	6.0643	-.25	14.8
math achievement test	HS grad or less	38	10.0877	5.61297	.91054	8.2428	11.9326	1.00	22.7
	Some College	16	14.3958	4.66544	1.16636	11.9098	16.8819	5.00	23.7
	BS or More	19	16.3509	7.40918	1.69978	12.7798	19.9221	1.00	23.7
	Total	73	12.6621	6.49659	.76037	11.1463	14.1779	1.00	23.7

Test of Homogeneity of Variances

	Levene Statistic	df1	df2	Sig.
grades in h.s.	1.546	2	70	.220
visualization test	1.926	2	70	.153
math achievement test	3.157	2	70	.049

Note: This tests an assumption of ANOVA, not the main hypothesis. The Levene test is significant for *math achievement* so the <u>variances</u> of the three groups are significantly different, indicating that the assumption is violated.

ANOVA

		Sum of Squares	df	Mean Square	F	Sig.
grades in h.s.	Between Groups	18.143	2	9.071	4.091	.021
	Within Groups	155.227	70	2.218		
	Total	173.370	72			
visualization test	Between Groups	22.505	2	11.252	.763	.470
	Within Groups	1032.480	70	14.750		
	Total	1054.985	72			
math achievement test	Between Groups	558.481	2	279.240	7.881	.001
	Within Groups	2480.324	70	35.433		
	Total	3038.804	72			

These are the degrees of freedom: 2, 70.

The between-groups differences for *grades in high school* and *math achievement* are statistically significant ($p < .05$) whereas those for *visualization* are not significantly different.

Interpretation of Output 11.1

The first table, **Descriptives,** provides familiar descriptive statistics for the three father's education groups on each of the three dependent variables (*grades in h.s.*, *visualization test,* and *math achievement*) that we requested for these analyses. Remember that, although these three dependent variables appear together in each of the tables, we have really computed three separate one-way ANOVAs.

The second table (**Test of Homogeneity of Variances**) provides the Levene's test to check the assumption that the variances of the three *father's education* groups are equal for each of the dependent variables. Notice that for *grades in h.s.* ($p = .220$) and *visualization test* ($p = .153$) the Levene's tests are *not* significant. Thus, the assumption is *not* violated. However, for *math achievement, $p = .049$*; therefore, the Levene's test is significant and thus the assumption of equal variances is violated. In this latter case, we could use the similar nonparametric test (Kruskal–Wallis). Or, if the overall F is significant (as you can see it was in the ANOVA table), you could use a post hoc test designed for situations in which the variances are unequal. We will do the latter in Problem 2 and the former in Problem 3 for *math achievement*.

The **ANOVA** table in Output 11.1 is the key table because it shows whether the overall Fs for these three ANOVAs were statistically significant. Note that the three *father's education* groups differ on *grades in h.s.* and *math achievement* but not *visualization test*. When reporting these findings one should write, for example, $F(2, 70) = 4.09$, $p = .021$, for *grades in h.s.* The 2, 70 (circled for *grades in h.s.* in the ANOVA table) are the degrees of freedom (*df*) for the between-groups "effect" and within-groups "error," respectively. *F tables* also usually include the mean squares, which indicate the amount of variance (sums of squares) for that "effect" divided by the degrees of freedom for that "effect." You also should report the means (and SDs) so that one can see which groups were high and low. Remember, however, that if you have three or more groups you will not know which specific pairs of means are significantly different unless you do a priori (beforehand) contrasts (see Fig. 11.1) or post hoc tests, as shown in Problem 11.2. We provide an example of appropriate APA-format tables and how to write about these ANOVAs after Problem 11.2.

Problem 11.2: Post Hoc Multiple Comparison Tests

Now we will introduce the concept of **post hoc multiple comparisons**, sometimes called **follow-up tests**. When you compare three or more group means, you know that there will be a statistically significant difference somewhere if the **ANOVA F** (sometimes called the **overall F** or **omnibus F**) is significant.

However, we would usually like to know which specific means are different from which other ones. In order to know this, you can use *one* of several post hoc tests that are built into the one-way ANOVA program. The **LSD** post hoc test is quite liberal and the **Scheffe** test is quite conservative so many statisticians recommend a more middle of the road test, such as the **Tukey HSD** (honestly significant differences) test, if the Levene's test was not statistically significant, or the **Games–Howell** test, if the Levene's test was significant. Ordinarily, you do post hoc tests only if the overall F is statistically significant. For this reason, we have separated Problems 11.1 and 11.2, which could have been done in one step. Fig. 11.3 shows the steps one should use in deciding whether to use post hoc multiple comparison tests.

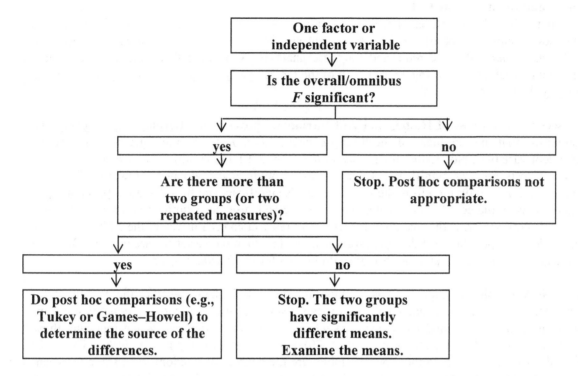

Fig. 11.3. Schematic representation of when to use post hoc multiple comparisons with a one-way ANOVA.

11.2.   If the overall F is statistically significant, which pairs of means are significantly different?

After you have examined Output 11.1 to see if the overall F (ANOVA) for each variable was statistically significant, you will do appropriate post hoc multiple comparisons for these variables. We will use the **Tukey HSD** if variances can be assumed to be equal (i.e., the Levene's test is *not* statistically significant) and the **Games–Howell** if the assumption of equal variances cannot be justified (i.e., the Levene's test is significant).

First we will do the Tukey HSD for *grades in h.s.* Open the **One-Way ANOVA** dialog box *again* by doing the following:

- Select **Analyze → Compare Means → One-Way ANOVA…** to see Fig. 11.1 again.
- Move *visualization test* out of the **Dependent List:** by highlighting it and clicking on the arrow pointing left because the overall F for *visualization test* was not significant. (See interpretation of Output 11.1.)
- Also move *math achievement* to the left (out of the **Dependent List:** box) because the Levene's test for it <u>was</u> statistically significant. (We will use it later.)
- Keep *grades* in the **Dependent List:** because it had a significant ANOVA, and the Levene's test was not statistically significant.
- Insure that *father's educ revised* is in the **Factor** box.
- Your window should look like Fig. 11.4.

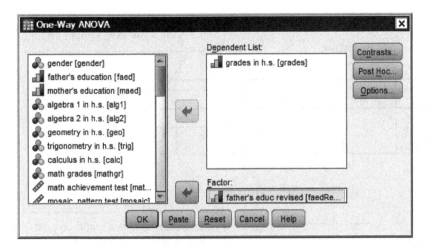

Fig. 11.4. One-Way ANOVA.

- Next, click on **Options...** and remove the check for **Descriptive** and **Homogeneity of variance test** (in Fig. 11.2) because we do not need to do them again; they would be the same.
- Click on **Continue**.
- Then, in the main dialogue box (Fig. 11.1), click on **Post Hoc...** to get Fig. 11.5.
- Check **Tukey** because, for *grades in h.s.,* the Levene's test was not significant so we can assume that the variances are approximately equal.

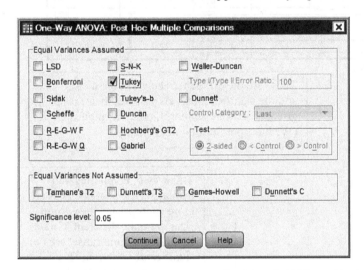

Fig. 11.5. One-way ANOVA: Post hoc multiple comparisons.

- Click on **Continue** and then **OK** to run this post hoc test.

Compare your output to Output 11.2a.

Output 11.2a: Tukey HSD Post Hoc Tests

```
ONEWAY grades BY faedRevis
  /MISSING ANALYSIS
  /POSTHOC = TUKEY ALPHA(0.05).
```

Oneway

ANOVA

grades in h.s.

	Sum of Squares	df	Mean Square	F	Sig.
Between Groups	18.143	2	9.071	4.091	.021
Within Groups	155.227	70	2.218		
Total	173.370	72			

> This is the same as in Output 10.1.

Post Hoc Tests

Multiple Comparisons

> The Tukey HSD is a common post hoc test to use when variances are equal. This table is most appropriate when the group *ns* are similar. Here they are quite different. See below.

Dependent Variable: grades in h.s.
Tukey HSD

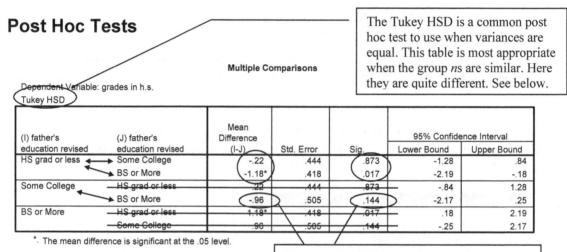

(I) father's education revised	(J) father's education revised	Mean Difference (I-J)	Std. Error	Sig.	95% Confidence Interval	
					Lower Bound	Upper Bound
HS grad or less	Some College	-.22	.444	.873	-1.28	.84
	BS or More	-1.18*	.418	.017	-2.19	-.18
Some College	HS grad or less	.22	.444	.873	-.84	1.28
	BS or More	-.96	.505	.144	-2.17	.25
BS or More	HS grad or less	1.18*	.418	.017	.18	2.19
	Some College	.96	.505	.144	-.25	2.17

*. The mean difference is significant at the .05 level.

> These are the differences between the means and the significance levels you would use if the group sizes were similar. Ignore the duplicates. (We have put lines through them.)

Homogeneous Subset

grades in h.s.

Tukey HSD[a,b]

father's education revised	N	Subset for alpha = .05	
		1	2
HS grad or less	38	5.34	
Some College	16	5.56	5.56
BS or More	19		6.53
Sig.		.880	.096

Means for groups in homogeneous subsets are displayed.

a. Uses Harmonic Mean Sample Size = 21.209.

b. The group sizes are unequal. The harmonic mean of the group sizes is used. Type I error levels are not guaranteed.

> This way of computing and displaying the post hoc tests is more appropriate when group sizes are quite different. Groups listed in the same subset are not significantly different. Thus, the grades of students whose fathers were *HS grads or less* are not different from those whose fathers had *some college*. Likewise, those with *some college* are not different from those with a *BS or more*, but *HS grads or less* are different from those with a *BS or more*. This is the same conclusion from the **Post Hoc Tests** table.

After you do the Tukey test, let's go back and do **Games–Howell**. Follow these steps:

- Select **Analyze → Compare Means → One-Way ANOVA…**
- Move *grades in h.s.* out of the **Dependent List:** by highlighting it and clicking on the arrow pointing left.
- Move *math achievement* into the **Dependent List:** box.
- Insure that *father's educ revised* is still in the **Factor:** box.
- In the main dialogue box (Fig. 11.1), click on **Post Hoc…** to get Fig. 11.4.
- Check **Games–Howell** because equal variances cannot be assumed for *math achievement*.
- <u>Remove</u> the check mark from Tukey.
- Click on **Continue** and then **OK** to run this post hoc test.
- Compare your syntax and output to Output 11.2b.

Output 11.2b: Games–Howell Post Hoc Test

```
ONEWAY mathach BY faedRevis
  /MISSING ANALYSIS
  /POSTHOC = GH ALPHA(0.05).
```

Oneway

ANOVA

math achievement test

	Sum of Squares	df	Mean Square	F	Sig.
Between Groups	558.481	2	279.240	7.881	.001
Within Groups	2480.324	70	35.433		
Total	3038.804	72			

Post Hoc Tests

Multiple Comparisons

We used Games–Howell because the Levene's test indicated that the variances are unequal.

Dependent Variable: math achievement test

Games-Howell

(I) father's education revised	(J) father's education revised	Mean Difference (I-J)	Std. Error	Sig.	95% Confidence Interval	
					Lower Bound	Upper Bound
HS grad or less	Some College	-4.3081*	1.47969	.017	-7.9351	-.6811
	BS or More	-6.2632*	1.92830	.008	-11.0284	-1.4980
Some College	HS grad or less	4.3081*	1.47969	.017	.6811	7.9351
	BS or More	-1.9551	2.06147	.614	-7.0308	3.1205
BS or More	HS grad or less	6.2632*	1.92830	.008	1.4980	11.0284
	Some College	1.9551	2.06147	.614	-3.1205	7.0308

*. The mean difference is significant at the .05 level.

Interpretation of Output 11.2
The first table in both Outputs 11.2a and 11.2b repeats appropriate parts of the **ANOVA** table from Output 11.1. The second table in Output 11.2a shows the **Tukey HSD** test for *grades in h.s.* that you would use if the three group sizes (n = 38, 16, 19 from the first table in Output 11.1) had been similar. For *grades in h.s.*, this Tukey table indicates that there is only a small not statistically significant mean difference (.22) between the mean grades of students whose fathers were *high school grads or less* (M = 5.34 from Output 11.1) and those fathers who had *some college* (M = 5.56). The **Homogeneous Subsets** table shows an <u>adjusted Tukey</u> that is appropriate when group sizes are not similar, as in this case. Note that there is <u>not</u> a statistically significant difference (p = .880) between the grades of students whose fathers were *high school grads or less* (low education) and those with *some college* (medium education) because <u>their means are both shown in **Subset 1.**</u> In **Subset 2,** the medium and high education group means are shown, indicating that they are not significantly different (p = .096). By examining the two subset boxes, we can see that the low education group (M = 5.34) is different from the high education group (M = 6.53) because these two means do not appear in the same subset. Output 11.2b shows, for *math achievement,* the **Games–Howell** test, used for variables that have unequal variances. Note that each comparison is presented twice. The **Mean Difference** between students whose fathers were *high school grads or less* and those with fathers who had *some college* was -4.31. The **Sig.** (p = .017) indicates that this is a statistically significant difference. We can also tell that this difference is statistically significant because the confidence interval's lower and upper bounds both have the same sign, a minus, so zero (no difference) is not included in the confidence interval. Similarly, students whose fathers had a *B.S. degree* were significantly different on *math achievement* from those whose fathers had a *high school degree or less* (p = .008).

An Example of How to Write about Outputs 11.1 and 11.2.
Results
A statistically significant difference was found among the three levels of father's education on grades in high school, $F(2, 70) = 4.09$, $p = .021$, and on math achievement, $F(2, 70) = 7.88$, $p = .001$. Table 11.2a shows that the mean grade in high school is 5.34 for students whose fathers had low education, 5.56 for students whose fathers attended some college (medium), and 6.53 for students whose fathers received a BS or more (high). Post hoc Tukey HSD tests indicate that the low education group and high education group differed significantly in their grades with a large effect size ($p < .05$, $d = .85$). Likewise, there were also statistically significant mean differences on math achievement between the low education and both the medium education group ($p < .017$, $d = .80$) and the high education group ($p = .008$, $d = 1.0$) using the Games–Howell post hoc test.

Table 11.2a

Means and Standard Deviations Comparing Three Father's Education Groups

Father's education	n	Grades in H.S.		Math achievement		Visualization	
		M	SD	M	SD	M	SD
HS grad or less (low)	38	5.34	1.48	10.09	5.61	4.67	3.96
Some college (medium)	16	5.56	1.79	14.40	4.67	6.02	4.56
BS or more (high)	19	6.53	1.22	16.35	7.41	5.46	2.79
Total	73	5.70	1.55	12.66	6.50	5.17	3.83

Table 11.2b

One-Way Analysis of Variance Summary Table Comparing Father's Education Groups on Grades in High School, Math Achievement, and Visualization Test

Source	df	SS	MS	F	p
Grades in high school					
Between groups	2	18.14	9.07	4.09	.021
Within groups	70	155.23	2.22		
Total	72	173.37			
Math achievement					
Between groups	2	558.48	279.24	7.88	.001
Within groups	70	2480.32	35.43		
Total	72	3038.80			
Visualization test					
Between groups	2	22.51	11.25	.76	.470
Within groups	70	1032.48	14.75		
Total	72	1054.99			

Problem 11.3: Nonparametric Kruskal–Wallis Test

What else can you do if the homogeneity of variance assumption is violated (or if your data are ordinal or highly skewed)? One answer is a nonparametric statistic. Let's make comparisons similar to Problem 11.1, assuming that the data are ordinal or the assumption of equality of group variances is violated. Remember that the variances for the three fathers' education groups were statistically significantly different on *math achievement*, and the *competence* scale was not normally distributed (see Chapter 4). The assumptions of the Kruskal–Wallis test are the same as for the Mann–Whitney test (see Chapter 10).

11.3. Are there statistically significant differences among the three father's education groups on *math achievement* and the *competence scale?*

Follow these commands:
- **Analyze → Nonparametric Tests → Legacy Dialogs → K Independent Samples…**
- Move the dependent variables of *math achievement* and *competence* to the **Test Variable List:** (see Fig. 11.6).

- Move the independent variable *father's educ revised* to the **Grouping Variable** box.
- Click on **Define Range** and insert **1** and **3** into the **minimum** and **maximum** boxes (Fig. 11.7) because *faedRevis* has values of 1, 2, and 3.
- Click on **Continue**.
- Ensure that **Kruskal–Wallis H** (under **Test Type**) in the main dialogue box is checked.
- Then click on **OK**. Do your results look like Output 11.3?

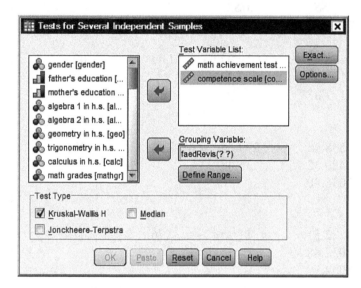

Fig. 11.6. Tests for several independent samples.

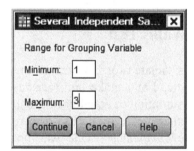

Fig. 11.7. Define range.

Output 11.3: Kruskal–Wallis Nonparametric Tests

```
NPAR TESTS
  /K-W=mathach competence   BY faedRevis(1 3)
  /MISSING ANALYSIS.
```

NPar Tests

Kruskal–Wallis Test

High mean ranks indicate high *math achievement* and *competence* scores.

Ranks

	father's education revised	N	Mean Rank
math achievement test	HS grad or less	38	28.43
	Some College	16	43.78
	BS or More	19	48.42
	Total	73	
Competence scale	HS grad or less	37	36.04
	Some College	16	35.78
	BS or More	18	36.11
	Total	71	

Test Statistics [a,b]

	math achievement test	competence scale
Chi-Square	13.384	.003
df	2	2
Asymp. Sig.	.001	.999

a. Kruskal Wallis Test

b. Grouping Variable: father's educ revised

Interpretation of Output 11.3

As in the case of the Mann-Whitney test (Chapter 10), the **Ranks** table provides **Mean Ranks** for the two dependent variables, *math achievement* and *competence*. In this case, the **Kruskal–Wallis** (K–W) test will compare the mean ranks for the three *father's education* groups.

The **Test Statistics** table shows whether there is an overall difference among the three groups. Notice that the p (Asymp. Sig.) value for *math achievement* is .001, which is the same as it was in Output 11.1 using the one-way ANOVA. This is because K–W and ANOVA have similar power to detect a difference. Note also that there is not a statistically significant difference among the father's education groups on the *competence scale* ($p = .999$).

Unfortunately, there are no post hoc tests built into the K–W test, as there are for the one-way ANOVA. Thus, you cannot tell which of the pairs of father's education means are different on *math achievement*. One method to check this would be to run three Mann–Whitney (M–W) tests comparing each pair of *father's education* mean ranks (see Problem 10.3). Note you would only do the post hoc M–W tests if the K–W test was statistically significant; thus, you would not do the M–W for *competence*. It also would be prudent to adjust the significance level by dividing .05 by 3 (the Bonferonni correction) so that you would require that the M–W Sig. be < .017 to be statistically significant. For the box about how to write about this output, we have computed the three M-W tests and r effect size measures, as demonstrated in Problem 10.3. Note that the Mean Rank when comparing two groups are different than when comparing all three groups.

How to Write About Output 11.3

Results

A Kruskal–Wallis nonparametric test was conducted to test for statistically significant differences between father's education groups in math achievement because there were unequal variances and ns across groups. The test indicated that the three father's education groups differed on math achievement, χ^2 (2, $N = 73$) = 13.38, $p = .001$. Post hoc Mann–Whitney tests compared the three pairs of fathers' education groups on math achievement, using a Bonferonni corrected p value of .017 to indicate statistical significance. The mean rank for math achievement of students whose fathers had some college (36.59, $n = 16$) was significantly higher than that of students whose fathers were high school graduates or less (23.67, $n = 38$), $z = 2.76$, $p = .006$, $r = .38$, a medium to large effect size according to Cohen (1988). Also, the mean rank for math achievement of students whose fathers had a bachelor's degree or more (38.47, $n = 19$) was higher than that of students whose fathers were high school graduates or less (24.26, $n = 38$), $z = 3.05$, $p = .002$, $r = .40$, a statistically significant difference with a medium to large effect size. There was not a statistically significant difference on math achievement between students whose fathers had some college and those whose fathers had a bachelor's degree or more, $z = -1.23$, $p = .23$.

Problem 11.4: Two-Way (or Factorial) ANOVA

In previous problems, we compared two or more groups based on the levels of only one independent variable or factor using t tests (Chapter 10) and one-way ANOVA (this chapter). These were called single factor designs. In this problem, we will compare groups based on *two* independent variables. The appropriate statistic for this is called a two-way or factorial ANOVA. This statistic is used when there are two different independent variables, each of which classifies participants with respect to a particular characteristic, with each participant being in one level of each of the independent variables (completely crossed design). An individual could be classified, based on the variables of gender and education level as, for example, a female college graduate. In this chapter, we provide an introduction to this complex difference statistic; a more in-depth treatment is provided in Leech et al., 2011.

11.4.   Do *math grades* and *gender* each seem to have a statistically significant effect on *math achievement*, and do the effects of *math grades* on *math achievement* depend on whether the person is male or female (i.e., on the interaction of *math grades* with *gender*)?

Follow these commands:

- **Analyze → General Linear Model → Univariate…**
- Move *math achievement* to the **Dependent Variable:** box.
- Move the first independent variable, *math grades* (not *grades in h.s.*), to the **Fixed Factor(s):** box.
- Then also move the second independent variable, *gender*, to the **Fixed Factor(s):** box (see Fig. 11.8).

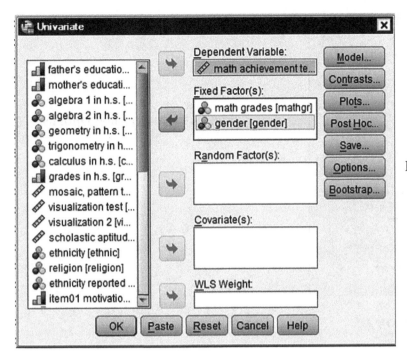

Fig. 11.8. GLM -Univariate.

Now that we know the variables we will be dealing with, let's determine our options.

*   Click on **Plots** and move *mathgr* to the **Horizontal Axis:** and *gender* to **Separate Lines:** box.
*   Then press **Add**. Your window should <u>now</u> look like Fig. 11.9.
*   Click on **Continue** to get back to Fig. 11.8.

Fig. 11.9. Univariate: Profile plots.

*   Select **Options** and click **Descriptive statistics** and **Estimates of effect size**. See Fig. 11.10.
*   Click on **Continue**.
*   Click on **OK**. Compare your syntax and output to Output 11.4.

Fig. 11.10. Univariate: Options.

Output 11.4: Two-Way ANOVA

```
UNIANOVA mathach  BY mathgr gender
  /METHOD = SSTYPE(3)
  /INTERCEPT = INCLUDE
  /PLOT = PROFILE(mathgr*gender )
  /PRINT = DESCRIPTIVE ETASQ
  /CRITERIA = ALPHA(.05)
  /DESIGN = mathgr gender mathgr*gender
```

Between-Subjects Factors

		Value Label	N
math grades	0	less A-B	44
	1	most A-B	31
gender	0	male	34
	1	female	41

Descriptive Statistics

Dependent Variable: math achievement test

math grades	gender	Mean	Std. Deviation	N
less A-B	male	12.8751	5.73136	24
	female	8.3333	5.32563	20
	Total	10.8106	5.94438	44
most A-B	male	19.2667	4.17182	10
	female	13.0476	7.16577	21
	Total	15.0538	6.94168	31
Total	male	14.7550	6.03154	34
	female	10.7479	6.69612	41
	Total	12.5645	6.67031	75

The cell means are important for interpreting factorial ANOVAs and describing the results.

These *F*s and significance levels tell you important information about differences between means and the interaction.

Tests of Between-Subjects Effects

Dependent Variable: math achievement test

Source	Type III Sum of Squares	df	Mean Square	F	Sig.	Partial Eta Squared
Corrected Model	814.481[a]	3	271.494	7.779	.000	.247
Intercept	11971.773	1	11971.773	343.017	.000	.829
MATHGR	515.463	1	515.463	14.769	.000	.172
GEND	483.929	1	483.929	13.866	.000	.163
MATHGR * GEND	11.756	1	11.756	.337	.563	.005
Error	2478.000	71	34.901			
Total	15132.393	75				
Corrected Total	3292.481	74				

a. R Squared = .247 (Adjusted R Squared = .216)

Percent of variance in *math achievement* predictable from both independent variables and the interaction.

Eta squared is an index of the effect size for each independent variable and the interaction. Thus, about 17% of the variance in *math achievement* can be predicted from *math grades*.

Profile Plots

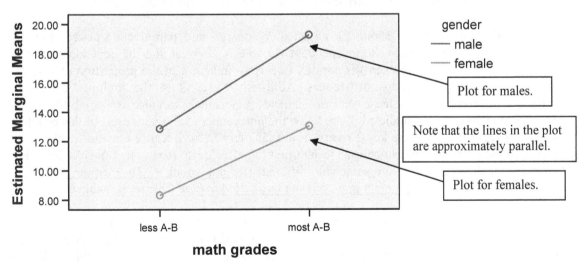

Estimated Marginal Means of math achievement test

gender
— male
— female

Plot for males.

Note that the lines in the plot are approximately parallel.

Plot for females.

Interpretation of Output 11.4

The GLM Univariate program allows you to print the means for each subgroup (cell) representing the interaction between the two independent variables. It also provides measures of effect size (eta^2) and plots the interaction, which is helpful in interpreting it. The first table in Output 11.4 shows that 75 participants (44 with less than A–B math grades and 31 mostly A–B math grades) are included in the analysis because they had data on all of the variables. The **Descriptive Statistics** table shows the cell and marginal (total) means; both are very important for interpreting the ANOVA table and explaining the results of the test for the interaction.

The ANOVA table, called **Tests of Between-Subjects Effects**, is the key table. Note that the word "effect" in the title of the table can be misleading because this study was not a randomized experiment. Thus, you cannot say in your report that the differences in the dependent variable were *caused* by or were the effect of the independent variable. Usually you will ignore the lines in the table labeled "corrected model" (which just summarizes all "effects" taken together) and intercept (which is needed to fit the best fit regression line to the data) and skip down to the interaction F(***mathgr * gender***) which, in this case, is not statistically significant, $F(1, 71) = .337$, $p = .563$. If the interaction were significant, we would need to be cautious about the interpretation of the main effects because they could be misleading.

Next we examine the main effects of *math grades* and of *gender*. Note that both are statistically significant. The significant F for *math grades* means that students with fewer As and Bs in math scored lower ($M = 10.81$ vs. 15.05) on *math achievement* than those with high math grades, and this difference is statistically significant ($p < .001$). *Gender* is also statistically significant ($p < .001$). Because the interaction is not statistically significant, the "effect" of *math grades* on *math achievement* is about the same for both genders. If the interaction were statistically significant, we would say that the "effect" of math grades depended on which gender you were considering. For example, it might be large for boys and small for girls. If the interaction is statistically significant, you should also analyze the differences between cell means (the simple effects). Leech et al. (2011) shows how to do this and discusses more about how to interpret statistically significant interactions. The profile plots may be helpful in visualizing the interaction, but you should not discuss statistically nonsignificant differences because the plots may be misleading.

Note also the callout boxes about the adjusted R squared and partial eta squared. Eta, the correlation ratio, is used when the independent variable is *nominal* and the dependent variable (*math achievement* in this problem) is normal. Eta^2 is an indicator of the proportion of variance that is due to between-groups differences. Adjusted R^2 refers to the multiple correlation coefficient squared. Like r^2, these statistics indicate how much variance or variability in the dependent variable can be predicted if you know the independent variable scores. In this problem, the eta^2 percentages for these key Fs vary from 0.5% to 17.2%. Because eta and R, like r, are indexes of association, they can be used to interpret the effect size. However, Cohen's guidelines for small, medium, and large are somewhat different (for eta, small = .10, medium = .24, and large = .37; for R, small = .14, medium = .36, and large = .51). (See Chapter 6, Table 6.5.)

In this example, eta (not squared) for *math grades* is about .41 and thus a large effect. Eta for *gender* is about .40, also a large effect. The overall adjusted R is about .46, a large effect. Notice that the adjusted R^2 is lower than the unadjusted (.22 versus .25). The reason for this is that the adjusted R^2 takes into account (and adjusts for) the fact that not just one variable but three (*math grades, gender*, and the interaction) were used to predict *math achievement*.

An important point to remember is that statistical significance depends heavily on the sample size, so that with 1,000 subjects a much lower F or r will be significant than if the sample is 10 or even 100. Statistical significance just tells you that you can be quite sure that there is at least a little relationship between the independent and dependent variables. Effect size measures, which are more independent of sample size, tell you how strong the relationship is and thus give you some indication of its importance.

The **profile plots** of cell means (which follow the table of between-subjects effects) help us to visualize the nature of a significant interaction when one exists. When the lines on the profile plot are parallel, there is not a significant interaction. Note that we requested that the separate lines represent the two genders because we felt that this would make a significant interaction easier to interpret than if the two lines represented predominant level of grades. However, really, either independent variable could have been represented in either part of the graph.

An Example of How to Write About Output 11.4
Results

To assess whether *math grades* and *gender* each seem to have a statistically significant effect on *math achievement*, and if the effects of *math grades* on *math achievement* depend on whether the person is male or female (i.e., on the interaction of *math grades* with *gender*) a two-way ANOVA was conducted.

Table 11.4a shows the means and standard deviations for math achievement for the two genders and for the two math grades groups. Table 11.4b shows that there was not a significant interaction between gender and math grades on math achievement ($p = .563$). There was, however, a statistically significant main effect of gender on math achievement, $F(1, 71) = 13.87$, $p < .001$. Eta for gender was .40, which, according to Cohen (1988), is a large effect. Furthermore, there was a statistically significant main effect of math grades on math achievement, $F(1, 71) = 14.77$, $p < .001$. Eta for math grades was about .41, also a large effect.

Table 11.4a

Means, Standard Deviations, and n for Math Achievement as a Function of Gender and Math Grades

Math Grade	Males			Females			Total	
	n	M	SD	n	M	SD	M	SD
Less A–B	24	12.88	5.73	20	8.33	5.33	10.81	5.94
Most A–B	10	19.27	4.17	21	13.05	7.17	15.05	6.94
Total	34	14.76	6.03	41	10.75	6.70	12.56	6.67

Table 11.4b

Analysis of Variance for Math Achievement as a Function of Gender and Math Grades

Variable and source	df	MS	F	p	η^2
Math grades	1	515.46	14.77	<.001	.172
Gender	1	483.93	13.87	<.001	.163
Math grades× gender	1	11.76	.34	.563	.005
Error	71	34.90			

Interpretation Questions

11.1. In Output 11.1: (a) Describe the *F*, *df,* and *p* values for each dependent variable as you would in an article. (b) Describe the results in nontechnical terms for visualization and grades. Use the group means in your description.

11.2. In Outputs 11.2 a and b, what pairs of means were significantly different?

11.3. In Output 11.3, interpret the meaning of the sig. values for math achievement and competence. What would you conclude, based on this information, about differences between groups on each of these variables?

11.4. Compare Outputs 11.1 and 11.3 with regard to math achievement. What are the most important differences and similarities?

11.5. In Output 11.4: (a) Is the interaction significant? (b) Examine the profile plot of the cell means that illustrates the interaction. Describe it in words. (c) Is the main effect of gender significant? Interpret the eta squared. (d) How about the "effect" of math grades? (e) Why did we put the word effect in quotes? (f) Under what conditions would focusing on the main effects be misleading?

Extra SPSS Problems

Using your College Student data file, do the following problems. Print your outputs after typing your interpretations on them. Please circle the key parts of the output that you use for your interpretation.

11.1. Identify an example of a variable measured at the scale/normally distributed level for which there is a statistically significant overall difference (F) between the three marital status groups. Complete the analysis and interpret the results. Do appropriate post hoc tests.

11.2. Use the Kruskal–Wallis test, with Mann–Whitney post hoc follow-up tests if needed, to run the same problem as 11.1. Compare the results.

11.3. Do students' heights differ depending on gender and marital status, and do gender and marital status interact? Run the appropriate analysis and interpret the results.

11.4. Do gender and having children interact and does either seem to affect current GPA?

11.5. Are there differences between the age groups in regard to the average number of hours they (a) study, (b) work, and (c) watch TV?

APPENDIX A

Getting Started and Other Useful SPSS Procedures

Don Quick
Colorado State University

This section includes step-by-step instructions for procedures related to getting started with SPSS: (a) making a working file, (b) opening and starting SPSS and getting familiar with the **SPSS data editor**, (c) setting your computer so that SPSS will print the **syntax** or **log** along with each output, (d) saving syntax and later using it to rerun statistics, (e) editing your output, (f) importing data and exporting results, (g) converting variables to standardized variables, (h) selecting cases, (i) splitting files,(j) merging files, and (k) case summaries.

Copy the Data Files from the Web Site

The data sets are available to **download** from **http://www.routledge.com/9781848729827**. They are contained in a Zip file under the **Downloads** tab. The ZIP file contains:

    hsbdata.sav (11KB)   **DataFemales.sav (10KB)**
    college student data.sav (4KB)   **DataMales.sav (10KB)**
    Chapter Seven Data.sav (6KB)
    Alternative hsbdataB.sav (13KB) (to use if you skip Chapter 5 or make an error doing it)
Note: you may not see the file extension (.sav) depending on your computer setup.
Download these files to a working folder on your personal flash or network drive.

Open and Start the SPSS Application

- If an **SPSS icon** is available on the desktop, double click on it (see Fig. A.1).
- If there is no icon, click **Start → All Programs → IBM SPSS Statistics → SPSS → IBM SPSS Statistics 20** (see Fig. A.1). If **IBM SPSS Inc** is not listed in the **All Programs** menu, it will need to be installed on your computer. <u>It is not part of the Microsoft Windows package or the Web site for this book</u> and must be loaded separately.

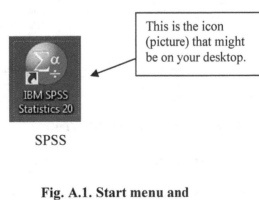

This is the icon (picture) that might be on your desktop.

SPSS

Fig. A.1. Start menu and SPSS icon.

After you start the program, you will see the **SPSS startup screen**. Notice that in the Startup screen, there is a list of SPSS files available on your computer.

- Click the SPSS file you wish to use *OR*
- If no files are listed, click OK to bring up the **Open File** dialogue box to search for the file you want to open. You can also use the **Open File** dialogue box to open SPSS syntax or output files if you want to open those types of files. *OR*
- Click the **Cancel** button, which will bring up a new SPSS desktop screen, called the **SPSS Data Editor,** as shown later in Figs. A.3 and A.4.

Files also can be opened from the program's **Data Editor** screen. In this screen, there are two tabs at the bottom left side of the screen; the **Data View** tab and the **Variable View** tab (see Fig. A.2). Please refer to your SPSS Help menu for further information on how to do this in earlier versions.

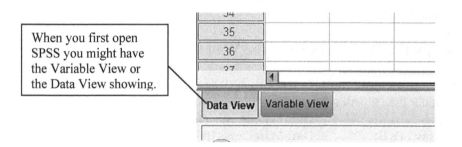

When you first open SPSS you might have the Variable View or the Data View showing.

Fig. A.2. View tabs.

Although the toolbar at the top of the data editor screen is the same for both the Variable and Data View screens, it is important to notice the *subtle* differences in desktop features between these two screens found within the data editor (compare Fig. A.3 and Fig. A.4).

- Click on the **Variable View** tab (see Fig. A.2) in the data editor screen to produce Fig. A.3.

Notice the column headers are those in Fig. A.3 (i.e., Name, Type, Width, etc.). One creates (defines and labels) new variables using the **Variable View** (see Chapter 2).

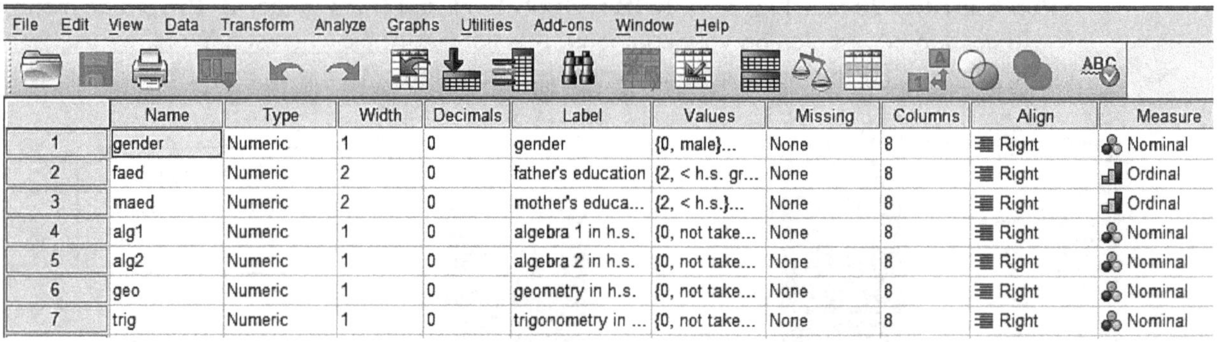

	Name	Type	Width	Decimals	Label	Values	Missing	Columns	Align	Measure
1	gender	Numeric	1	0	gender	{0, male}...	None	8	≡ Right	Nominal
2	faed	Numeric	2	0	father's education	{2, < h.s. gr...	None	8	≡ Right	Ordinal
3	maed	Numeric	2	0	mother's educa...	{2, < h.s.}...	None	8	≡ Right	Ordinal
4	alg1	Numeric	1	0	algebra 1 in h.s.	{0, not take...	None	8	≡ Right	Nominal
5	alg2	Numeric	1	0	algebra 2 in h.s.	{0, not take...	None	8	≡ Right	Nominal
6	geo	Numeric	1	0	geometry in h.s.	{0, not take...	None	8	≡ Right	Nominal
7	trig	Numeric	1	0	trigonometry in ...	{0, not take...	None	8	≡ Right	Nominal

Fig. A.3. SPSS data editor: Variable View.

- Click on the **Data View** tab in the data editor to produce Fig. A.4.

Notice the column headers change to **var** or to the names of your variables if you have already entered them (see Fig. A.4). One enters (inputs) data using the **Data View**.

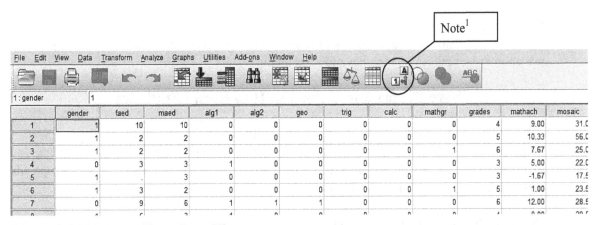

Fig. A.4. SPSS data editor: Data View.

Set Your Computer to Print the SPSS Syntax (Log)

With the current version of the program, your computer will automatically print the SPSS commands on your output, as shown throughout this book. If you are using an earlier version, you may need to turn this function on. To do so, set your computer using the following:

- Click on **Edit → Options.**
- Click on the **Viewer** tab near the top left of the **Options** window to get Fig. A.5 (see the circled tab in Fig. A.5).

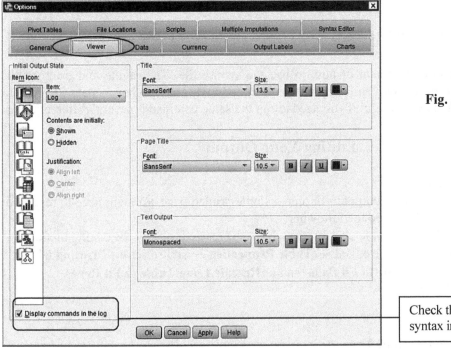

Fig. A.5. Edit: Options.

- Check **Display commands in the log** near the lower left of the window (see oval).

---

[1] If the values for gender are shown as female or male, the value labels rather than the numerals are being displayed. In that case, click on the circled symbol to change the format to show only the numeric values for each variable.

- Leave the other defaults as is.
- Click on **OK.** Doing this will always print the syntax on your output on this computer. If you use another computer you may have to set it again.

Save Syntax and Later Use It to Rerun Statistics

To save and later use syntax to rerun statistics, you will need to do the following:
- Click on **File** → **New** → **Syntax.** Copy and paste the syntax into the syntax editor that you just opened and click **File** → **Save as.** This will save as a **Syntax File (*.sps)** → type file name in dialog box → **Save (**see Figure A.6).

To open a saved syntax file, from the menu choose:
- **File** → **Open** → **Syntax.**
- Select a syntax file → and click **Open**. Navigate to where you saved the syntax file.
- Once a syntax file is open, from the menu choose **Run** → **Selection.**

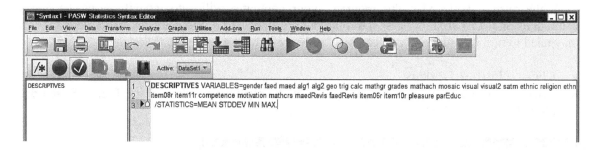

Fig. A.6. SPSS Syntax Editor.

Note: This is a simplified version of how to use the syntax file. The saving and using of the syntax file may be different on your computer depending on whether you have a data file open or not. However, it can be very useful if you need to run the same commands several different times.

Editing Your Output

Resize/Rescale to Print
In order for larger tables in the output to fit onto a single printed page, you will need to rescale or shrink especially wide tables. Do the following:
- From the SPSS Viewer, double click on the table to be resized to enter the editing mode.
- Right click on the table to be edited → **Table Properties** → and select the **Printing** tab.
- Check **Rescale Wide Table to Fit Page** (and/or **Rescale Long Table to Fit Page**).
- Click on **OK.** Close window.
- Print.

Editing Tables, Charts, and Text
When using the SPSS viewer, editing outputs can be done in a variety of ways by either double clicking on any item within the table or chart, or by choosing **Edit** from the menu and scrolling down to **Options**.

- Double click on any item within a table or chart. This will allow you to edit the text size, font, color, change the look of a table, or pivot the table. After double clicking, you can do the following:

To edit text size, font, and color:
- From the menu choose **View** → **Toolbar**. This will activate the **Formatting Toolbar** if it hasn't already been activated.

To customize a table, including text, alignment, shading, footnotes, cell formats, borders, and printing options:
- From the menu choose **Format** → **Table Properties**.

To change the look of a table:
- From the menu choose **Format** → **TableLooks.**
- The **TableLooks** dialog box will appear listing a variety of predefined styles.
- A style can be previewed in the Sample window to the right of the TableLooks dialog box. (See Appendix C on making tables.)

To modify the table layouts and data order:
- From the menu choose **Pivot.**
- The **Pivoting Trays** window will appear which provides a way to move data between columns, rows, and layers.

Most of the table editing procedures can also be completed by choosing **Edit**, then scrolling down to **Options** in the SPSS viewer menu or by right clicking what you want to edit.

Importing Data and Exporting Results

SPSS allows you to import data from Microsoft Access or Excel (or other ODBC data sources) and export results outputs to Microsoft Excel and Word, or other file types.

To import from MS Access or Excel
- From the SPSS viewer menu choose **File** → **Open Database** → **New Query**
- The **Database Wizard** will guide you through the process of importing data.

To export results
- When the output you wish to export is open, from the SPSS viewer menu choose **File** → **Export**. The **Export Output** window will appear (see Figure A.7).
- Under **Type** you must choose the file type that you want.
- Under **File Name**, you can click on the **Browse...** button to choose where to save the new file and change its name if you want.
- Click **OK** to generate the file.

Note: You can also export individual elements of the output by right clicking on the element and selecting **Export.**

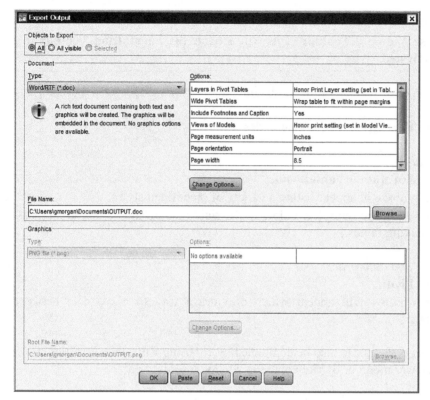

Fig. A.7. Export output.

Converting Variables into Standardized Variables (z Scores)

This procedure transforms the data for one variable to a standard score that has a mean of zero and a standard deviation of one. Standardized scores are used when you want to compute a summated scale score made up of variables with quite different means and standard deviations. They are also used to compare apples and oranges, for example, achievement on a math test and an English test. Next we will make the *math achievement* scores into z scores.

- Click on **Analyze →Descriptive Statistics → Descriptives…**
- Select the variable *math achievement.*
- Click the arrow in the middle of the dialog box to move the variable to the **Variables** box.
- Check the box **Save Standardized Values as Variables.**
- Click **OK.** An output window will appear with the descriptive statistics. The z score for each subject will be included as a new variable (*Zmathach*) in the last column of the SPSS Data Editor. The variable *Zmathach* and the first few z scores are shown in Fig. A.8.

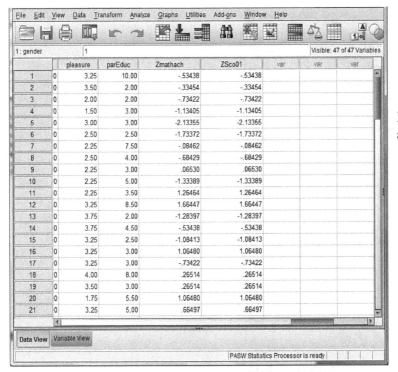

Fig. A.8. *z* scores for math achievement.

Selecting Cases

The select cases command permits the analysis of a specific subset of the data. Once a subset is selected and used for the analysis, the user can either revert to the entire data set by clicking on reset, or you can delete the unselected cases to create a new data file of the selected cases. If you want to do the same analysis separately on all subsets of data, then **Split File** should be used instead of **Select Cases** (see below). It is advisable to <u>save your work before deleting cases</u>, just in case you change your mind! To select cases:

- Click on **Data → Select Cases.**
- Choose the method of selecting cases you prefer: (a) **If condition is satisfied** (a conditional expression is used to select cases), (b) **Random sample of cases** (cases are selected randomly based on a percent or number of cases), (c) **Based on time or case range** (case selection is based on a range of case numbers or a range of dates/time), or (d) **Use filter variable** (a numeric variable can be used as the filter—any cases with a value other than 0 or missing are selected). **Unselected cases** may be **Filtered** (remain in the data file but are excluded in the analysis) or **Deleted** (removed from the working data file and cannot be recovered if the data file is saved after the deletion). (See Fig. A.9.)
- For example, if you wanted to select only males, you would use **If condition is satisfied** and click on the **If...** button.
- Then type gender = 0 and click **Continue**. Your window should look like Fig. A.9.
- Click on **OK.**

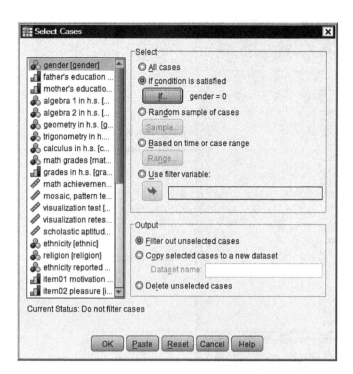

Fig. A.9. Select cases.

Splitting Files

Split Files splits the data file into separate groups for analysis based on the values of one or more grouping variables. Data can be displayed for group comparisons, or data can be displayed separately for each group (see Fig. A.10). This is a very useful tool, but <u>be sure to reset **Split File** after doing the analyses you want split, or all further analyses will be split in the same way</u>. In this example, we will split the hsbdata.sav file into two files, one with the data for the males and one with the data for the females.

- **Data → Split File**.
- Select the appropriate radio button for the desired display option (**Compare groups** or **Organize output by groups**). Be sure the **Sort the file by grouping variables** is selected. The window should look like Figure A.10.
- Click on **OK**.

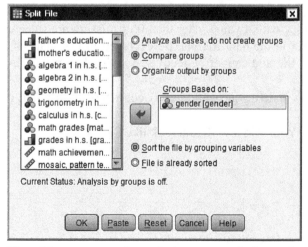

Fig. A.10. Split file.

Note: Now you can do statistics separately for males and females.

Merging Files

Merge files allows the working data file to be combined with a second data file that contains (a) the *same variables but different cases* or (b) the *same cases but different variables*.

To Add Cases
An example of merging files with the same variables but different cases might be if you had all the males for the hsbdata set in one file and all the females in another. In order to compare males and females, these two data files need to be merged.

- Open both data files you want to merge. In this example, open DataMales.sav and DataFemales.sav. (They are on the Web site for this book.)
- In the DataFemales.sav file, click on **Data → Merge Files → Add Cases**.
- The **Add Cases to DataFemales.sav [DataSet2]** window will open (see Fig. A.11).
- Highlight **DataMales.sav [DataSet1]** and then click on **Continue**.

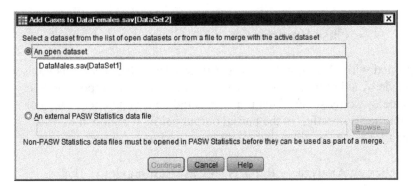

Fig. A.11. Add cases to DataFemales.sav [DataSet1].

- The **Add Cases from DataMales.sav [DataSet1]** will open. (See Fig. A.12.)

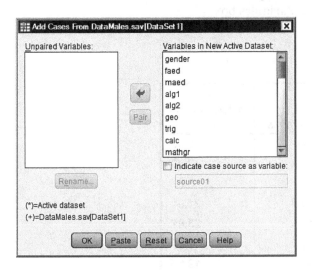

Fig. A.12. Add cases from DataMales.sav [DataSet1].

- Click on **OK.** The data from the DataMales.sav file will be added to the DataFemales.sav file.

Using a similar procedure, you can merge two files that have the same, or at least overlapping cases but different variables.

To Add Variables

Before you add <u>variables</u> to a file using this method, you should first make sure that each participant who has data in both data sets is identified by the same ID number in both files. Then, you should use **Sort Cases** to sort each file (by itself), sequentially in ascending order, saving each file once it is sorted. You should make sure that you open the data file <u>first</u> that has the correct values of any variables that exist in both data sets. SPSS will save only one copy of each variable, and that will be the one that is in the first (working data) file.

- Click on **Data → Merge Files → Add Variables.**
- In the **Add Variables to...** window (similar to Fig. A.11), select the dataset you want to add a variable from and click **Continue**.
- In the **Add Variables from...** window (similar to Fig. A.12), select **Match cases on key variables in sorted files** to select a key variable. A key variable must be a variable common to both datasets (such as a participant ID) which SPSS will use to match the participants from the two datasets. Choices for a key variable will appear in the **Excluded Variables:** box.
- Click on such a variable and move it into the **Key Variables:** box.
- Click on **OK**.

Case Summaries

A useful report that can be printed with SPSS is called **Case Summaries**. This report lets you see the data for several variables side by side for each participant. You can have the report include all participants or, as we have below, only some. This function could be used to check whether you have computed a transformation correctly. In the partial output below we show how you could visually examine the data for three variables that might be related to *math achievement*.

- In the DataMales.sav file, click on **Analyze → Reports → Case Summaries...** The **Summarize Cases** window will open.
- Select the variables *father's education, math grades, grades in h.s., and math achievement.*
- Click the arrow to move the variables to the **Variables** box.
- Change the "Limit cases to first" box to **10**.
- Click on **OK**.

a

	father's education	math grades	grades in h.s.	math achievement test
1	h.s. grad	less A-B	half CD	5.00
2	master's	less A-B	mostly B	12.00
3	coll grad	less A-B	half BC	3.67
4	h.s. grad	less A-B	mostly B	21.00
5	coll grad	most A-B	mostly A	23.67
6	< 2 yrs coll	less A-B	mostly D	9.00
7	.	most A-B	half AB	19.67
8	h.s. grad	less A-B	half AB	7.67
9	master's	less A-B	half BC	14.33
10	h.s. grad	most A-B	mostly B	14.33

Limited to first 10 cases.

APPENDIX B

Writing Research Problems and Questions

Frameworks for Stating Research Problems

A common definition of a research problem is that it is a statement that asks what relationship exists between two or more variables. However, most research problems are more complex than this definition implies. The research problem should be a broad statement that covers several more specific research questions to be investigated, perhaps by using summary terms that stand for several variables. Several ways to state the research problem are provided in this appendix. Underlines indicate that you fill in the appropriate name for the variable or group of variables.

Format

One way that you could phrase the problem is as follows: The research problem is to investigate whether (put independent variable 1 or group of variables here) (and independent variable 2, if any, here) (and independent variable 3, if any) are related to (dependent variable 1, here) (and dependent variable 2, if any) in (population here).

Except in a totally descriptive study, there always must be at least two variables (one is usually called the independent variable and one the dependent variable). However, there can be two or more of each, and there often are. In the statement of the problem, in contrast to the research questions/hypotheses, it is desirable to use broad descriptors for groups of similar variables. For example, in the hsb data demographics might cover four variables: gender, mother's and father's education, and ethnicity. Spatial performance might include a mosaic pattern test score and a visualization score. Likewise, grades and mathematics attitudes could each refer to more than one variable. Concepts such as self-esteem or teaching style have several aspects that usually result in more than one variable.

Examples

If your study uses the randomized experimental approach, you could phrase the problem as:

1. The research problem is to investigate the effect of a new curriculum on grades, math attitudes, and spatial performance in high school students.

For other studies that compare groups or associate/relate variables, you could phrase the problem as follows:

2. The problem is to investigate whether gender and grades are related to mathematics attitudes and achievement in high school students.

If you have several *independent variables* and want to predict some outcome, you could say:

3. The problem is to investigate the variables that predict or *seem* to influence mathematics achievement.

This latter format is especially useful when the approach is a complex (several independent variables) associational one that will use multiple regression.

Framework for Stating Research Questions/Hypotheses

Although it is okay to phrase a randomized experimental research problem (in the format of the first example earlier) as a "study of the effect of ...," we think when a study is not a randomized experiment, it is best to phrase your research questions or hypotheses so that they do not appear to imply cause and effect (i.e., as *difference* or *associational* questions/hypotheses and/or as *descriptive* questions). The former are answered with inferential statistics, and descriptive questions are answered with descriptive statistics. There are several reasonable ways to state research questions. In the following, we show one way to state each type of question, which we have found useful and, hopefully, clear for our students.

Descriptive Questions

Basic descriptive questions. Descriptive questions ask about the central tendency, frequency distribution, percentage in each category, variability, or shape of the distribution of a variable. Some descriptive questions are intended to test assumptions. Some questions simply describe the sample demographics; others describe a dependent variable. A few *examples* are:

1. Is mathematics achievement distributed approximately normally?
2. What percentage of participants is of each gender?
3. What are the mean, mode, and median of the mathematics achievement scores?

Complex descriptive questions. These questions deal with two or more variables at a time, but do not involve inferential statistics. Cross-tabulations of two categorical variables, factor analysis, and measures of reliability (e.g., Cronbach's alpha) are examples.

Two *examples* are:
1. What is the internal consistency reliability of the pleasure scale items?
2. What are the percentages of males and females in each of the three main religious groups (Protestant, Catholic, not religious)?

Difference Questions/Hypotheses

Basic difference questions. The *format* is:

Are there statistically significant differences between the (insert number) levels of (put the independent variable name here) (you could name the levels here in parentheses) in regard to the average (put the dependent variable name here) scores? Another acceptable format is shown in example 2.

Two *examples* are:
1. Are there statistically significant differences between the three levels (high, medium, and low) of father's education in regard to the average mathematics achievement scores of the students?
2. Is there a statistically significant difference between males and females on the visualization score?

Appropriate analyses: One-way ANOVA (see Chapter 10). A *t* test could be used if there were only two levels of the independent variable, as in example 2 (see Chapter 9).

Complex difference and interaction questions. When you have two categorical independent variables considered together, you will have *three* research questions or hypotheses. There are advantages to considering two or three independent variables at a time. See Chapter 10 for an introduction about how to interpret the *interaction* question. Sample *formats* for a set of three questions answered by *one* 2-way ANOVA are as follows:

1. Is there a statistically significant difference between (<u>insert the levels of independent variable 1</u>) in regard to the average (<u>put dependent variable 1 here</u>) scores?
2. Is there a statistically significant difference between (<u>insert the levels of independent variable 2</u>) in regard to the average (<u>dependent variable 1</u>) scores?
3. Is there a statistically significant interaction of (<u>independent **variable 1**</u>) and (<u>independent **variable 2**</u>) in regard to the (<u>**dependent** variable 1</u>)?

(Repeat these three questions, for the second dependent variable, if there is more than one.) An *example* is as follows:

1. Is there a statistically significant difference between students who have high versus low math grades in regard to their average mathematics achievement scores?
2. Is there a statistically significant difference between male and female students in regard to their average math achievement scores?
3. Is there a statistically significant interaction between mathematics grades and gender in regard to math achievement?

Note that the first question states the *levels* or categories of the first independent variable; that is, it states the groups that are to be compared (high vs. low math grade students). The second question does the same for the second independent variable; that is, it states the *levels* (male and female) to be compared. However, the third (interaction) question asks whether the first *variable* itself (mathematics grades) interacts with the second variable (gender). No mention is made, in the interaction question, of the values or levels or groups.

An appropriate analysis: Factorial ANOVA (see Chapter 10).

Associational/Relationship Questions/Hypotheses

Basic associational questions. When both variables are ordered and essentially continuous (i.e., have five or more ordered categories), we consider the approach and research question to be associational. There are two main types of basic associational statistics: correlation and regression.

The *format* for a correlation is as follows:

Is there a statistically significant association between (<u>variable 1</u>) and (<u>variable 2</u>)?

In this case, it is arbitrary which variable is independent or antecedent and which is dependent or outcome unless one occurs before the other in time; see example 3. An *example* for a single association or relationship is as follows:

1. Is there a statistically significant association between grades in high school and mathematics achievement?

If there are more than two variables, which is common, and each pair of variables is associated separately, you can have a series of questions asking whether there is an association between *each* variable and every other variable. This would produce a *correlation matrix*.

An *example* that would produce a correlation matrix is as follows:
2.   Are there statistically significant associations among the <u>three</u> mathematics attitude scale scores?

Note that what is said to be associated in these questions is the variable itself; no mention is made of the levels or values here.

If one variable is clearly the independent, antecedent, or predictor, you would phrase the question as follows and use *bivariate regression* analyses:

3. How well can we predict math achievement test scores (the dependent variable) from grades in high school (the independent variable)?

Appropriate analyses: Bivariate regression if there is a clear independent or antecedent variable and you want to make a prediction; correlation if there is no clear independent variable (see Chapter 8).

Complex associational questions. In the associational approach, when two or more *independent* variables are considered together, rather than separately, as in the previous basic format, you get a new kind of question. The *format* can be phrased something like:

How well does the combination of (<u>list the several specific independent variables here</u>) predict (<u>put dependent variable here</u>)?

Two *examples* are as follows:
1.   How well does the combination of number of mathematics courses taken, gender, and father's education predict mathematics achievement?
2.   How well does a combination of H.S. ACT, GPA, and rank in class predict first year college GPA?

An appropriate analysis: Multiple regression (see Chapter 8).

The first complex question above also could be expanded, into a set of questions, to help you understand more fully. This set first asks about the association of each of the predictors (or independent) variables and the dependent (or outcome) variable and then states the complex or combination question as earlier.

For *example*:
1.   Is there a statistically significant association between the number of mathematics courses taken and mathematics achievement test scores?
2.   Is there a statistically significant association between gender and mathematics achievement?
3.   Is there a statistically significant association between father's education and mathematics achievement?
4.   How well does the combination of the number of mathematics courses taken, gender, and father's education predict mathematics achievement test scores?

Appropriate analysis: The multiple regression output will provide you with the three bivariate, Pearson correlations in a matrix as well as the multiple regression statistics (see, for example, Output 8.6).

APPENDIX C

Answers to Odd Numbered Interpretation Questions

Chapter 1

1.1 Compare the terms active independent variable and attribute independent variable. What are the similarities and differences?

An *attribute independent variable* is a characteristic or a "part" of the participants, whether or not the study takes place. It is not manipulated by the researcher. Some common attribute variables, such as ethnicity, gender, and IQ, are not easily changed. Other attributes, such as age, income, job title, personality traits, and attitudes, can change over time. The key characteristic of *attribute independent variables* is that they are *measured, not manipulated*. An *active independent variable* is manipulated or caused to vary systematically. The treatment or condition that the group receives may be determined by the experimenter or sometimes by someone else, often a group (school, clinic, etc.). The researcher or other person actively gives different groups different treatments, and the differences between groups that have different treatments are usually the focus of the study. The most common active variable is when an experimental and comparison group receive different treatments (curricula, interventions, etc). The participants might be randomly assigned to groups or already be in intact groups such as school classes.

1.3. What is the difference between the independent variable and the dependent variable?

In the classic definition of the independent variable, it is the variable that is manipulated; however, in this book and commonly in the field, the term "independent variable" is used more broadly to mean the *presumed cause* of differences in the outcome variable. The scores or values for the dependent variable "depend on" the level of the independent variable. For example, you might have an experiment in which you are testing the effectiveness of a new weight reduction plan, say reduced carbohydrates. The independent variable involves whether or not the participant was on the low carbohydrate diet. One group (one level of the independent variable) is given and follows a low carbohydrate diet, whereas the other group (the other level of the independent variable) eats their normal diet. Then to determine if the low carbohydrate system works, the researcher might make weight measurements before the low carbohydrate diet is initiated and again following a certain period of time (during which one group was on the low carbohydrate diet and one was not). The weight measurements serve as the dependent variable. Thus, the researcher is hoping that the low carbohydrate treatment (the independent variable) affects a change in weight (the dependent variable).

1.5 Write a research question and a corresponding hypothesis regarding variables of interest to you but not in the HSB data set. Is it an associational, difference, or descriptive question?

Of course the answers to this question will vary greatly. An associational question will most likely involve the relation between two normally distributed variables, for example, "Is there an association between IQ scores and SAT scores for high school seniors?" Difference questions usually compare two to four groups on some outcome variable. For example, "Are there differences between three different weight loss programs in regard to the average weight loss?"

Although it should be the easiest, often students misunderstand descriptive questions. Descriptive questions do NOT try to make inferences about the larger population and group differences are associations that exist generally. They are limited to trying to understand the distributional characteristics of the data for the specific group of people who were studied. You might ask, "What is the average weight loss of all participants in the study?" Or, "What is the average age of all participants in the study?" Descriptive questions are not answered with inferential statistics such as a *t* test.

Chapter 2

2.1. What steps or actions should be taken after you collect data and before you run any analyses?

(a) Decide how to code each variable (i.e., what numbers/values to use with each type of response).
(b) Check the data (e.g., questionnaires) to see if participant responses can be coded consistently and accurately with your coding rules; fix any problems.
(c) Define and label variables with SPSS.
(d) Enter the data; the data can be entered directly from the original questionnaires or from a coding sheet. Some prefer to enter the data in a spreadsheet program first (e.g., Excel) then import it into SPSS.
(e) Compare the data that you entered with the original data (e.g., questionnaires).
(f) Finally, check by running a few simple descriptive statistics to look for errors in the data. For example, if you have a variable with scores ranging from 1 to 5, the maximum value in any field should not be greater than 5 nor less than 1.

2.3. Why would you print a codebook?

Codebooks serve as a dictionary for your data. It provides a way to check what was entered for each variable so that you understand the meaning of the variable and its levels, special missing value codes, and the level of measurement.

2.5. If the university in the example allowed for double majors in different colleges (such that it would actually be possible for a student to be in two colleges), how would you handle cases in which two colleges are checked? Why?

There are a number of possible correct answers to this question. One good answer would be to create another category, 4 = other (e.g., more than one college, undeclared college). Another would be to create a separate category for double majors across colleges: 4 = double major in two colleges. The first solution would be better if such double majors are rare (more participants would be included if the category were more inclusive). The second option would be better if double majors and/or undeclared colleges were common.

Chapter 3

3.1. If you have categorical, ordered data (such as low income, middle income, high income) what type of measurement would you have? Why?

The type of measurement you would have would be ordinal. The key here is that the data are ordered. Low income is clearly lower than middle income, but the data are not interval or normal because the distances between the low, middle, and high income categories are probably not equal, and our definition of approximately normal specifies that there be five or more ordered categories. This is a little tricky because the term categorical is often associated with nominal; however, if the categories are ordered, the variable is better treated as ordinal.

3.3. What percent of the area under the standard normal curve is between the mean and one standard deviation above (or below) the mean?

Approximately 34% above and 34% below. The exact percentage is 34.13. Approximately 32% of the scores lie more than one standard deviation away from the mean.

3.5. Why should you not use a frequency polygon if you have nominal data? What would be better to use to display nominal data?

Frequency polygons are designed for use with normally distributed or scale data because they are depicting the data as continuously increasing in value across the graph. Better ways to display nominal data would include the frequency distribution or the bar chart.

Chapter 4

4.1. Using Output 4.1: (a) What is the mean *visualization score*? (b) What is the skewness statistic for *math achievement*? What does this tell us? (c) What is the minimum score for the *mosaic pattern test*? How can that be?

(a) 5.24
(b) .044. This tells us that the variable is not very skewed (i.e., is approximately normally distributed).
(c) −4.0. At first this may seem like an error. However, if you check the codebook, you will see that visualization scores go from −4 to 16. The −4 score also verifies that at least one person scored the lowest possible score, which is probably negative due to a penalty for guessing wrong.

4.3. Using Output 4.2b: (a) How many participants have missing data? (b) What percentage of students has a valid (nonmissing) score for both motivation and competence? (c) Can you tell from Outputs 4.1 and 4.2b how many are missing both motivation and competence scores? How?

(a) 4
(b) 94.7%
(c) In Output 4.1b, you can see that there were 73 competence scale scores and 73 motivation scale scores. In Output 4.2b, you can see that only 71 had both of the scores. Therefore, no one is missing both motivation and competence scores, because two are missing each of the scores, and four are missing at least one of the scores.

4.5.   Using Output 4.5: (a) 9.6% of what group are Asian Americans? (b) What percentage of students has visualization 2 scores of 6? (c) What percent had scores of 6 or less?

(a)   This is the percentage of subjects in the study who made a valid answer to this question and listed themselves as Asian Americans. It does not include those who left the question blank or checked more than one ethnic group.

(b)   There are no missing data on this variable, so the valid percent and the percent are both the same, and the answer is 5.3%.

(c)   70.7%. This is read from the cumulative percent column.

Chapter 5

5.1.   Using your initial HSB data file (the file in Chapter 1), compare the original data to your new variables: (a) How many math courses did Participant 1 take? (b) What should *faedrRevis* be for Participants 2, 5, and 8? (c) What should the pleasure scale score be for Participant 1? (d) Why is comparing a few initial scores to transformed scores important?

(a)   None.

(b)   1, missing, and 2, respectively.

(c)   3.25.

(d)   It is easy to make an error in setting up the transformation command, thus giving you wrong data after transformation. Checking a few data points is reassuring and gives you confidence in your data. The computer will not make computation errors, but you might give it the wrong recoding or computing instructions.

5.3.   Why did you reverse Questions 6 and 10?

These two questions are worded such that higher scores on the item reflect lower amounts of the characteristic being measured by that subscale. Thus, for items 02 and 14, a 4 is high pleasure and 1 is low pleasure, but for these two (Items 06 and 10) it is the opposite. Therefore, we cannot add these four items together unless we reverse the coding on Items 06 and 10 so that a 4 = 1, 3 = 2, 2 = 3, and 1 = 4. Then all four items will have high pleasure equal to 4.

5.5.   When would you use the Mean function to compute an average? And when would the Mean function not be appropriate?

If participants have completed most items on a construct or scale composed of several questions, the SPSS "Mean" function allows you to compute the average score on that variable for *all the participants* by using the average of their responses for the items that they did answer.

When computing a multiple item scale, it is important *not to use* the Mean function if respondents only answered one or a few items. For example, if the construct of math anxiety was being measured and math anxiety was composed of responses to seven items, but some respondents only completed two or three of the seven items, the Mean function would give a biased answer.

Chapter 6

6.1. Compare and contrast a between-groups design and a within-subjects design.

In a *between-groups design,* different people get different treatments or have different levels of the independent variable. In other words, each level of the independent variable indicates a particular treatment that participants in that group received or a particular attribute participants share, and participants are classified into groups based on these differences. For example, you might want to see if one 8th grade math curriculum is more effective than another. Each level of the independent variable in this between-groups design would involve a different set of students.

In a *within-subjects design*, the same people get multiple treatments or are measured on the same variable at different times (or related/matched people get the same treatment or are measured on the same variable). This design is sometimes referred to as a repeated-measures design. The most common example of this design is a pretest posttest design. All students take the pretest and the same students take the posttest. Another example is when a group of people are being monitored over time. Twenty people might enter an exercise program and their blood pressure and cholesterol levels might be measured each week for 10 weeks. The independent variable in a within-subjects design is sometimes referred to as "time," and is used to assess how the dependent variable changes as a function of time (i.e., differences across different levels of the "time" variable in the dependent variable). For example, "was there a significant change in the cholesterol levels and blood pressure levels over the 10-week period?" is a within-subjects design question. It is also a within-subjects design if pairs of subjects are matched and then compared because the subjects are systematically related to each other and do not meet the assumptions of a between-subjects design. It is also a within-subjects design if there is a family link between participants. For example, is there a difference between students' height and students' same sex parent's height?

6.3.   Provide an example of a study, including identifying the variables, level of measurement, and hypotheses, for which a researcher could <u>appropriately</u> choose two different statistics to examine the relations between the same variables. Explain your answer.

Answers will vary. We have presented an example to assist in your understanding:
Hypothesis: More guilt-prone adults are more likely to help out a needy child than are less guilt-prone adults.
IV: guilt proneness on an ordered 5-point scale (20+ adults at each level)
DV: helping behavior (normally distributed), measured by how much of the participant's prize money for participating in a study is donated to "a needy child" (jar with poster of child and a sign requesting help).
One could use ANOVA to compare the five groups, with each level of guilt proneness creating a separate group of participants. Post hoc tests would allow one to determine whether each pair of guilt levels differ; the hypothesis predicts that high (e.g., levels 4 and 5) guilt-prone adults would help more than low (e.g., levels 1 and 2) guilt-prone persons. Because both variables have five or more levels, one could also use correlation to examine this if one thought that there should be a linear relation between guilt proneness and altruism.

6.5. Interpret the following related to effect size:

(a) $d = .25$ Small or smaller than typical
(b) $r = .35$ Medium or typical
(c) $R = .53$ Large or larger than typical
(d) $r = .13$ Small or smaller than typical
(e) $d = 1.15$ Much larger than typical
(f) eta $= .38$ Large or larger than typical

6.7. What statistic would you use if you had two independent variables, income group (< $10,000, $10,000–$30,000, > $30,000) and ethnic group (Hispanic, Caucasian, African-American), and one normally distributed dependent variable (self-efficacy at work).

Factorial ANOVA (This would be a 3 × 3 factorial ANOVA.).

6.9. What statistic would you use if you had three normally distributed (scale) independent variables (weight of participants, age of participants, and height of participants), plus one dichotomous independent variable (gender) and one dependent variable (positive self-image), which is normally distributed?

Multiple regression.

Chapter 7

7.1. Write an additional sentence or two that you might include in a detailed research report describing the disagreements in Output 7.1. Why are these disagreements important to consider?

There were six disagreements between the ethnicity reported in the school records and the ethnicity reported by the student. These included one student whose record indicated they were Euro-American, but who self-identified as African-American; three students whose record indicated they were African-American but two self-identified as Euro-American and one as Latino-American; and two students who self-identified as African-American but whose school's record showed they were Latino-American and Asian-American.

These disagreements are important to consider since they may be errors in the school's record or errors in the self-identified data. Or, the student may self-identify themselves based on different criteria.

7.3 In Output 7.3 which factor explained the most variance? Why is this important?

Factor 1 explained the most variance (21.55%). This is important to consider because if there is one factor that explains most of the variance, then the scale may only have one factor to consider.

7.5. If you had to delete one question from the analysis in Output 7.3a, which one would you delete?

By looking at the Item-Total Statistics table, the last column under "Cronbach's Alpha if Item Deleted," one can see that item 05 reversed would decrease the alpha the most if it were deleted so you wouldn't want to delete it. Item 11 reversed is the best one to delete if we had to delete one because deleting it would increase Cronbach's alpha from .856 to .869.

Chapter 8

8.1.   In Output 8.1: (a) What do the terms "count" and "expected count" mean? (b) What does the difference between them tell you?

(a) The count is the actual number of subjects in that cell. For example, in this output, 24 males and 20 females had low math grades. The expected count is what you would expect to find in the cell given the marginal totals (the values in the "total" column and row) if there were no relationship between the variables.

(b) If the expected count and the actual count are similar, there is probably not a significant difference between males and females in this data set. If, however, there is a large difference between expected and actual count, you would expect to find a significant chi-square.

8.3.   In Output 8.2: (a) How is the risk ratio calculated? What does it tell you? (b) How is the odds ratio calculated and what does it tell you? (c) How could information about the odds ratio be useful to people wanting to know the practical importance of research results? (d) What are some limitations of the odds ratio as an effect size measure?

(a) The risk ratio for students with low math grades is the percentage of those students who didn't take algebra 2 who have low math grades (70%), divided by the percentage of those students who did take algebra 2 who have low math grades (45%). In this case, students who don't take algebra 2 are about 1½ times as likely to have low math grades as those who do take algebra 2.
(b) The odds ratio is the ratio of the risk ratios for students with low and with high math grades. It tells you that one is almost three times as likely to get low grades as high grades if one didn't take algebra 2.
(c) The odds ratio is useful because it describes the likelihood that people will have a certain outcome given a certain other condition. One can then judge whether or not these odds justify the intervention/ treatment.
(d) Unfortunately, there are no agreed upon standards as to what is a large odds ratio.

8.5.   In Output 8.4: (a) How do you know which is the appropriate value of eta? (b) Do you think it is high or low? Why? (c) How would you describe the results?

(a) The eta with math courses taken as the dependent variable is the appropriate eta, because we are thinking of gender as predicting math courses taken, rather than the reverse.
(b) It is medium (average) to large, using Cohen's criteria; however, gender does not explain very much variance (.11) in how many math courses are taken.
(c) The results indicate that boys are likely to take more math courses than are girls.

Chapter 9

9.1.   Why would we graph scatterplots and regression lines?

The most important reason is to check for violations in the assumptions of correlation and regression. Both the Pearson correlation and regression statistic assume a linear relationship. Viewing the scatterplot lines allows the researcher to check to see if there are marked violations of linearity (e.g., the data may be curvilinear). In regression, there may be better fitting lines such as a quadratic (one bend) or cubic (two bends) that would explain the data more accurately. Graphing the data also allows you to easily see outliers.

9.3.   In Output 9.3, how many of the Pearson correlation coefficients are significant? Write an interpretation of (a) one of the significant and (b) one of the nonsignificant correlations in Output 8.3. Include whether or not the correlation is significant, your decision about the null hypothesis, and a sentence or two describing the correlations in nontechnical terms. Include comments related to the sign (direction) and to the effect size.

There are five significant correlations: (1) visualization with scholastic aptitude test – math, (2) visualization with math achievement test, (3) scholastic aptitude test – math and grades in high school, (4) scholastic aptitude test – math with math achievement, and (5) grades in high school with math achievement. There are several possible answers to the rest of this question; we present two examples.

(a)   There was a significant positive association between scores on a math achievement test and grades in high school ($r_{(73)} = .504$, $p < .001$). In general, those who scored high on the math achievement test also had higher grades in high school. Likewise, those who did not score well on the math achievement test did not do as well on their high school grades. The effect size ($r = .50$) was larger than typical. The null hypothesis stating that there was no relationship can be rejected.

(b)   There was not a significant relationship between the visualization test scores and grades in high school ($r_{(73)} = .127$, $p = .279$). Although this could be said to be a very small positive effect size, the direction of the relationship and effect size should not be discussed because the magnitude of this correlation is so low (and nonsignificant) that it can be viewed as a chance deviation from zero. There is little evidence from this data set to support a relationship between these two variables. The null hypothesis is not rejected.

9.4.   Using Output 9.5, find the regression weight (B) and the standardized regression (beta) weight. (a) How do these compare to the correlation between the same variables in Output 9.2? (b) What does the regression weight tell you? (c) Give an example of a research problem in which Pearson correlation would be more appropriate than bivariate regression, and one in which bivariate regression would be more appropriate than Pearson correlation.

(a)   The term regression weight refers to the unstandardized (B) coefficient for grades, which is 2.142. The *bivariate* correlation (R on the output, but actually r because it is bivariate) and the standardized (beta) coefficient are the same, in this case .504. This is also the same as the Pearson correlation in Ouput 9.3. So with two variables the correlation ($r = .504$) and the standardized bivariate regression weight ($\beta = .504$) are the same.

(b)   The unstandardized coefficient (B) allows you to build a formula to predict math achievement based upon grades. B is the slope of the best fit regression line.

(c) The key here is that bivariate regression gives you the ability to predict from one variable to another, where correlation shows the strength of the relationship but does not involve prediction. Correlation is more appropriate than bivariate regression when there is no clear independent or antecedent variable (perhaps both variables were assessed at the same time) and there was no intention to predict. So an example of a situation in which a Pearson correlation would be more appropriate would be if one wanted to assess the relations between a person's height and his/her weight. One does not in any way assume that weight causes height or height causes weight; nor was there any intent to predict one variable from the other. In contrast, one might prefer a regression if one wanted to predict math grades in college from SAT quantitative scores. The idea in this case is to know, before a student attends college, whether or not she or he is likely to succeed in the math course, so a regression is more appropriate.

Chapter 10

10.1. (a) Under what conditions would you use a one-sample t test?
      (b) Provide another possible example of its use from the HSB data.

(a) It is not uncommon to want to compare the mean of a variable in your data set to another mean for which you do not have the individuals' scores. One example of this is comparing a sample with the national norm. You could also compare the mean of your sample to that from a different study. For example, you might want to replicate a study involving GPA, and ask how the GPA in your study this year compares to the GPA in the replicated study of 10 years ago, but you only have the mean GPA (not the raw data) from that study.

(b) We could compare the mean in the HSB data set with national norms for the visualization test, the mosaic pattern test, or the math achievement test. Comparing our data with national norms could help us justify that the HSB data set is similar to all students or tell us that there is a significant difference between our HSB data and national norms.

10.3. (a) Compare the results of Output 10.2 and 10.3.
      (b) When would you use the Mann–Whitney U test?

(a) Note that, although the two tests are based on different assumptions, the significance levels (i.e., p values) and results were similar for the t test and the M–W that used the same variables. Males and females were significantly different on math achievement ($p = .009$ and .010, respectively) and on visualization scores ($p = .020$ and .040), but there was not a significant difference between males and females on grades in high school ($p = .369$ and .413).

(b) The Mann–Whitney U is used to compare two groups, as is a t test, but you should use the M–W when you have ordinal (not normally distributed) dependent variable data. The M–W can also be used when the assumption of equal group variances is violated.

10.5. (a) Compare the results of Output 10.4 and 10.5.
      (b) When would you use the Wilcoxon test?

(a) The paired *t* test for father's and mother's education gives similar statistical significance results ($p = .019$) to the Wilcoxon ($p = 037$) for the same variables.

(b) The Wilcoxon test would be used when the variables are not normally distributed.

Chapter 11

11.1. In Output 11.1: (a) Describe the *F*, *df*, and *p* values for each dependent variable as you would in an article. (b) Describe the results in nontechnical terms for visualization and grades. Use the group means in your discussion.

(a) There is a significant difference between father's education groups on students' grades in high school, $F(2, 70) = 4.09$, $p = .021$ and on their math achievement scores, $F(2, 70) = 7.88$, $p = .001$. In order to fully interpret these results, you need to do additional comparisons between specific groups to see if differences are significant. There is not a significant difference between father's education groups on students' visualization scores. Note that between-groups degrees of freedom is 2 because there are 3 groups, $3 - 1 = 2$. The degrees of freedom within is the total minus the number of groups or $73 - 3 = 70$.

(b) There is not a significant difference in average student visualization scores among the groups of students who have fathers with a high school or less education, with some college education, or with a B.S. or more. There is one or more significant differences among the father's educational level groups in regard to their child's grades in high school. Students who had parents with a B.S. or better received average grades of 6.53, which, using the codebook, is approximately a 3.25 GPA, halfway between mostly Bs and half As and half Bs. Students who had parents with some college had mean grades of 5.56, about a 2.75 GPA. Students whose parents had a high school degree or less (mean = 5.34) had an average about 2.65.

In Output 11.1 we did not run post hoc tests. To see if these group differences are statistically significant, we would need to use a post hoc test as we did in Output 11.2.

11.3. In Output 11.3, interpret the meaning of the sig. values for math achievement and competence. What would you conclude, based on this information, about differences between groups on each of these variables?

Using the Kruskal–Wallis test, there is a significant difference somewhere among the three parental educational levels on math achievement (chi-square = 13.384, $df = 2$, $N = 73$, $p = .001$). There are no differences on the competence scores among the parental education groups.

If you review the Mean Rank table, it is fairly clear to see that the mean ranks for competence scales are similar (36.04, 35.78, and 36.11). It also appears that the mean ranks on math achievement are quite different (28.43, 43.78, and 48.42). Students who had parents with a B.S. or more seemed to score higher on math achievement than did those who had parents with a high school degree or less. However, it is less clear if there are significant differences between the group in the middle (some college) and the one above or below it. To test these comparisons statistically would require post hoc analysis, probably with Mann–Whitney tests.

11.5. In Output 11.4: (a) Is the interaction significant? (b) Examine the profile plot of the cell means that illustrates the interaction. Describe it in words. (c) Is the main effect of gender significant? Interpret the eta squared. (d) How about the "effect" of math grades? (e)

Why did we put the word effect in quotes? (f) Under what conditions would focusing on the main effects be misleading?

(a) No. $F = .34$, $p = .563$. This indicates that we can interpret the main effects without concern that they might be misleading.

(b) Males did better than females regardless of whether they had high or low high school math grades. Note that the lines are nearly parallel, indicating that the difference is about the same for the less than A–B math grades group and the mostly A–B math grades group.

(c) Gender is significant ($F = 13.87$, $p < .001$). Eta squared is .163. This indicates that about 16% of the variance in math achievement can be predicted by gender. Taking the square root of eta squared you get eta = .415, which is a larger than typical effect. Males had higher math achievement, on average, than did females.

(d) The math grades "effect" is also statistically significant ($F = 14.77$, $p < .001$). By looking at the total means or the plot, we can see that students with high (most A–B) math grades had higher average math achievement scores.

(e) We put "effect" in quotes because this is not a randomized experiment so we cannot know if either of these variables is the *cause* of higher math achievement.

(f) If there is an interaction, you must interpret the interaction first, as the interaction can make the results of the main effects misleading.

For Further Reading

American Educational Research Association (2006). Standards for reporting on empirical social science research in AERA publications. *Educational Researcher*, *35*(6), 33–40.

American Psychological Association (APA). (2010). *Publication manual of the American Psychological Association* (6th ed.). Washington, DC: Author.

Chen, P. Y., & Popovich P. M. (2002). *Correlation: Parametric and nonparametric measures.* Sage University Papers Series on Quantitative Applications in the Social Sciences, 07–139. Thousand Oaks, CA: Sage.

Cohen, J. (1988). *Statistical power and analysis for the behavioral sciences* (2nd ed.). Hillsdale, NJ: Lawrence Erlbaum Associates.

DeVellis, R. F. (2012). *Scale development: Theory and applications* (3rd ed.). Los Angeles, CA: Sage.

Fink, A. (2009). *How to conduct surveys: A step-by-step guide* (4th ed.). Thousand Oaks, CA: Sage.

Gliner, J. A., Morgan, G. A., & Leech, N. A. (2009). *Research methods in applied settings: An integrated approach to design and analysis* (2nd ed.). New York, NY: Routledge/Taylor & Francis.

Huck, S. J. (2012). *Reading statistics and research* (6th ed.). Boston, MA: Allyn & Bacon.

Leech, N. A., Barrett, K. C., & Morgan, G. A. (2011). *IBM SPSS for intermediate statistics: Use and interpretation* (4th ed.). New York, NY: Routledge/Taylor & Francis Group.

Morgan, G. A., Gliner, J. A., & Harmon, R. J. (2006). *Understanding and evaluating research in applied and clinical setting.* Mahwah, NJ: Lawrence Erlbaum Associates.

Morgan, S. E., Reichart T., & Harrison T. R. (2002). *From numbers to words: Reporting statistical results for the social sciences.* Boston, MA: Allyn & Bacon.

Newton, R. R., & Rudestam, K. E. (1999). *Your statistical consultant: Answers to your data analysis questions.* Thousand Oaks, CA: Sage.

Nicol, A. A. M., & Pexman, P. M. (2010). *Presenting your findings: A practical guide for creating tables* (6th ed.). Washington, DC: American Psychological Association.

Nicol, A. A. M, & Pexman, P. M. (2010). *Displaying your findings: A practical guide for creating figures, posters, and presentations* (6th ed.). Washington, DC: American Psychological Association.

Rudestam, K. E., & Newton, R. R. (2007). *Surviving your dissertation: A comprehensive guide to content and process* (3rd ed.). Thousand Oaks, CA: Sage.

Thompson, B. (2006). *Foundations of behavioral statistics: An insight-based approach.* New York, NY: The Guilford Press.

Vaske, J. J., Gliner, J. A., & Morgan, G. A. (2002). Communicating judgments about practical significance: Effect sizes, confidence intervals, and odds ratios. *Human Dimensions of Wildlife, 7*, 287–300.

Vogt, W. P. (2011). *Dictionary of statistics and methodology* (4rd ed.). Thousand Oaks, CA: Sage.

Wilkinson, L., & The APA Task Force on Statistical Inference. (1999). Statistical methods in psychology journals: Guidelines and explanations. *American Psychologist, 54*, 594–604.

Index[1]

---

[1] Commands or terms used by SPSS but less common in statistics or research methods books are in bold.

Related IBM SPSS Manuals:

- *IBM SPSS for Intermediate Statistics, 4th ed* Leech, Barrett & Morgan (May, 2011) Pb ISBN: 978-0-415-88047-3
- *Multilevel Modeling of Categorical Outcomes Using IBM SPSS* Heck, Thomas, & Tabata (April, 2012) Pb ISBN: 978-1-84872-956-8
- *Multilevel and Longitudinal Modeling with IBM SPSS* Heck, Thomas, & Tabata (April, 2010) Pb ISBN: 978-1-84872-863-9

Related Introductory and Intermediate Statistics books:

- *Understanding the New Statistics: Effect Sizes, Confidence Intervals, and Meta-Analysis* Cumming (July, 2011) Pb ISBN: 978-0-415-87968-2
- *Statistics in Plain English, 3rd ed* Urdan (May, 2010) Pb ISBN: 978-0-415-87291-1
- *An Introduction to Statistical Concepts, 3rd ed* Lomax & Hahs-Vaughn (February, 2012) Hb ISBN: 978-0-415-88005-3
- *Statistical Concepts: A Second Course, 4th ed* Lomax & Hahs-Vaughn (February, 2012) Pb ISBN: 978-0-415-88007-7
- *Data Analysis: A Model Comparison Approach, 2nd ed* Judd, McClelland, & Carey (August, 2008) Hb ISBN: 978-0-8058-3388-1
- *Statistical Misconceptions* Huck (November, 2008) Pb ISBN: 978-0-8058-5904-1
- *Learning from Data, 3rd ed* Glenberg & Andrzejewski (August, 2007) Hb ISBN: 978-0-8058-4921-9
- *Intermediate Statistics, 3rd ed* Stevens (February, 2007) Pb ISBN: 978-0-8058-5466-4
- *Statistics as Principled Argument* Abelson (March, 1995) PB ISBN: 978-0-8058-0528-4

Related Research Methods and/or Experimental Design books:

- *Research Design and Statistical Analysis, 3rd ed* Myers, Well & Lorch (May, 2010) Hb ISBN: 978-0-8058-6431-1
- *Handbook of Ethics in Quantitative Methodology* Panter & Sterba (January, 2010) Pb ISBN: 978-1-84872-855-4
- *Research Methods in Applied Settings, 2nd ed* Gliner, Morgan & Leech (June, 2009) Hb ISBN: 978-0-8058-6434-2
- *Understanding & Evaluating Research in Applied & Clinical Settings* Morgan, Gliner, & Harmon (August, 2006) Pb ISBN: 978-0-8058-5332-2
- *Strategies & Tactics of Behavioral Research, 3rd ed* Johnston & Pennypacker (2008) Hb ISBN: 978-0-8058-5882-2
- *International Handbook of Survey Methodology* de Leeuw, Hox, & Dillman (January, 2008) Pb ISBN: 978-0-8058-5753-5
- *Designing Experiments and Analyzing Data, 2nd ed* Maxwell & Delaney (July, 2003) Hb ISBN: 978-0-8058-3718-6
- *Principles and Methods of Social Research, 2nd ed* Crano & Brewer (November, 2001) Pb ISBN: 978-0-8058-3904-3

For details about any of these books please visit:
www.researchmethodsarena.com or www.psypress.com.